IRELAND
TRAVELBOOK™

SECOND EDITION

AAA

President & CEO: Robert Darbelnet
Executive Vice President, Publishing &
 Administration: Rick Rinner
Managing Director, Travel Information: Bob
 Hopkins

Director, Product Development: Bill Wood
Director, Sales & Marketing: John Coerper
Director, Purchasing & Corporate Services:
 Becky Barrett
Director, Business Development: Gary Sisco
Director, Tourism Information Development
 (TID): Michael Petrone
Director, Travel Information: Jeff
 Zimmerman
Director, Publishing Operations: Susan Sears
Director, GIS/Cartography: Jan Coyne
Director, Publishing/GIS Systems &
 Development: Ramin Kalhor

Managing Editor, Product Development:
 Margaret Cavanaugh
Development Editor: Greg Weekes
Marketing Manager: Bart Peluso
AAA Travel Store & e-store Manager: Sharon
 Edwards

Manager, Product Support: Linda Indolfi
Manager, Electronic Media Design: Mike
 McCrary
Manager, Pre-Press & Quality Services: Tim
 Johnson

Published by AAA Publishing, 1000 AAA
Drive, Heathrow, Florida 32746

Northern Ireland mapping reproduced by
permission of the Director and Chief
Executive, Ordnance Survey of Northern
Ireland, acting on behalf of the Controller of
Her Majesty's Stationery Office
© Crown copyright 2002 (Permit No.
20162).

Republic of Ireland mapping reproduced by
permission of the Director of Ordnance
Survey Ireland © Ordnance Survey Ireland
and Government of Ireland 2002 (Permit
No. 7558).

Mapping produced by the Cartographic
Department of The Automobile
Association.

Traffic signs © Crown copyright.
Reproduced with the permission of the
Controller of Her Majesty's Stationery
Office.

The contents of this book are believed to be
correct at the time of printing. The
publishers are not responsible for changes
that occur after publication.

The *AAA Ireland TravelBook* was created
and produced for AAA Publishing by AA
Publishing, AA Developments Limited,
Millstream, Maidenhead Road, Windsor,
Berkshire SL4 5GD, England.

Written by Susan Poole
Second edition verified by Hilary Weston
Page make-up by Anton Graphics Ltd.

Cover photos
Main photo: County Cork
© H. Armstrong Roberts
Cover inset: Sheep farmer
© Index Stock
Spine: St. Colman's Cathedral in Cobh
© H. Armstrong Roberts

ISBN 1-56251-821-6

Cataloging-in-Publication Data is on file
with the Library of Congress.

Color separations by Leo Reprographic
Ltd., Hong Kong

Printed in Dubai by Oriental Press

A01235

Experience fun and good conversation wherever the Irish gather

FOREWORD

Welcome to the AAA Ireland TravelBook!

When you're planning your trip to Ireland, let this book whet your appetite for the pleasures in store for you in this unique and beautiful land. Introduce yourself to historic Dublin, with its buzzing streets, stately Georgian buildings and haunting echoes of turbulent Irish history. Explore Belfast, with its thriving industry and appealing city-center areas enlivened with street entertainers. Discover the scenic magnificence of the countryside: The wild, dramatic coastline of the west, the splendors of Munster, the beauty of Achill Island and the eerie limestone landscapes of the Burren.

This is a land that wears its personalities on its sleeve. Sligo echoes the poetry of William Butler Yeats. The day of Ireland's patron, St. Patrick, brings the whole population and compatriots throughout the world into a festive mood. Shadows of literary giants such as James Joyce and Jonathan Swift fall on Dublin's streets where the literary heritage is still flourishing. Folk heroes like Finn MacCool permeate the Irish psyche.

But, most of all, let the author's enthusiasm for Ireland introduce you to its best attraction – its people. Enjoy them at their most relaxed – celebrating at festivals, and at folk and music and sporting events held all over the country. The Irish are among the most smiling and welcoming people you'll find.

Let the AAA TravelBook, with its informative text and colorful illustrations, stir your imagination. Practical information will help you get your bearings and decide what you want to do. There are maps to help you find your way and useful suggestions for eating, drinking and shopping; everything to help you get the most out of your trip to Ireland.

IRELAND TRAVELBOOK™

CONTENTS

The National Stud Farm in Kildare

INTRODUCTION TO IRELAND

"AN Irishman was once asked if there was an an equivalent Irish word to mañana. 'Oh no,' he replied, 'we have nothing with that sense of urgency!'"

St. Mary's Abbey at Trim silhouetted against the dappled evening sky

IRELAND

Capturing the essence of Ireland in mere words is a daunting task. In 1842, William Thackeray wrote an English friend: "I am beginning to find out now that a man ought to be 40 years in this country, and then he wouldn't be able to write about it!" Many a visitor would agree with him when struggling to reduce to words the emotional overload of Ireland's unique mix of scenic wonders and a people who are irrepressibly romantic and brushed with a hint of magic. A varied and most welcoming country awaits you.

The Mountains of Mourne sweep down to meet green pastures

THE EMERALD ISLE

The real Ireland only begins to come alive as you watch the delicate play of light and shade on the mountains from Glengarriff in County Cork to Kenmare in County Kerry, or pass through the lush greenness of County Waterford byways, or gaze in awe at the mystical moonscape of County Clare's Burren, or see a grassy hillside change from the brightest hue of green to silver-gray in the changing light, or view a cloud-studded sky so enormous it makes eternity seem small, or stand on the rocky shore at Ventry on the Dingle Peninsula, where legend says the "King of the World" went down to defeat at the hands of Fionn MacCumhaill (Finn MacCool, see page 199) and his Fianna warrior band. But most of all, it is the people who live among those scenic wonders and more than half-believe those ancient legends who defy description. Around every bend, that luminous, ever-changing landscape and the unique charm of the Irish cry out for the poet. Many a poet has answered its call but fallen short of the mark. Poor Thackeray – no wonder he was so frustrated!

Geographically Speaking

To get the statistics out of the way: Ireland covers 32,524 square miles (about the size of New Hampshire, Vermont and Massachusetts combined), 302 miles at its longest point and 189 miles at its widest. It's the "last parish before America," the most westerly island of Europe, and its bowl-shaped contours are formed by a great limestone plain surrounded by mountains (Kerry's Carrantuohill is the highest at 3,414 feet). The many jagged peninsulas create a coastline that measures more than 3,000 miles and encircles 9,000 miles of rivers (the 230-mile Shannon is the longest) and 800 lakes, the largest of which is Lough Neagh (153 square miles).

From its early history, Ireland's 32 counties have been divided into the four provinces of Leinster, Munster, Connacht and Ulster (those "Four Green Fields" of song and story). Since 1921, Ulster has been divided into the

Locals and tourists enjoy the sunshine and friendly atmosphere in Kinvarra

six counties that form Northern Ireland – Londonderry, Antrim, Armagh, Down, Fermanagh and Tyrone, and three that lie in the Republic – Donegal, Monaghan and Cavan.

All That Rain

You certainly wouldn't come to Ireland for a suntan. However, the Gulf Stream's warming currents create a friendly climate that deals in moderation rather than extremes – seldom more than 65 degrees in July, 40 degrees in January. That famous (or infamous) rainfall is heaviest and most frequent in the mountains of the west, and frequent enough in the rest of the country to keep at least 40 shades of green glowing. To see more sun than rain, you'll generally find it in May everywhere except in the midlands and southeast; June is apt to be sunnier.

the Pat-and-Mike scenario in gleeful anticipation of an entertaining tale for the lads in the local pub.

A Complex People

If it's hard to find words for Ireland itself, it's nearly impossible to capture the complexities of the Irish personality. Complex they most certainly are – warm-hearted, witty, sometimes argumentative, often talkative, great at listening and most of all friendly. There's a certain panache about the Irish that so charms the visitor. True, the Irish will seldom bowl you over with all that charm – if there's anything they're not, it's intrusive. But ask the first question, make the first comment, and you're off and running. Your American accent invites instant interest in where you live, where you're going and what you think of their country.

"The English gave us their language," the Irish will tell you with a sly grin, "then we showed them how to use it." There's truth in that – they have turned out a staggering number of extraordinary writers, and even average Irish men and women tend to embellish everyday conversation with colorful phrases that would make any writer weep with envy. And they string them together in yarns that may be wildly fanciful, but are never dull, the words are delivered in the most melodic, lilting rendition of the English language. As for the celebrated Irish wit, more often than not it is directed at themselves, with a subtle blend of sly wording and a liberal dash of mischief.

There's more to the Irish, of course, than talk. There's the strong religious influence that passed from Celtic to Catholic rites without a hitch. And the fascinating mix of Celt, Viking, Norman and Saxon blood that has melded into an Irish race of brunettes, blonds and redheads.

About Those Stereotypes

Remember all those Pat-and-Mike "stage Irish" jokes and comedy skits you've heard? Don't look for their counterparts in Ireland. The only place you'll find them on their native turf is the comedy stage. Unless, that is, some canny Irishman, tempted beyond endurance by your expectation of finding those stereotypes, decides to play the complete buffoon and act out

Introduction to Ireland

When Irish monks began their laborious transcribing in the sixth century, they drew on a bardic oral storytelling tradition that reached back into prehistory. Their first recorded stories came from the glorious tales of fierce battles, passionate love affairs and heroic deeds that had been passed from generation to generation in both prose and poetry.

George Bernard Shaw at work

A WAY WITH WORDS

Tain Bo Cuailgne (The Cattle Raid of Cooley), Lebor na Huidre (The Dun Cow) and Lebor Laigen (The Book of Leinster) preserve the exploits, triumphs and tragedies of such legendary figures as Finn MacCool (see page 199), Cuchulainn, Oisin and the beautiful Deirdre.

Brian Merriman's *Cuirt an Mhean Oiche (The Midnight Court)* is a masterful satire on the attitudes of Irish men to marriage, while the *Annals of the Four Masters,* written by Franciscan monks, and Geoffrey Keating's *Foras Feasa ar Eirinn (History of Ireland)* deal with Irish history. Those early works were written in Irish, as was most of Irish literature until the 17th century. During that same period, works on a much lighter note came from the witty poet Raftery and the roguish Owen Roe O'Sullivan.

By the end of the 17th century, the Anglo-Irish literary movement was well established. Irish writers Oliver Goldsmith and Richard Brinsley Sheridan penned English-style drawing-room comedies and English manners novels, while Jonathan Swift, then dean of St. Patrick's Cathedral, was verbally flaying the English with his knife-edged satires.

Maria Edgeworth joined the ranks of outstanding Anglo-Irish writers in the 1800s, along with Thomas Moore, Gerald Griffin, William Carleton and Oscar Wilde. Toward the end of that century, dramatist George Bernard Shaw and novelist George Moore began brilliant careers that were to spill over into the next, as did poet William Butler Yeats and playwright John Millington Synge. Edith Somerville and her cousin Violet Martin were busy turning out comic sketches of Protestant life in rural Ireland, and novelist Bram Stoker's Dracula was let loose on the literary public.

The 20th century brought about a veritable explosion of Irish literary talent, whose vitality never flagged, despite the oppressive Censorship Act that drove many Irish writers to foreign publishers. Sean O'Casey's controversial plays put him in the forefront of Irish dramatists; Samuel Beckett was awarded the Nobel Prize while living in exile; James Joyce wrote knowingly of life in Dublin (and is considered by many to be the greatest Irish writer of the 20th century); and Brendan Behan enjoyed an all-too-short burst of literary fame.

Other writers who loom large on the Irish literary scene include playwrights Hugh Leonard, Brian Friel, Bernard Farrell and John B. Keane; novelists and short story writers Ben Kiely, James Plunkett, Mary Lavin, John Banville, Edna O'Brien, Dermot Bolger and Elizabeth Bowen; and poets Patrick Kavanagh, Thomas Kinsella, John Montague and Seamus Heaney (also a Nobel Prize winner). As impressive as that long list is, it is by no means complete. Today, scores of talented Irish writers are hard at work, most to an extraordinarily high standard. So, browse the bookshops, pick up any titles you find intriguing, and who knows – you may well discover the next famous Irish writer.

An abandoned cottage in fields near Rosmuck, County Galway

ABOUT THE PAST

The landscape of Ireland is haunted by its history. Its ghosts lurk along every road, around every bend, behind every bush. Relics are sprinkled across the land, some left in ruins, others authentically restored. Visit the reconstructed crannog at Craggaunowen in County Clare, and Bronze Age men and women will almost materialize before your eyes. Great monastic crosses and ruined abbeys speak of early Christians, while Norman spirits inhabit ruined castles that squat along riverbanks, atop lofty cliffs and in lonely fields.

In the Beginning

The earliest inhabitants to have left traces of their existence in Ireland probably arrived from Scotland in 6000 or 7000 BC. It wasn't until about 2000 BC that Neolithic people arrived, bringing along farming expertise and beginning Ireland's long tradition of farming and cattle raising. They cremated their dead and created communal burial chambers beneath stone cairns or inside earthen, tunnel-filled mounds like those at Newgrange in the Boyne Valley. They were followed by Bronze Age metal workers and artisans, who fashioned the exquisite ornaments that fill today's museums and left a wealth of megalithic stone structures. Believed to be descendants of the fertility goddess Eire (Noble), they transferred her name to this small island country.

In the fourth century BC, tall, fair-skinned, red-haired Celts, a fierce warlike people, arrived bearing iron weapons and military skills that soon established them as rulers of the land. A high king of Ireland ruled from Tara, but the countryside rang with battle cries as regional kings embarked on expansionary expeditions, and the high king of the moment never sat easy on his honorary throne. Nevertheless, there was unity in the strong bonds of a common culture and traditions held together by a common language. Tribes honored traveling bards, above all the Druids, who performed sacred ceremonies and rituals.

St. Patrick Arrives

It was the strange Celtic mixture of barbarous warring and a highly developed culture that greeted the arrival of Patrick in the fifth century carrying the message of Christianity. Although the Celts showed faint regard for the edicts of Rome (their Easter fell on a date different from that proclaimed by the Pope, for instance), his reception by the war-loving Celts was surprisingly cordial, and conversions came swiftly. By the time of St. Patrick's death in 461, the new religion was firmly established.

Viking Invaders

Viking raiders came by sea in AD 795, making lightning-fast strikes along the coastline and taking away plunder and captives. Their superior mail battle dress and heavy arms made easy victims of even the most stout-hearted Irish. Their raids moved farther and farther inland, with rich monastic settlements yielding the most valuable prizes. Churchmen retreated from the danger to tall, round towers with the only entrance high above the ground. Today you'll find one of the best preserved at the Rock of Cashel in County Tipperary.

Eventually turning to peaceful trading and, in a pattern to be followed by subsequent "conquerors," the Vikings were soon intermarrying with natives and becoming as Irish as the Irish themselves. Vestiges of their city walls, gates and fortifications remain to this day – Reginald's Tower in Waterford Quay is one of the most perfect examples.

The Normans Enter

In 1014, Irish High King Brian Ború won a decisive victory against the Vikings. Ború ascended into the rarefied stratosphere of Ireland's most revered heroes, but his death was followed by a century and a half of kingly tug-of-war to establish one central authority. Dermot MacMurrough, king of Leinster, committed the grave error of stealing the wife of the king of Breffni, who promptly hounded him out of Leinster. MacMurrough persuaded England's King Henry II to send Norman troops to win back Dermot's lost throne. When Rory O'Connor, the last high king of Ireland (buried at Clonmacnois, County Offaly) was defeated, MacMurrough's power began to rival that of King Henry. Alarmed, Henry elicited vows of fealty from many Irish kings who were anxious to hold onto their territories. For the next 350 years, territorial claims kept Anglo-Norman and Irish lords growling at each other as Normans acquired title to more than half of the country, building most of those sturdy castles in which you'll sightsee, banquet or spend the night during your visit.

To Hell or Connaught

By the time Elizabeth I became queen, the Reformation was firmly entrenched in England and the staunchly Catholic Irish found themselves fighting for their religion with even more fervor than they had fought for their lands. Having lost several long and bloody battles, Irish chieftains went into hiding, their lands now confiscated by the British Crown and resettled by loyal English and Scottish Protestants.

Arriving in 1649 and driven by religious fervor as well as political motives, Puritan Oliver Cromwell's campaign across the country left a trail of destruction. The Irish who escaped were shipped as slave labor to English plantations in the Sugar Islands (a virtual "hell") or driven to the bleak stony hills of Connaught. To his loyal

The Romans rampaging in southern Britain never did get around to conquering Ireland, but in the fifth century a conquest of quite another nature took place. A pagan religion that had flourished for centuries surprisingly embraced the doctrines and rites of Christianity that landed on Irish shores with Patrick. Born *Patricius* in Britain as a Roman Empire citizen, in his youth the budding saint had tended swine in Ulster as a slave, escaped and made his way back to the Continent, where he entered religious life before returning to his former captors as a missionary in 432.

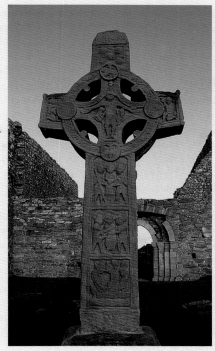

A 13-foot stone cross stands outside
St. Finghin Church

SAINTS AND SCHOLARS

Retaining just enough pagan customs to avoid hostile resistance, St. Patrick managed to transplant rites and superstitions into Christian soil without a murmur. The healing powers of many Irish "holy wells," for example, are those attributed to them by ancient Celts long before St. Patrick arrived on the scene. His firsthand knowledge of Celtic love of the mystical, especially when applied to the natural world, perhaps inspired him to use the native shamrock to symbolize the Holy Trinity and thereby make it Ireland's most enduring national symbol. Irish king after Irish king listened to the missionary and led his subjects into the new religion, although none went so far as to abandon such distinctly Celtic pastimes as intra-kingdom warfare and riotous revelry within his own court.

With the coming of Christianity, Celtic culture took a giant step forward. Already deeply respectful of learning in its higher forms, the Irish devoted themselves to a cloistered life within great monasteries that taught all the learning of their time, both Celtic and Roman. As Europe entered its culturally deprived Dark Ages, Ireland's monastic universities kept the lights of philosophy, theology, astronomy, literature, poetry and science brightly burning. Artistic achievement hit new heights inside their walls, as the exquisitely illustrated *Book of Kells* demonstrates. Until the end of the eighth century, Ireland's Golden Age was the brightest beacon in the Western world.

Away from these seats of learning, monks also moved out to more remote parts of the country. There they lived austere lives of meditation, building the beehive-shaped stone dwellings still intact today and marvelously engineered little stone churches such as Dingle's Gallarus Oratory (see page 132), constructed entirely without mortar and watertight for the past 1,500 years. The impressive stone Celtic crosses that dot the landscape had their origins in the seventh century.

Eventually, Europe's age of darkness retreated, helped by returning European scholars and Irish monks who left home to carry their teachings into cathedrals, royal courts and universities.

soldiers, Cromwell awarded vast estates in the fertile counties of the country. In the end, less than one-ninth of Irish soil remained in the hands of natives.

King Billy, the Treaty of Limerick and Penal Laws

Irish spirits rose once more when a Catholic, James II, ascended to the English throne in 1688. Deposed by William of Orange – King Billy – James fled to Ireland in 1689, where the Irish took up arms in his defense. King Billy arrived to lead a resounding victory in the Battle of the Boyne, after which James once more took flight. The Irish fought on until October 1691, when they signed the Treaty of Limerick, which allegedly allowed them to retain both their religion and their land. Parliament, however, instituted a series of measures so oppressive they became known as the Penal Laws. Catholics were stripped of all civil and political rights and forced to work the estates of absentee English landlords. Irish farmers paid enormous rents for the privilege of building primitive huts and using a small plot of ground to raise the potatoes that kept their families from starving.

United Irishmen

Anglo-Irish Protestants gradually came to feel a stronger allegiance to Ireland than to England and, demanding greater independence, got a token Irish Parliament in 1782. Forming the Society of United Irishmen to work for a totally independent Irish republic, and enlisting military aid from France, revolutionist Wolfe Tone led a full-fledged insurrection in 1798. Disaster on the battlefield became even greater than the disaster in the halls of the English Parliament. In 1800 the Act of Union was passed and Ireland became an extension of British soil. It was

Daniel O'Connell (affectionately named "The Liberator") who, on getting elected to Parliament in 1828, restored all Catholic civil rights, accomplished a total repeal of the Penal Laws and embarked on a campaign for repeal of the Act of Union.

Just as members of the Young Ireland movement were beginning to be heard, potato blight gripped the country and the Irish goal became one of simple survival. By 1849 a population of nearly 9 million people was reduced to little more than 6 million. Those that did not die of starvation and disease escaped on ships to the United States and Canada, but the vessels were so overcrowded and disease infested that they were little more than floating coffins.

The Land League, Home Rule and Sinn Fein

By 1879 Irish tenant farmers were so frustrated by oppressive land rentals that they eagerly joined with Charles Stewart Parnell's Land League. Farmers organized strikes by "boycott" against any landlord who evicted tenants – so called for Captain Boycott against whom it was first used. Parnell's energetic campaign for Home Rule also granted limited independence, but it wasn't until the eve of World War I that such a measure was adopted by the British.

Outnumbered by Catholics, Unionists in Ulster feared Home Rule would become Rome Rule, and put up armed resistance against the equally determined Irish Republican Army. The IRA is the military arm of Sinn Fein, a republican political party whose name is pronounced "shin fain," and means ourselves alone. The country was fairly bristling with arms when everything was put on hold by the urgency of World War I.

Folk musicians playing traditional instruments at an Irish pub

"AND ALL THEIR SONGS ARE SAD"

So said G. K. Chesterton about the Irish, having just asserted, "All their wars are merry." He may have been half right, but their songs are most assuredly not all sad. The Irish have celebrated, mourned, exalted, damned and lamented everything in their lives through music. Until the 1690s and the Englishman Oliver Cromwell, songs and ballads were composed entirely in Irish. After that, English was the only legal language, imposed as an attempt to help erase any remaining traces of nationalism. Even the Penal Laws were unable to do that, however, for the wily Irish praised their country under the guise of singing about their sweethearts: *Roisin Dubh* and *Kathleen Huallachain* spoke of loved ones, but every Irishman knew they really were odes to Ireland herself. Those traditional songs and airs are still played frequently today. If you listen closely to modern Irish ballads, you'll notice that a few are still concerned with celebrating or mourning, exalting some facet of Irish life.

The tones that spring from the harp, *uilleann* (elbow) pipes – played sitting down and some say developed to get around English law that forbade the playing of any instrument while standing in order to prevent the pipes from playing troops into battle, the *bodhrán* – a drum made of goatskin stretched tightly over a round wooden frame, the tin whistle, fiddle and accordion mix in a unique harmony that can break your heart or send your spirits soaring.

In Ireland, native music has become trendy in recent years, and pubs often feature "trad" groups or local lads aiming in that direction. Even if a pub is not known for music, the lyrical Irish spirit frequently bursts forth in pubs as the evening progresses. You are likely to hear the familiar twang of American country music as often as the impassioned lyrics of Ireland's traditional songs.

Culturlann na hEireann (pronounced "Kultur-arn na-Airan"), based in the Dublin suburb of Monkstown, organizes year-round traditional entertainment including *ceilis* (pronounced "kay-lees," traditional set dancing) in hotels, pubs and at local branch meetings, which are all open to the public. During the last weekend in August, look for the All-Ireland Fleadh, pronounced "flah." It's a three-day traditional music and song festival held each year in a different town. Worldwide music lovers congregate in pubs, hotels, private houses and streets to play, sing and just listen to this special brand of music. The Fleadh Nua on the last weekend in May is another showcase for the best in traditional music.

Introduction to Ireland

THE WINDS OF CHANGE

The Irish treasure their cultural heritage, but are nowadays using it as a solid base for swiftly moving changes in manners and mores of this dynamic era. With an economy labeled "The Celtic Tiger" and recognized as the fastest growing in the European Union, the country is awash with signs of prosperity and affluence. Lifestyles are changing at a fast clip, but the winds of change are nothing new for the Irish.

With centuries of flexibility in meeting new circumstances, current changes are a piece of cake! The basic elements of Irishness – courtesy, compassion and the ability to laugh at the absurdities of life – are still very much alive and well, even as high-tech industries invade the country and young people leave traditional pursuits for higher pay and city life.

Until the last decade of the 20th century, hard times in Ireland spawned youthful emigration. In the wake of hard-won reversal of fortunes, an ever increasing number are returning. This influx of returnees and the dramatic decrease in young people leaving for foreign shores has resulted in a large youthful population. Such a vibrant, well-educated and young work force is luring more and more international companies to use Ireland as their gateway to European markets.

On the social front, Ireland has embraced change with breathtaking speed: politically, male domination is fast disappearing and Ireland now has its second woman president.

Ireland's modernity belies the "quaint" label so often applied and makes for a memorable holiday.

An exhilarating way of exploring County Galway's pristine coastline

wondrous to behold. Sunday afternoon matches are regular events all around the country, and it's great fun to mingle with the local fans.

While organized Gaelic football matches date back only about a century, the game undoubtedly evolved from fierce tribal rivalries. None of the fervor of participants or spectators has been lost in the shift. An amateur field game, it is played by two teams of 15 and incorporates elements of both soccer and rugby (some say it's more exciting than either). Weekend local matches are great to watch, and for sheer excitement nothing quite matches that of the All Ireland finals in early September as more than 90,000 fans in Dublin's Croke Park roar support for their county teams. "Football" in Ireland often means soccer, and American football is only beginning to take hold in Ireland and mainland Europe.

Hands-on Sports

If there's such a thing as a fisherman's heaven, it must be Ireland! Irish waters are home to such freshwater fish (coarse fishing) as bream, dace, pike, perch and various hybrids in rivers, streams and lakes. Or you may elect to stalk the famous Irish salmon from January through September in coastal rivers, their stillwaters and headwaters. Sea trout and brown trout are among other challenging game fish.

Sea anglers will find plentiful supplies of bass, whiting, mullet, flounder, plaice, pollack and coalfish from shore casting on rocks, piers, beaches and promontories. Deep-sea fishing for shark, skate, dogfish, pollack, ling and conger is yours for incredibly low costs all around the coast.

Other water sports include surfing, water skiing and windsurfing. And, of course, there are lovely beaches for swimmers who don't demand summer

temperatures much above 70 degrees. It is positively rejuvenating to commune with sea and sun on long stretches when there's not another soul in sight. Seaside resorts can also be fun, from the

The ancient game of hurling is fast and furious

lively, crowded Tramore in County Waterford to the quieter Kilkee in County Clare.

For golf enthusiasts, more than 360 superb golf courses dot the Irish countryside, and a growing number of hotels now have their own course or access to local courses. Visiting golfers are very welcome. Caddies are not generally available, although they can be booked ahead at some of the larger courses. And don't look for golf carts – the closest you'll find is a pull-cart. Many courses have clubs for rent, but some do not. Irish golfing vacations can be arranged to include accommodations, golf clinics, and special weekends with groups. Tourist offices can provide you with lists of locations and specific information on what's available at each course.

Equestrians of any age or level of expertise will never have to look far for stables offering riding instruction, as well as trail riding, guided point-to-point treks with overnight accommodations or hunting.

TIMELINE

circa 3000 BC	Neolithic farmers construct sacred burial chambers at Newgrange and Knowth in the Boyne Valley. Bronze Age metal workers come seeking copper and gold.
600	Celts arrive, bringing iron weapons and the Gaelic language.
AD 456	Patrick begins his Christian conversion of Irish tribes.
circa 795	Vikings plunder monasteries and found cities of Dublin, Wexford, Waterford, Cork and Limerick.
1014	Brian Ború defeats the Vikings at Battle of Clontarf.
1169	Normans, led by Strongbow, begin England's long domination of Ireland.
1608	Leading Irish chieftains flee in the "Flight of the Earls."
1609	Plantations in Ulster begin as English and Scottish Protestants occupy Irish farms.
1649	Lord Protector Oliver Cromwell sweeps through Ireland to subdue the rebellious Irish.
1690	Catholic defeat at the Battle of the Boyne begins a century of Catholic oppression under the Penal Laws.
1791	Wolfe Tone founds the United Irishmen.
1798	Insurrection led by Tone, Robert Emmet and others squelched by English forces.
1800	The Act of Union was passed handing direct rule of Ireland over to London Parliament.

A "TERRIBLE BEAUTY IS BORN"

On Easter Monday of 1916, the whole question of Irish independence was put right back on the front burner. Leading a scruffy and poorly armed little band of patriots, Padraic Pearse and James Connolly took occupation of Dublin's General Post Office in the name of a provisional government. Pearse read "The Proclamation of the Irish Republic to the People of Ireland," and for the next six days, the Post Office stood embattled under the ancient symbol of Ireland (a golden harp on a pennant of brilliant green) and the Sinn Fein banner of green, white and orange.

In the end the rebels surrendered, and Pearse, Connolly and 14 others were executed by firing squad. Irish loyalties became united behind their new republic and the ideal of Irish independence. It was at that moment – as the executioners' gunsmoke cleared in Kilmainham Gaol's yard – that the poet Yeats proclaimed "A terrible beauty is born."

In 1919 Sinn Fein set up the National Parliament of Ireland in Dublin. Bitter bloodshed followed. The Anglo-Irish Treaty was signed naming 26 counties the Irish Free State. Six counties in Ulster would remain – as they wished – an integral part of Great Britain. In 1948 Ireland was formally declared outside the Commonwealth, and Ireland was made a Republic.

1845–51	The Great Potato Famine causes widespread starvation and more than 1 million Irish emigrate, chiefly to America.
1879	Charles Stewart Parnell and Michael Davitt found the Land League to secure tenant land ownership.
1905–08	Sinn Fein political party evolves, with Irish independence its primary goal.
1912	Home Rule goes into effect; Ulster Volunteers founded by loyalists; Irish Republican Army established as military adjunct of Sinn Fein.
1916	Padraic Pearse, James Connolly and others lead Easter Monday uprising; their execution unites Irish and world public opinion in support of Irish independence.
1921	Dominion status granted to 26 counties as Irish Free State; partition leaves six Ulster counties as part of Great Britain; civil war rages until 1923.
1937	New constitution put forth by Eamon De Valera.
1948	Twenty-six of Ireland's counties become a republic with no constitutional ties to Britain.
1968	Violence breaks out in Northern Ireland when British troops fire on peaceful Catholic civil rights demonstration in Londonderry.
1969	Beginning of "The Troubles" in Northern Ireland when Britain stations military force to protect the peace.
1973	The Republic of Ireland joins the European Economic Community.
1986	Anglo-Irish Agreement gives Republic limited input in Northern Ireland affairs.
1994	IRA declares an end to military operations; Loyalist paramilitaries issue similar cease-fire.
1995	Ireland approves the European Union; British and Irish governments issue New Framework for Agreement; President Clinton makes his historic visit to Ireland.
1996	IRA resumes campaign of violence as peace talks collapse.
1997	IRA declares new cease-fire and enters all-party peace talks chaired by United States Congressman George Mitchell.
1998	Good Friday Agreement affirmed by referenda in the Republic, and Northern Ireland paves the way for a Northern Ireland Assembly; sporadic violence continues in Northern Ireland.
2000	Northern Ireland executive committee suspended after meeting only 10 weeks when United Unionist Party demands IRA disarm in advance of Good Friday Agreement deadline of May 2000, but reconvenes when compromise is reached.
2002	Launched in January, the euro becomes the official currency of the Republic of Ireland.

SURVIVAL GUIDE

- Consider basing yourself in one location for three or four days. Ireland is a small, compact country and lends itself to day trips from a central regional base. While you'll always be made welcome at any pub in the country, when you return a second night, you'll automatically become a "regular" and the locals will delight in hearing what you've done and seen during the day, as well as have a load of "insider" tips for the next day.

- Plan to vary your accommodations between hotels, guesthouses and bed-and-breakfast homes. Ireland has an incredible array of high-quality places to stay. Self-catering accommodations are also an attractive alternative – not only are they money-savers when it comes to meals, but trips to local grocery shops for essentials will add another dimension to your Irish experience.

- If you're traveling with children or if you exult in the glories of country life, book into a farmhouse for a few days. Hospitality seems to take on an even keener edge out in the country, and most hosts will delight in showing you around a working farm. Children especially respond to close-up contact with farm animals.

- Keep your daytime activities flexible enough to stop and spend some time if you come across a street fair, cattle mart or horse fair. County Waterford's annual horse fair in Tallow is a great opportunity to watch such age-old practices as rural people bargaining for horses and sealing a deal with a handshake. Remember, in Ireland time is made for *you,* not you for time!

- Be sure to bring a raincoat, not only for Ireland's magical rain but for an evening wrap when the temperature drops, and as a dressing gown when accommodations have the bathroom down the hall.

- Plan at least one picnic. The Irish landscape beckons to picnickers to spread a lunch on a deserted beach, under a tree on the edge of a field, on a picnic table at a scenic overlook or any place looking out to mountains. Besides, it's great fun to shop for picnic makings in shops that often stock locally made cheeses and fresh bread.

- Make your main meal a late lunch (after a gigantic Irish breakfast, you won't want lunch until 2 or 2:30 p.m.) Lunch in even the most expensive restaurants costs a fraction of the same meal in the evening. Most pubs serve hot plates heaped with home-cooked meats and vegetables, as well as excellent cold salad plates of ham or chicken.

- Be sure to inquire about discounts at sightseeing attractions for families, senior citizens and students. They're not always posted and can amount to a considerable saving. Any identification will be helpful.

- Ireland's highways and secondary roads are rapidly improving, but especially in the west drivers should be on the lookout for potholes. Major highways connect most tourist destinations, but it's worth a detour or two to drive down tree-shaded rural roads that bring you right into the landscape. When off the main roads, expect to encounter farmers driving cattle or sheep to and from fields in the early morning and late afternoon – just stop the car and wait for the animals to sweep past you.

- The plethora of Irish "roundabouts" (traffic circles) seems to present all

Dublin with no Guinness is like earth with no air

sorts of difficulties for American drivers. The cardinal rule is: The driver on the right has the right of way. If you miss your exit, just go around again and be sure you're in the correct lane to exit.

- A few conversation tips: Politics and religion are both very serious subjects in Ireland, and it is best to avoid any discussion of either. The status of Northern Ireland is also a touchy and complex subject. Be careful in expressing any judgment to people you meet in Ireland.

- As tempting as the sight of a broad deserted beach is, resist swimming when there's no one else around, especially from Atlantic beaches in the west, where tides are strong and currents can be treacherous. Always swim at more populated beaches.

- Be sure to stock up with plenty of film before leaving home. It will cost less, and you may not be able to get the exact film you need. Ireland is a *very* scenic country, and with the "perfect shot" around every bend in the road, you're likely to need more film than you might anticipate. Also be sensitive when taking pictures inside churches or at family occasions. If in doubt, ask for permission to take a picture or shoot video.

- Be aware that some conveniences you're accustomed to at home will not be on hand everywhere in Ireland, and some Irish customs are going to differ from those with which you are familiar. Just relax and enjoy the differences.

CONNACHT

" ***C*** *ONNACHT probably comes closer to the popular perception of Ireland. Its bleak, stony Atlantic landscape has a stark beauty, blending softly to the green and fertile inland counties.* *"*

Brightly painted boats rest on the shores of Lough Conn

CONNACHT

Connacht's counties – Galway, Leitrim, Mayo, Roscommon, Sligo – form a large portion of Ireland's West, a region of which James Joyce's poet-surgeon friend Oliver St. John Gogarty wrote,

There's something sleeping in my breast
That wakens only in the West;
There's something in the core of me
That needs the West to set it free.

That "something" undoubtedly springs from a long history of hardships stoically endured and rebelliously resisted.

Within the boundaries of counties Galway and Mayo lie such distinct geographic divisions as Connemara, the Aran Islands and Achill Island. Galway's landscape in the east is made up of flat, fertile plains that reach from Lough Derg and the Shannon Valley north to County Roscommon, while to the northwest, lumpy mountains push the mainland into a great elbow bent against the Atlantic. Connemara's stony landscape is bounded by a coastline dotted with wonderful, mostly uncrowded beaches. Lough Corrib stretches its 27 miles along an invisible line that marks the change. Some 30 miles offshore, the Aran Islands are an outpost of rugged, self-sufficient fishermen and their families. These people have kept alive many aspects of

In the heart of Connemara – the peaks of Twelve Pins seen from Roundstone Bay

A mural decorates a storefront in the small town of Kinvarra, Galway

their ancient culture even as they move into easier lifestyles of modern Ireland. Pre-Christian stone forts rub shoulders with early Christian round towers, oratories and tiny churches. The musical Gaelic language of their ancestors is that of today's islanders. Menfolk still fish the sea as they have

done over the ages, while their womenfolk spin and weave and knit the clothing that is so distinctly theirs, all the while welcoming and providing for a steady stream of visitors who come by steamer or small aircraft.

Eastern County Mayo is flat. It was near Cong, on the Plain of Southern Moytura, that a prehistoric battle raged between Tuatha De Danann and the Firbolgs, ending in the first defeat of the Firbolgs, who declined in power until they were crushed forever seven years later in Sligo. Northeast of Cong is the small village of Knock, a shrine to the many reported visions and a place of pilgrimage for thousands of Christians. A 20,000-seat circular church was built here in 1876, and pilgrims gather on the last Sunday in July each year to walk barefoot in the steps of St. Patrick. Their path takes

The dock at Leenane village on the inner reaches of Killary Harbour

them to the summit of Croagh Patrick on Clew Bay's southern shore.

Connected to the mainland by a causeway, Achill Island presents a mountainous face to the sea, its feet surrounded by golden sandy strands. Along the western part of County Sligo are the heathery slopes of the Ox Mountains; the north holds high, flat-topped limestone hills like Yeats'

beloved Benbulben. Farther north, the long, narrow finger of Killary Harbour marks the County Mayo border.

Out of season, most of Connacht is quiet with many attractions closed. If you don't want to drive, the best base is Galway city, which has plenty to do all year and opportunities for nearby sightseeing excursions, which can be arranged by your hotel or tourist office.

GALWAY

Galway may have begun its life as a small village that grew from a fishing camp at the only possible ford of the River Corrib, but over the centuries it has blossomed into a thriving, lively city that breathes new life into the entire region. It has become a center for the arts, drama, music and all manner of creative activities that draw visitors from around the world, many of whom elect to stay on as permanent residents in an environment that nurtures talent.

Galway owes its existence to the grief of Breasail, an ancient Celtic chieftain. After his daughter drowned in the River Corrib, he established a permanent riverbank camp that grew into the tiny fishing village of the Claddagh (see page 33). When the Normans arrived, they recognized the potential of the excellent harbor, developed a thriving maritime trade between Galway, Spain and France, and eventually enclosed the fine medieval town with stone walls. The 14 "Tribes of Galway" were composed of the town's most prosperous merchant families. At the height of the Great Famine in the mid-1800s, the city was filled with starving men, women and children who fought to board the infamous "coffin ships" in a desperate attempt to escape to America and a new life.

Today Ireland's fourth largest city is still a prosperous commercial center, a delightful blend of ancient and modern that welcomes visitors with open arms. Traces of its history abound with the oldest parts clustering around the harbor and riverside quays: the Spanish Arch, a gateway of the old city walls; Lynch's Castle, a 14th-century town house that is now a branch of the Allied Irish Bank; tiny cobblestone streets and lanes; the Long Walk along the banks of the Corrib, a much-loved waterside promenade for centuries and Galway's version of the "Left Bank" (the High

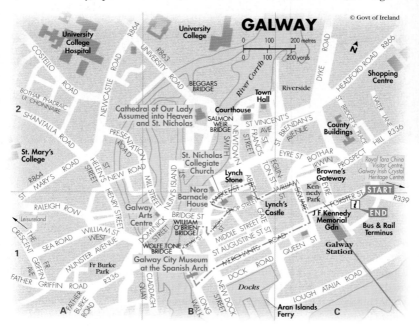

GALWAY
© Govt of Ireland

Galway's modern St. Nicholas's Cathedral

Street and Quay Street quarter of old buildings has been given a new life these days).

While all that ancient history is revered by Galway natives, they are busily creating a modern history that embraces the arts in all forms. Gaelic drama flourishes at the Taibhdhearc Theatre, while the Town Hall Theatre features avant-garde, new Irish and Anglo-Irish classic theater. Galway pubs ring with the sounds of traditional Irish music one night, rock 'n' roll the next, and aspiring (sometimes quite professional) musicians provide street entertainment aplenty.

Then there are the festivals. Galway's Arts Festival rages for 12 entertainment-filled days in July, with all sorts of stage plays, concerts and street entertainment, as well as a massive, offbeat parade that's a highlight.

At the end of July and the beginning of August, the six-day Galway Race Week draws the cream of the local and international horsey sets. When not at the track, horse owners, trainers and "punters" (the betting folk) are never idle – private parties warmly welcome complete strangers, and the track grounds are lined with food stalls and

Claddagh Rings

The design of these silver or gold rings originated in the Claddagh. Once a Gaelic-speaking fishing community outside Galway's old city walls by the western mouth of the river, it is now a neat suburb. Claddagh rings depict two hands holding a heart surmounted by a crown, symbolizing a promise, or a hope, or eternal love and friendship. The precious heirlooms were handed down the family's female line and depending which way round the ring was worn, showed whether a girl was engaged or still on the marriage market.

Connacht

street entertainers. Meanwhile, Galway's pubs are at their liveliest.

In mid-August (weather permitting) there's the Blessing of the Sea, when a procession of fishing boats sail out to sea led by a priest-filled boat whose ecclesiastical passengers implore heavenly powers to grant safe and profitable voyages as the herring season opens.

Hordes of Irish people from around the country descend on Galway in September to take part in the Oyster Festival, which they consider to be the festival to end all festivals. The Lord Mayor of Galway opens and eats the first oyster of the season, inaugurating a

weekend of sheer, unashamed gluttony. Oyster-openers from around the world gather for lively competitions in opening the most oysters in the shortest time, and although some wash the bivalves down with champagne, the overwhelming drink of preference is "the black stuff" (Guinness).

Galway is an upbeat, vivacious and enjoyable city that is good for shopping, especially secondhand books and classy crafts. Besides its own attractions, the city is a convenient base for exploring local areas – Connemara, Lough Corrib, the Aran Islands and the Burren in County Clare.

ESSENTIAL INFORMATION

TOURIST INFORMATION

Ireland West Tourism (serving counties Galway, Mayo and Roscommon), Áras Fáilte, Forster Street ☎ 091 537 700; fax 091 537 733; www.irelandwest.ie
The office will make reservations for accommodations, excursions, ferry services and bicycle and car rentals.
A tip: be sure to get a city map – it may well save your sanity as you wander this ancient city's narrow, winding streets, which often change names every few blocks.

URBAN TRANSPORTATION

Galway's local bus service, running from the Bus Eireann Travel Centre, Ceannt Station (☎ 091 562 000) just off Eyre Square, reaches most suburbs, including Salthill and other neighborhoods. From here there are good connections to almost anywhere in the country. Bus Eireann runs several worthwhile day tours from Galway and Salthill: Clew Bay and Killary Harbour; the Maam Valley and Cong. Some are half-day trips; others last the entire day. All are moderately priced, and you can book a tour at the tourist office in Galway or the railway station. The most central taxi stand is at Eyre Square. You can also call Galway Taxi Co-op ☎ 091 561 111. The first thing to be said about driving in Galway city is don't. The network of tiny lanes, alleyways

and medieval passageways make city driving a nightmare. Parking can also be a problem – street parking operates on the disk system, and the few multistory parking garages are expensive and often fill up early in the day. It's best to leave your car at your hotel, take a bus into the town center, and walk – those same little streets are a joy to wander.
There's direct rail service between Galway and Dublin. While there are connecting services to other major destinations around the country, they often involve time-consuming, multi-change schedules. In Galway, trains arrive and depart from Ceannt Station (☎ 091 561 444) just off Eyre Square (down from the Great Southern Hotel). Several ferry companies operate regular services to the outlying Aran Islands, departing from Galway docks, a 90-minute voyage, or Rossaveal (20 miles west of Galway city on R336, the Barna road), with shuttle service to the ferry from the city), which takes 40 minutes. Make reservations at the tourist office the day before your visit.

AIRPORT INFORMATION

Daily Aer Lingus flights between Dublin and Galway use Galway Airport (☎ 091 752 874) in Carnmore, about 6.5 miles east of Galway city. Aer Arann flies from Connemara Airport (on the Monivea road 4 miles from Galway) to Kilronan, Inis Mór's main port town.

CLIMATE – Average highs and lows

	JAN.	FEB.	MAR.	APR.	MAY	JUN.	JUL.	AUG.	SEP.	OCT.	NOV.	DEC.
	8°C	8°C	10°C	12°C	14°C	16°C	17°C	17°C	16°C	14°C	11°C	9°C
	46°F	46°F	50°F	54°F	57°F	61°F	63°F	63°F	61°F	57°F	52°F	48°F
	4°C	4°C	5°C	6°C	8°C	10°C	12°C	12°C	11°C	8°C	6°C	5°C
	39°F	39°F	41°F	43°F	46°F	50°F	54°F	54°F	52°F	46°F	43°F	41°F

GALWAY SIGHTS

Key to symbols

➕ map coordinates refer to the Galway map on page 32; sights below are highlighted in yellow on the map

✉ address or location ☎ telephone number

◷ opening times 🚌 nearest bus route

🍴 restaurant on site or nearby

💺 admission charge: $$$ more than €6, $$ €4 to €6, $ less than €4

ℹ information

CATHEDRAL OF OUR LADY ASSUMED INTO HEAVEN AND ST. NICHOLAS

This Roman Catholic cathedral is a striking city landmark. Its tall spire visible from almost any point in the city, the cathedral is often used by residents as a designated meeting place. Set beside the Salmon Weir Bridge on the River Corrib and constructed from native limestone with Connemara marble flooring, the Renaissance-style building topped by a copper dome is a showcase for mosaics, statues and stained-glass windows created by contemporary Irish artisans. It was completed in 1965 after seven years of construction.

Shoals of salmon leap the falls by the Salmon Weir Bridge as they swim upstream to spawn from mid-April to early July.

➕ B2 ✉ University and Gaol roads ☎ 091 563 577 ◷ Daily 8:30–6:30; phone for additional evening opening 🍴 Restaurant 🚌 2, 4, 5 💺 Free (donations welcome)

GALWAY ARTS CENTRE

This was once the townhouse of Lady Augusta Gregory (1859–1932), a wealthy widow who nurtured a generation of Irish writers and poets, and who founded the Abbey Theatre in Dublin (see page 66). Later, Galway Corporation took it over for office space. These days, it once more nurtures Irish figures such as Fiona Murray and Charles Lamb, as well as presenting international artists through concerts, literary readings and exhibitions.

➕ B1 ✉ 47 Dominick Street and 23 Nuns Island

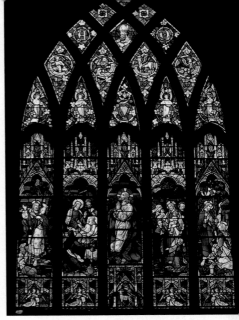

Intricate stained glass in Galway's cathedral

☎ 091 565 886 ◷ Mon.–Sat. 10–6 🚌 2, 4, 5 💺 Concerts: $$–$$$; exhibits: free

GALWAY CITY MUSEUM AT THE SPANISH ARCH

Dating from 1584, the days when trade between Galway and Spain led to the city's prosperous development, the Spanish Arch is a fitting setting for this small museum. In addition to historic photographs and documents, there are examples of medieval stonework and a fascinating map of the city in 1651.

➕ B1 ✉ Spanish Arch, The Quay ☎ 091 567 641 ◷ Daily 10–1 and 2–5, Apr.–Sep.; Wed.–Fri. 10–1, Oct.–Mar. 🚌 City Centre 💺 $$

GALWAY IRISH CRYSTAL HERITAGE CENTRE

A tour of this Heritage Centre situated on the outskirts of town includes displays of master craftspeople blowing, shaping and hand-cutting distinctive Galway crystal patterns. An audiovisual presentation, "Life in Galway," supplements the marvelous exhibits depicting the beginnings of Claddagh village from which Galway grew.

➕ C2 ✉ Merlin Park, Dublin Road (N6) ☎ 091 757 311 ◷ Mon.–Sat. 9–6, Sun. 10–6, Apr.–Sep.;

Mon.–Fri. 9–5:30, Sat. 10–5:30, Sun. 11–5:30, rest of year. Closed Jan. 1, Mar. 17, Dec. 24–26 and 31 🍴 Restaurant 🚇 Merlin Park Service 💲 Free; tours $$ 🛈 Showroom features Belleek Pottery, Aynsley China and Galway Irish Crystal

LEISURELAND

Give the kids – and yourself – a break from sightseeing by reserving purely recreational time at Leisureland. There's a heated indoor pool, a tropical beach pool and treasure cove. Most popular of all is the 200-foot waterslide. Many other diversions such as crazy golf and an amusement park will keep you and your youngsters occupied.
➕ A1 ✉ Salthill ☎ 091 521 455 🕐 Daily 8 a.m.–10 p.m., Jul.–Aug.; 10–5, rest of year 🍴 Poolside restaurant 🚇 1 💲 $$

NORA BARNACLE HOUSE

This tiny cottage is the girlhood home of James Joyce's lady love, later his wife and life-long inspiration, Nora Barnacle. It can be found in a quiet steet close to the city center and was built around the beginning of the 20th century. Literary enthusiasts will enjoy perusing an interesting and enlightening collection of photographs and other exhibits pertaining to the Joyce's connections with Galway (the Joyces were one of the ancient tribes that founded the city).
➕ B2 ✉ 8 Bowling Green ☎ 091 564 743 🕐 Mon.–Sat. 10–5, May–Sep. 🚇 City Centre 💲 $

ROYAL TARA CHINA VISITOR CENTRE

You can tour the Royal Tara China factory and watch master craftspeople creating fine bone china as each piece passes through no fewer than 10 stages of production. Set in Tara Hall, a lovely Queen Anne-Georgian style mansion, the center has a wide variety including exclusive handpainted pieces and a barrelmen collection that will evoke a smile. For considerable price savings, it's worth taking a look at the slightly imperfect pieces.
➕ C2 ✉ Tara Hall, Mervue ☎ 091 751 301;

Festivities in Eyre Square, Galway

fax 091 757 574 🕐 Daily 9–8, Jul.–Sep.; 9–6, rest of year 🍴 Coffee shop 🚇 Half-hourly buses from Eyre Square to Mervue 💲 Free 🛈 Free tours conducted every hour 9:30–3:30

ST. NICHOLAS COLLEGIATE CHURCH

Tradition has it that Christopher Columbus worshipped here in 1477 during a stopover on his way to discover the New World. That would be quite appropriate, since this church is dedicated to the patron saint of all travelers. Built in 1320 on the site of an earlier chapel, this is Ireland's largest medieval church still in constant use. The church's unique shape came about when extensions were made in the 16th century. Cromwellian forces headquartered in the church in 1652 destroyed many of its features. Still intact, however, are tombstones from the 12th to 20th centuries, including that of a Norman crusader's tomb from the 12th or 13th century. Other outstanding relics are the unique free-standing holy water holder (*benitier*) and a carved font from the 16th or 17th century.
➕ B1 ✉ Lombard Street ☎ 091 564 648 🕐 Mon.–Sat. 9–5:45, Sun. 1–5:45, Apr.–Sep.; Mon.–Sat. 10–4, Sun. 1–4, rest of year 🚇 City Centre 💲 Free (donations welcome)

WALK: STROLL BACK IN TIME

Refer to route marked on city map on page 32.

There's hardly a street or lane in Galway city center that doesn't hark back to some facet of the city's history; take time to soak up the very spirit of the place. Allow 1 to 2 hours.

Leaving the tourist office, head along Forster Street to Eyre Square.
At the far end of the square on the left side, the Bank of Ireland dates to 1836, but the site reaches back to 1312 or earlier when the priory of the Knights Templars sat there. Inside a fine silver civic sword and great mace are on display. The sword was made in Galway in 1610 and the mace was made in Dublin 100 years later.

Leave the bank, cross the street and walk into Eyre Square.
This is the heart of the city and the setting for all kinds of street entertainment. Originally called the Fair Green, it was presented to the town in 1710 by Mayor Edward Eyre. President John F. Kennedy spoke to the people of Galway here in 1963, and its name was officially changed to John F. Kennedy Park, although you're not likely to hear it called anything other than Eyre Square.

The rusting sails of the fountain symbolize the dark brown sails of the Galway Hookers and Púcáns of the Claddagh fishing fleet. The most beloved statue in the square is that of Gaelic writer Padraic O'Conaire, a delightful storyteller who is portrayed, hat and pipe in place, sitting on a limestone wall and writing away in his notebook.

Turn left at the top corner of the square and continue down Williams Street to Shop Street.
Lynch's Castle stands on the corner of Shop and Abbeygate streets, its stone facade bearing coats of arms (including those of the Earl of Kildare and King Henry VII), gargoyles and exotic escutcheons.

Continue down Shop Street to Abbeygate Street, turn right down the street and left onto Market Street.
Around the corner, look for the Lynch Memorial Window, a marble plaque over a Gothic doorway commemorating a legend that historians dispute but others defend as the true origin of the expression "Lynch law." This is where in 1493 Mayor James Lynch carried out "stern and unbending justice" when he condemned his 19-year-old son, Walter, to death when he pleaded guilty to murder. Walter was held in such high esteem, however, that the town executioner refused to carry out the execution. The sorrowing elder Lynch embraced his son and did the deed himself. Hence, some say, the entry of justice by "Lynch law" into common use.

Just across the street, No. 8 Bowling Green is the Nora Barnacle House (see page 36).

Go back across Market Street and turn right.
On Market Street, keep an eye out for "marriage stones" set into some house walls, which display the coats of arms of two families united in marriage. Also look for the main gates of the Collegiate Church of St. Nicholas (see page 36).

Turn left into Churchyard Street and cross the intersection of Shop and Mainguard streets to High Street.
On your left you'll see the King's Head Pub. An ideal stop for refreshment and a look at the magnificently carved 1612 chimneypiece. Some say that the pub is haunted by King Charles I's restless spirit.

Continue down High Street to Cross Street, turn right, then take a short left into Kirwan's Lane. At the bottom of the lane turn right into Quay Street.
Continuing right, you enter the area known as Spanish Parade in memory of the Spanish merchant ships that once docked here. The air in the Fishmarket across the road once rang with the sound of Claddagh women selling their wares.

By the river, a sculpture commemorates Christopher Columbus' landing in 1477. Farther along is the Spanish Arch, a fine example of medieval walling. On the other side of the river across Wolfe Tone Bridge is the Claddagh (see page 35), much changed since its beginnings as a tiny village. Galway City Museum is next door to the Spanish Arch through which you can reach the pleasant quayside Long Walk.

Walk to the end of Merchant's Road, turn left and first right. Continue along Forster Street to return to the tourist office.

Connacht

REGIONAL SIGHTS

Key to symbols

✚ map coordinates refer to the region map on page 29; sights below are highlighted in yellow on the map

✉ address or location ☎ telephone number

🕐 opening times 🍴 restaurant on site or nearby

💲 admission charge: $$$ more than €6, $$ €4 to €6, $ less than €4 ℹ information

THE ARAN ISLANDS

Lying some 29 miles offshore almost directly across the mouth of Galway Bay, the three inhabited Aran Islands are Inishere (Inisírr, or eastern island), the smallest and nearest to the mainland (only 6 miles from Doolin, County, Clare); Inishmaan (Inis Meáin, or middle island); and Inishmore (Inis Mór, or big island), 7 miles from the Connemara coast. Ferries dock at Kilronan (Cill Rónan), the only safe harbor. Bleak and virtually treeless and with no significant hills or mountains, these three remote islands on the edge of Europe are linked geologically with the Burren in County Clare. The sheets of gray rock are reminiscent of a moonscape (see page 134).

The cracked limestone islands are steeped in tales of the hardy fishermen and farmers who developed a culture of self-sufficiency that reaches back before recorded history. Traces of the past remain in one of the most dramatic stone forts in western Europe, Dún Aengus. Early Christians left tiny churches and

A traditional alternative to modern transportation in Kilronan, the capital of Inishmore

oratories. And the daily use of the Gaelic language is still alive today.

Mere survival was an everyday challenge for those early inhabitants: for generations, fishermen braved the seas in frail wood-and-canvas curraghs (keel-less rowing boats), while those who stayed at home laboriously collected seaweed and sand to enrich the rocky soil and support enough produce to keep body and soul intact. They also built stout stone walls as protection from the strong Atlantic winds.

With the advent of electricity, modern plumbing and improved travel to and from the mainland, the centuries-old isolation of the islands has lifted and everyday life is easier. Day-to-day necessities arrive daily instead of monthly; larger, safer fishing vessels now augment catches of curraghs that still sail to sea, but in more limited numbers. And the traditional dress of the islanders is reserved for special occasions. Probably the most important attack on isolation has been the arrival of tourism, with the consequent opening of island homes and restaurants to accommodate visitors.

Upon arrival at Kilronan pier on Inishmore, you'll be greeted by lines of cars and minibuses for hire to explore the island with delightful and informative narratives by your driver-guide. There are bikes for rent as well. If you're a walker, this is the place for it, with stops to chat a bit with an old man smoking his pipe in an open doorway or a housewife hurrying along a lane to the village.

The Aran Way comprises three separate walks on each of the three islands: the Inis Mor Way (21 miles), the Inis Meain Way (5 miles) and the Inis Oirr Way (6.5 miles). The highest point is Baile na mBrocht at 400 feet.

Although Gaelic is the everyday language, the courteous islanders will speak to you in English. No matter how you choose to explore the island, don't miss the islands chief attraction, Dún Aengus. Dramatically perched some 300 feet above the sea, this 11-acre cliff-top stone fort inhabits one of the most peaceful spots in Ireland. Don't miss the cluster of ecclesiastical ruins known as the Seven Churches, and you can also visit

The Aran Islands – at the edge of Western Europe

Aran's Heritage Centre to see Robert Flaherty's 1934 "Man from Aran" film, which vividly depicts the harsh life of islanders in the past.

If you have a yen to visit Inishere or Inishmaan (where you're much more likely to see the traditional Aran style of dress than on Inishmore), ask any of the fishermen at the Kilronan pier and they'll arrange to take you over by curragh or other small boat. Both islands have small fortresses, churches and folk museums. And if you're really taken with the islands, the tourist office in Galway lists several good accommodations.

Several ferry companies serve the islands from Galway, Rossaveal and Doolin. Aer Arann fly small aircraft to all three islands. All transport services may be affected by weather and it is best to check schedules before your visit.

✚ A1

Tourist information ✉ Ireland West Tourism, Forster Street, Galway ☎ 091 537 700 🕐 Mon.–Sat. all year

Aer Arann ✉ Connemara Regional Airport, Inverin, Co. Galway ☎ 091 593 034; fax 091 593 238

Doolin Ferries ✉ Doolin, County Clare ☎ 065 707 4455; fax 065 707 4417

Island Ferries ✉ 4 Forster Street, Galway ☎ 091 568 903; fax 091 568 538

O'Brien Shipping (contact Galway tourist information ☎ 091 537 700)

Twelfth-century remains of the Cistercian abbey at Boyle

BOYLE

The Cistercian abbey that stands beside the rushing River Boyle in the heart of Boyle is the main reason to visit this quiet town. Dating from the late 12th century, it was founded as a daughter-house of Mellifont Abbey (see page 62). Unsuccessful in their efforts to keep the world's violence at bay, however, the abbey's monks were slaughtered and its walls torn down, leaving these impressive ruins to tell the grim story. The nave, with its Romanesque and Gothic arches, as well as the choir and transepts are still in good condition, and the restored 16th- to 17th-century gatehouse houses an interpretive center.

In the beautifully restored King House, with its delightful setting overlooking the River Boyle, historical exhibitions give the 18th-century mansion, home of the Earls of Kingston, an intriguing hands-on museum quality. Historical happenings from 1603 to 1957 are explained by the King family in one exhibit. In another you get to beat a regimental drum as you hear the exploits of the Connaught Rangers army regiment barracked here. In yet another, try your hand at building a brick vault as instructed by craftsmen who built and later restored King House. You can write with quill and ink, as well as join a clan feast in still another.

A short distance east of Boyle is Lough Key Forest, a mixed woodland of 850 acres and one of the country's loveliest parks. Especially interesting is the bog garden, with heathers and other small peat-growing plants, and the dozen or so islands in the lake: Trinity Island holds the ruins of a McDermott castle and a medieval priory, and Church Island also holds the remains of a medieval priory. Wildlife thrives in the park's varied habitats. Amenities include nature trails, ring forts, a central viewing tower, pony-and-cart rides, boats (the lake is navigable from the River Shannon via the River Boyle) and picnic grounds. Lovers of traditional music may want to make a pilgrimage to Keadue village (4 miles northeast of Lough Key). The blind harpist Turlough O'Carolan lies in Kilronan Abbey cemetery just west of the village. On the cemetery's arched gateway is inscribed: "Within this

Lough Key, a naturalist's paradise northeast of Boyle

churchyard lie the remains of Carolan, the last of the Irish bards who departed this life 25th March, 1738. R.I.P."

The nearby Tullyboy Farm is a marvelous treat for children. Centered around an 18th-century farmhouse, this family-run working farm has the usual animals plus some exotic breeds such as llamas, Jacob sheep, ostriches and Angora and Anglo Nubian goats. Soda bread is baked on the open hearth of the old kitchen, and there's a vintage threshing mill for the oats. There are pony rides, a playground and a picnic area to keep youngsters occupied.

⊞ C2
Tourist information ✉ King House, Boyle
☎ 079 62145 🕐 Daily 10–6, May–Sep.
Boyle Abbey ✉ N4 to Garrick ☎ 079 62604
🕐 Daily 10–6, Easter–Oct. 🖐 $
King House ✉ Main Street ☎ 079 63242; fax 079 63243 🕐 Daily 10–6, May–mid-Oct.; Sat.–Sun. 10–6, Apr. and late Oct.; pre-booked groups rest of year
☎ 079 63242; fax 079 68031 🍴 Coffee shop 🖐 $$
🛈 Children's activities and crafts shop
Lough Key Forest Park ✉ N4, just east of Boyle

☎ 079 62212 🕐 Daily dawn–dusk 🍴 Tearooms overlook the lake 🖐 $$ for parking
Kilronan Abbey ✉ 4 miles northeast of Lough Key
Tullyboy Animal Farm ✉ Tullyboy, 2 miles south of Boyle on N61, Boyle – Roscommon road ☎ 079 68031; fax 079 68031 🕐 Mon.–Sat. 10:30–6, Sun. noon–6, Easter–Sep. 🍴 Café 🖐 $$

CASTLEBAR

Castlebar is the county town of County Mayo; its most notable attraction is the Museum of Country Life. Housed in a carefully renovated 18th-century building, along with purpose-built extensions, this is the first branch of the National Museum to be located outside Dublin. Innovative displays, utilizing 50,000 items – crafts, household utensils, tools and clothing – reflect the lives of Ireland's people and their trades and illustrate the social history of Ireland over the past 200 years.

⊞ B2
✉ Turlough Park House ☎ 1890 687 386
🕐 Tue.–Sat. 10–5, Sun. 2–5 🍴 Restaurant 🖐 Free

The attractive grounds of Ashford Castle are a match for its exuberant architecture

CASTLEREA

The most impressive site in this unassuming town is Clonalis House, the home of the O'Conor Don, chieftain of the Clan O'Conor, one-time high kings of Ireland, traditional kings of Connaught and Europe's oldest family. Their ancestors can be traced back through 60 generations to 1100 BC. The house was built in 1878 and is largely furnished with Sheraton and Louis XV pieces. The house is richly furnished, and has an impressive collection of artifacts includes the harp of the bard Turlough O'Carolan (1670–1738), rare glass and china, paintings, antique lace, the ancient O'Conor inauguration stone and Gaelic manuscripts.

✚ B2

Clonalis House ✉ On the Roscommon–Castlebar road (N60) just west of Castlerea ☎ 0907 20014 ⏲ Daily 11–5, Jun.–mid-Sep. ▣ $$

CONG

Successive generations of Americans have loved Ireland as a direct result of the antics of John Wayne, Maureen O'Hara and Barry Fitzgerald as they romped through "The Quiet Man," the 1952 film that has become a classic. The main village street scenes took place near the cross in the market square of Cong, and the nearby general store was transformed into Cohan's Bar for the film. Many of the exterior shots were taken on the grounds of Ashford Castle – including the woodlands, the church, Squire Danaher's house and the salmon river with its arched bridge. The Heritage Centre has re-created a typical Irish cottage of the 1920s, and exhibitions in the Archaeological and Historical Interpretative Centre detail the plethora of relics in the Cong area.

Enter Cong's Augustinian abbey through this impessive stone doorway

The marvelous, fairyland architectural concoction that is Ashford Castle makes a superb luxury hotel much favored by international celebrities (President and Mrs. Reagan stayed here during their 1984 visit). No less marvelous are its grounds, with beautifully landscaped lawns sloping down to the island-dotted lake. The castle was originally built by the de Burgoes in 1228, and since then a French chateau-style mansion of the early 1700s and Sir Benjamin Guinness' additions in the mid-1800s have been incorporated – eccentric, to say the least.

At the edge of this picturesque little village is the Royal Abbey of Cong. This was built in 1120 by Turlough Mor O'Connor, high king of Ireland, and is the final resting place of Rory O'Connor, last high king, who died in 1198. Situated on the site of an earlier seventh-century St. Fechin community, this was an important ecclesiastical center for more than 700

years, and as many as 3,000 people once lived here.

Immediately east of Cong toward Cross lies the Plain of Moytura, where you'll find the Ballymagibbon Cairn. Dating from about 3,000 BC, the 60-foot-high, 287-foot-circumference cairn was erected to commemorate a fierce prehistoric battle between the Firbolg and de Danann tribes. It seems that the Firbolgs carried the day during the early fighting, and each warrior presented a stone and the head of a Danann to his king, who used the stones to build the cairn in honor of the grisly tribute.

On a happier note, nearby Moytura House (privately owned and not open to the public) was once the home of Sir William Wilde and wife Speranza, parents of Oscar Wilde.

 B2

Tourist information ✉ Abbey Street, Cong ☎ 092 46542 🕐 Mon.–Sat. 10–6, Mar.–Oct.; winter hours vary, phone to confirm

Quiet Man Heritage Cottage and Archaeological Historical Centre ✉ Circular Road, Cong ☎ 092 46089; fax 092 46448 🕐 Daily 10–5, Mar.–Oct.; otherwise by appointment 💲 $$

Ashford Castle ✉ Cong, .5 mile outside Cong on the right of the Galway Road ☎ 092 46003; fax 092 46260 🕐 Daily 10–5 💲 $$

Grand Tudor Gothic architecture at Kylemore Abbey

JOURNEY THROUGH SILENCE – CONNEMARA

To travel through Connemara is journeying through largely unpopulated spaces. The land-scape is constantly changed by shifting light and shade that generations of artists have struggled to capture on canvas. Rock-strewn fields contrast with glimpses of sandy strands at the sea's edge.

Natural Country Rhythms

Life is simple in Connemara. Keep your eyes open for turf being cut and dried in the boglands April through June. Especially along the coastal road you may see donkeys with loaded creels transporting the dried turf to be stacked against the winter's cold. Sheep-shearing is done by hand in June and July, often within the roofless walls of ruined cottages. Seaweed is traditionally harvested at the full and new moons. Thatchers are usually at work in September and October, and the biggest concentration of thatched cottages is between Ballyconneely and Roundstone and between Cleggan and the Clifden road by way of Claddaghduff.

At Roundstone and Cleggan, small trawlers fish year-round, with open lobster boats and curraghs setting out only in summer months. You may want to allow time to stroll two beautiful nearby beaches, Goirtin and Dog's Bay. If you're lucky, you'll happen on a curragh race in one of the coastal villages – be sure to stop and join in the conviviality.

Roundstone is also the home of master *bodhrán* maker Malachy Kearnes, whose

Connacht

workshop is in the IDA Craft Centre. The *bodhrán*, a one-sided goatskin frame drum, is an ancient Irish instrument, and Malachy's Celtic artist wife, Anne, decorates the finished *bodhráns* with colorful designs. A craftshop and Folk Instrument Museum are nearby.

You can be briefed on the shaping of Connemara from prehistoric times to the present in an audiovisual presentation at the Connemara Heritage and History Centre. There is a most spectacular view of Roundstone Bog, a 5,000-year-old burial site, a reconstruction of a *crannóg* (lake dwelling), ring fort and early Christian oratory.

Clifden

The August Connemara Pony Show is in Clifden, where the spirited bidding for the sturdy little animals takes on an air of ritual in a country-fair atmosphere. This is a great family day of eating, drinking and visiting with like-minded horse lovers. Summer evenings also bring traditional music in many of Clifden's hotel bars and pubs; check with the tourist office or the hotel's front desk.

One thing you won't want to miss in Clifden is the spectacular Sky Drive, a cliff road that forms a 9-mile circle around a peninsula and opens up vast seascapes. It's well signposted from Clifden. Boats are also available (through most accommodations) for deep-sea fishing expeditions for mackerel, blue shark, conger, cod, ling and many other varieties.

North of Clifden, Cleggan is the mainland departure point for Inishbofin Island, a place of great tranquility, wide beaches and stunning views.

Mountains and Moors

Stretching south near the 19th-century Quaker village of Letterfrack is the 3,800-acre Connemara National Park, encompassing mountains, bogs, heaths and grasslands, and crisscrossed by nature walks through beautiful woodlands and surrounding hills. Irish red deer and herds of Connemara ponies roam these same grounds, and birdwatchers will delight in the variety of winged species. Allow time

to visit the park's visitor center with its informative audiovisual presentation and exhibition and perhaps walk one of its shorter nature trails.

To the east of Letterfrack is magnificent Kylemore Abbey with its picture-postcard setting of woodlands on the banks of Pollacappal Lough and impressive neo-Gothic facade reflected in the lake's mirror surface. The stone mansion dates from the 19th century, when it was built as a private residence. It is now home to an order of Benedictine nuns who have for many years conducted an international girls' school, a thriving pottery industry and crafts shop.

Not to be missed is the beautifully restored Gothic chapel, which can be reached by a footpath that goes along the lakeside. Their recently restored walled Victorian garden is the largest in Ireland and is accessed through a marvelous wilderness walk.

Coastal Views and Butterflies

Letterfrack's Oceans Alive Sealife Centre and Seaside Park bring alive the Connemara coastal oceans, most vividly through scenic and wildlife coastal cruises aboard the *Queen of Connemara*, and sealife exhibits and an aquarium. On the grounds are sandy coves, picnic areas, children's play areas and a craft shop. And on Sunday afternoons, there are children's plays and Irish music sessions.

Tourist information ✉ Galway Road, Clifden ☎ 095 21163; fax 095 21887 ⏰ Daily 9–5:45, Jun.–Aug.; phone for opening times Mar.–May and Sep.–Oct.
Roundstone Musical Instruments ✉ IDA Craft Centre, Roundstone ☎ 095 35808; fax 095 35980 ⏰ Daily 9–7, Mar.–Oct.; closed Sun., rest of year
Connemara National Park ✉ Letterfrack, Clifden-Westport Road (N59) ☎ 095 41054 ⏰ Park: open all year; visitors center: daily 10–6:30, Jul.–Aug.; 10–5:30, Apr.–Jun. and Sep. to mid-Oct. 🍴 Tearoom 🍷 $$
Kylemore Abbey and Garden ✉ Connemara, near Letterfrack ☎ 095 41146; fax 095 41145 ⏰ Abbey: daily 9–5:30. Gardens: daily 10:30–4:30, Easter–Oct. Closed Good Friday and Dec. 25–31 🍴 Restaurant, 🍷 $$
Ocean's Alive Sealife Centre and Seaside Park
✉ Renvyle Peninsula, Connemara ☎ 095 43473; fax 095 43911 ⏰ Daily 10–7 🍴 Café 🍷 $$

Connacht

The 16th-century tower house of Thoor Ballylee

GORT

Gort is surrounded by history, which includes the seventh-century monastic settlement of Kilmacduagh, and five castles within a 5-mile radius. The poet William Butler Yeats bought Thoor Ballylee, a 16th-century castle keep, for just £35 ($56) in 1917 when it was not much more than a ruin. After restoring it to a habitable state, he summered here until 1929. Poems written about or at Thoor Ballylee are included in his book of poems *The Tower*. His life and times are portrayed in an audiovisual presentation.

The town is much associated with Yeats' contemporary, Lady Augusta Gregory, whose house at Coole was demolished in the 1940s. There must always have been creative inspiration in this tranquil setting, for this patron of the arts and founder of the Abbey Theatre attracted many of Ireland's most illustrious literary figures – writers W. B. Yeats, George Bernard Shaw and Sean O'Casey all drew encouragement and nourishment from stimulating and appreciative conversations while visiting Coole House. Sadly, only ruins mark the place where the house once stood – the grounds are now a nature reserve. You can, however, take a look at the famous

"Autograph Tree" for carved names of literary guests.

Such literati also had links with Dunguaire Castle. In the early 1900s it was a country retreat for Irish writer Oliver St. John Gogarty, who held regular literary gatherings. Furnishings of the castle reflect its medieval beginnings, and the banquet and literary evening attractions are much more intimate than those at Bunratty and Knappogue (see page 144). The entertainment reflects Ireland's bardic tradition and celebrates the richness of this country's literary and musical past.

✚ B1

Tourist information ✉ Thoor Baliyee, Gort ☎ 091 631 436 🕐 Mon.–Sat.10–6, May–Sep.

Yeats Tower (Thoor Ballylee) ✉ Signposted near Gort, half a mile off N18 (Galway to Limerick road) and half a mile off N66 (Gort to Loughrea road) ☎ 091 631 436 May–Sep., 091 563 081 rest of year; fax 091 537 733 🕐 Daily 10–6, May.–Sep. 🚶 $$ ℹ Picnic area, tourist office and exchange bureau

Coole Park ✉ 2 miles north of Gort, due west of N18 ☎ 091 631 804 🕐 Vistors center: daily 10–6, Jun.–Aug.; 10–5 Sep.; Tue.–Sun. 10–5, Apr.–May. Grounds open all year 🚶 Visitors' center: $$; grounds: free

Dunguaire Castle ✉ Kinvarra 10 miles northwest of Gort on the N18 Galway road ☎ 061 360 788; fax 061 361 020 🕐 Daily 9:30–5:30 (last admission at 4:30), May–early Oct. 🚶 Castle: $$

Read the runes inscribed on Sligo's monument to W. B. Yeats

Connacht

SLIGO

Sligo (Sligeach, Shelly Place) grew up around a ford of the River Garavogue, which rises in Lough Gill and tumbles over swift rapids as it approaches its estuary. The town's strategic position gave it early prominence as a seaport, and as a religious center, it is the cathedral town of both a Catholic and Protestant diocese. While many come to Sligo for the sights associated with the poet William Butler Yeats, it would be a mistake not to see the hightlights of the old town itself.

Its streets are filled with quaint old shopfronts and 19th-century buildings. The ruins of the Dominican Abbey on Abbey Street represent the town's only surviving medieval building. Kings and princes of Sligo were brought for burial here, and the abbey often suffered raids, eventually closing in 1641. The altar here is one of the few surviving medieval altars in Ireland.

On Adelaide Street, the Cathedral of the Immaculate Conception is a massive limestone structure of Renaissance Romanesque style. St. John's Church on John Street dates from the mid-1700s and was designed by the same architect as Leinster House (see page 80), the seat of the Irish government in Dublin.

The Town Hall on Quay Street dates from 1865 – a graceful Italian Renaissance building that legend says stands on the site of a 17th-century Cromwellian fort. At Teeling and Chapel streets, the Courthouse incorporates part of an earlier courthouse. In 1832, when cholera swept over Sligo, the building housed coffin builders. You can't miss the impressive Pollexfen Ships Building at the corner of Adelaide and Wine streets; the large stone building originally belonged to the largest ship owners in Sligo. It was Yeats' grandfather who, on owning the building, added the tower as a lookout point for his ships returning to port.

There's no shortage of nighttime entertainment in Sligo. The Hawks Well Theatre was the first purpose-built theater in western Ireland, and it places a strong emphasis on Irish playwrights. Productions are performed by leading Irish theater companies, with an occasional evening of poetry, musical concerts and traditional song, dance, drama and comedy. It's fairly easy to find traditional music and ballads in Sligo pubs. However, since the schedule for such happenings is often a non-schedule, be sure to check with the tourist office for information

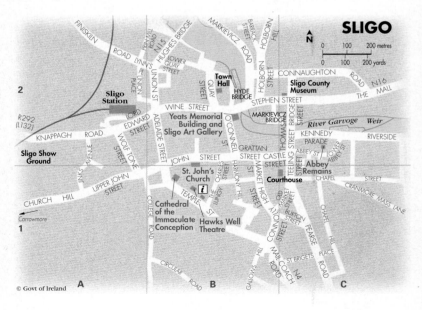

The graceful Italian Renaissance tower of Sligo Courthouse

about pubs which are likely to have musical entertainment.

For Yeats' devotees, it comes as no surprise that Sligo offers a wealth of information and memorabilia: For two weeks every August, Sligo breathes, eats and sleeps the incomparable poet as the Yeats International Summer School presents seminars, lectures, workshops, poetry readings and dramas that draw throngs of dedicated scholars from around the world. However, the ultimate source of information on W. B. Yeats can be found at the Yeats Society, headquartered in the red-brick 1895 Yeats Memorial Building on Hyde Bridge. Inside, the Sligo Art Gallery's plethora of exhibits relating to the poet include his complete works in first editions and his 1923 Nobel Prize for Literature.

Sligo has intrigued painters as much as writers, and Yeats had no family monopoly on fascination with this countryside – his painter brother, Jack Yeats, sought to capture it on canvas, and there's an extensive collection of his paintings and drawings.

County Sligo encompasses some of Ireland's most wondrous scenery – the sort of sea and mountains and far-flung vistas that shaped Yeats' life and work. From boyhood stays in Magheraboy with his grandparents to the end of his life when he was laid to rest in Drumcliff churchyard, Yeats' imagination was fired by local legends of ancient heroes who lived out their sagas in this part of Ireland and left the countryside strewn with mementos of their passing; cairns, dolmens, passage graves and prehistoric relics continue to bear silent witness to the lives that so engaged him.

Places associated with Yeats are marked by simple signposts inscribed with appropriate verses, but before rambling through Yeats Country, go by the tourist office or a Sligo bookshop and pick up the excellent booklet *The Yeats Country*, which tells you which poems were written about which places. The Yeats Country drive on pages 50–52 also takes you to some of these spots: beautiful Lough Gill, where you'll find his Isle of Inisfree, and the cairn at Knocknarea's summit where

according to "passionate Maeve is stony-still." His words about this mystical, magical part of Ireland cannot be bettered, and you will find yourself recalling them again and again.

Scattered over the face of the county are traces of the prehistoric races who lived here during three main periods: the Late Stone Age (Neolithic, 2500–2000 BC); the Bronze Age (2000–500 BC); and the Early Iron Age (500 BC to AD 500). The tourist office has a detailed leaflet, *Archaeology in County Sligo*, that tells you where to find the most important court cairns, portal dolmens, passage graves, ring forts and gallery graves. In the immediate vicinity of Sligo town, you'll find Carrowmore (south near Ballysodare), Ireland's largest group of megalithic tombs.

✚ C3 (regional map on page 29)

Tourist information ✚ B1 ✉ Temple Street ☎ 071 61201; fax 071 60360 ◷ Mon.–Fri. 9–7, Sun 10–6, late Jun.–Aug.; Mon.–Fri. 9–5, Sat 10–2, Apr.–late Jun., Sep.; Mon.–Fri. 9–5, rest of year

Sligo Art Gallery ✚ B2 ✉ Yeats Memorial Building, Hyde Bridge ☎ 071 42212 ◷ Mon.–Sat. 10–5:30 ▯ Free

Hawks Well Theatre ✚ B1 ✉ Temple Street ☎ 071 69802 ◷ Box office: Mon.–Sat. 10–6

Connacht

DRIVE: YEATS COUNTRY

Duration: 1–2 days

Steeped in echoes of the poet William Butler Yeats and prehistory, you'll find in this corner of Ireland a happy unison of wooded lakes, bare mountaintops and Atlantic seascapes. This 98-mile tour starts from the tourist office on Temple Street in Sligo.

Take the N15 for 5 miles to Drumcliff.
Under bare Ben Bulben's head
In Drumcliff churchyard Yeats is laid
An ancestor was rector there
Long years ago; a church stands near,
By the road an ancient cross,
No marble, no conventional phrase;
On limestone quarried near the spot,
By his command these words are cut:
Cast a cold eye
On life, on death,
Horseman, pass by!

Yeats' poem describes Drumcliff completely, and his grave can be found easily in the Protestant churchyard. Yeats died in 1939 in the south of France and was buried in a cemetery overlooking the Mediterranean Sea. His remains were brought home to his beloved Sligo in 1948 and placed here, as he wished, in the shadow of Benbulben. The road runs through a monastic site to the church where the poet's grandfather was rector.

Continue on the N15 and almost
immediately take a turn left for 4 miles
to Lissadell.

Yeats was a regular visitor to the Greek-revival style Lissadell House. The slightly forbidding classical facade hides the romance captured in his poem in memory of the Gore-Booth sisters, Eva (of whom he was particularly fond) and Constance, which begins:

The light of evening, Lissadell,
Great windows open to the south,
Two girls in silk kimonos, both
Beautiful, one a gazelle.

Constance became the Countess Markievicz, a leader in the Easter Rising of 1916, and the first woman to be elected to Westminster, although she never took her seat. The 1830s limestone mansion, still owned by the Gore-Booth family, has a charming music room and a dining room with intriguing murals. The striking two-story entrance hall is lined with Doric columns and features a beautiful double staircase. Among the multitude of family documents are diaries of Robert Gore-Booth, whose charity to the poor during famine years forced him to mortgage the estate. The house is set in fine parkland near the sea, supposedly the warmest bathing water in the country, where seals can be spotted basking on the sandbanks.

Drive through the parkland, rejoin the
road and turn left, then right at the fork.
Soon after that, turn right and continue

to the village of Grange. Turn left to rejoin the N15 for Bundoran.

Contrasting with the placid towns and coastal villages of the northwest, the busy seaside resort of Bundoran offers many attractions, a good beach and cliff walks. Southwest of Bundoran, at Streedagh, a small park commemorates the place where three vessels of the Spanish Armada foundered in 1588. Members of the crew who struggled ashore from the overladen ships found little help on land.

Take the R280 for 3 miles to Kinlough.

This attractive village at the north end of Lough Melvin is good for coarse and salmon fishing. On the shore is the ruins of Rossclogher Abbey, and on an artificial island are the remains of the MacClancy Castle (known as Rossclogher Castle), where nine survivors of the Armada were given refuge.

Follow the R281 along the Lough Melvin shore for 8 miles, then turn right onto the R282 for Manorhamilton.

This unassuming village in County Leitrim stands in an area of untouched mountain valleys with lofty peaks, lush fertile slopes, steep clefts and gray cliff walls. It's overlooked by a ruined castle that was built at the meeting of four mountain valleys by the Scottish 17th-century planter Sir Frederick Hamilton, who gave his name to the village.

Take the N16 for Sligo. After 7 miles turn right onto an unclassified road for Glencar Lake.

Glencar is a beautiful lake; the steep valley slopes are clothed with mixed woodland, a profusion of rare plants and luxuriously heathered mountaintops. Glencar waterfall, white with spray, cascades down from a rocky headland and is immortalized by Yeats in his poem *The Stolen Child*.

At the end of the lakeside road, turn right toward Sligo on the N16, then left to Parke's Castle Visitor Centre on the R286.

Although its name comes from the English family who moved in during the 1620 plantation of this part of Ireland, the beautifully restored Parke's Castle is a fortified manor house that was originally the home of the O'Rourke clan, rulers of the kingdom of Breffni. The audiovisual show not only tells this story (including how the Parke family unashamedly dismantled a neighboring castle for materials to use in

Glencar waterfall tumbles down through the trees and rocks

their own), but also includes a wealth of information on other points of interest in the area. From Parke's Castle, there is a superb view of Lough Gill, and to the southwest is the Isle of Innisfree for which Yeats yearned – "where peace comes dropping slow" – and to which you can take a cruise from Parke's Castle (including one at sunset). If you explore the lake, you'll find a sweat-house, medieval Ireland's answer to the sauna.

Continue on the R286, then turn right onto the R288 for Dromahair or Carrick-on-Shannon, then turn right on the R287 for Sligo. After 2.5 miles turn right again, following the R287 past the sign for Innisfree to Dooney Rock Forest, before rejoining the N4.

This corner of Lough Gill reveals forests and paths to satisfy any enthusiastic walker and great views of the lough. Dooney Rock Forest bears the vestiges of a once important oak forest. Here you can see the "twining branches," two linked oaks. Yeats wrote of "the Fiddler of Dooney," who made folk "dance like the waves of the sea." The poem has inspired a Fiddler of Dooney competition for the champion fiddler of Ireland. It's held in Sligo in July.

Cairns Hill Forest Park marks the two cairns on Belvoir and Cairns peaks. A legend holds that these cairns are the burial places

The Georgian Lissadell House, built in 1834 by Sir Robert Gore-Booth

of the warriors, Omra and Romra. Omra fell in love with Romra's daughter Gille, meaning beauty. When a mortal battle ensued after the lovers were discovered by Romra, Gille drowned herself, and Lough Gill was formed from the tears of her nursemaid.

Travel south on the N4, then turn right on the R292 for Rathcarrick and Strandhill.
Great Atlantic breakers crash onto the beach at Strandhill, making the small village a favored place for surfing championships. If you prefer calmer waters drive to Culleenamore where it is safer and quiet. The town nestles beneath the cairn-capped Knocknarea mountain. This is the great Misgaun Maeve, an unopened cairn about 200 feet in diameter and 80 feet high that archeologists believe covers a vast passage grave, but legend insists is the burial monument to Maeve, the warrior queen of Connacht. If you climb to the summit of Knocknarea, Sligo tradition suggests that you add a stone to the cairn as a protection against the fairies.

Among the fields below Knocknarea at Carrowmore is one of Europe's largest concentrations of megalithic tombs. Visitors are inevitably quite moved at the sight of this sacred burial place of more than 100 passage graves. The earliest tombs are said to predate the famous passage grave at Newgrange by about 700 years.

Take the R292 for 5 miles back to Sligo.

Lissadell House ✉ Drumcliff, off N15 (main Sligo to Donegal road) 8 miles north of Sligo ☎ 071 63150 ⏺ Mon.–Sat. 10:30–12:15 and 2–4:15, Jun. to mid-Sep. 🎫 $$
Parke's Castle ✉ Fivemile Bourne, Co. Leitrim, on the north shore of Lough Gill ☎ 071 64149 ⏺ Daily 10–6, Mar.–Oct. 🍴 Tearoom 🎫 $$
Carrowmore Megalithic Cemetery ✉ Carrowmore Visitors Centre. Signposted on N15 from Sligo, N4 from the south ☎ 071 61534 ⏺ Daily 10:30–4:45, May–Oct.; open to groups on request during winter months 🎫 $$

STROKESTOWN AND ROSCOMMON

Many Irish towns and villages reveal their Georgian origins in wide streets, but Strokestown, said to have the widest main street in Ireland, is exceptional in that it was originally modeled on Vienna's Ringstrasse. The town is little more than an adjunct to Strokestown Park House, one of Ireland's finest great houses, which lies beyond the Gothic triple arch on this main street. Dating from the early 1700s, the 45-room Palladian house incorporates parts of an earlier tower house. The reception rooms, galleried kitchen and some bedrooms and nurseries are furnished in its original style. The restored walled "pleasure garden" invites a stroll. Elaborate vaulted stables in the south wing of the house hold the fascinating Irish Famine Museum.

Roscommon Castle ruins date to 1269

Strokestown Park was the family seat of the Pakenham Mahon family from the 1600s to 1979, and family archives that were purchased with the house shed light on the heart-wrenching plight of the Irish poor during the devastating years of the potato famine. They also form an authentic platform for the museum's critical view of contemporary world poverty and hunger.

South of Strokestown, the county town of Roscommon also lies to the west of Lough Ree and has many fine old buildings, including several churches, the Old Military Barracks, the Court House and the Old Jail, which had an 18th-century female executioner called "Lady Betty." Condemned to death herself, allegedly for murdering her son, she volunteered to step into the breach when the hangman was ill on condition that her life be spared. She was subsequently appointed for the job with a salary and accommodation at the jail where she remained for about 30 years. She drew charcoal portraits of some of her clients, whom she dispatched from a hinged board outside her third-floor window.

Overlooking the town, ruins of drum towers are all that remain of the 13th-century castle that once stood here. After changing hands between the O'Kelly and O'Conor clans over the centuries, it finally fell into those of Cromwellian troops, who left behind the destruction of all but the towers. The remains of Félim O'Conor, 13th-century king of Connacht, rest in the ruins of a Dominican priory in a tomb decorated with effigies of gallowglasses (soldiers of fortune).

Three miles southwest of Roscommon, the ruins of Fuerty, a Franciscan church, mark the setting for the slaughter of 100 priests by a local tyrant. Among the interesting headstones in the graveyard is that of a blacksmith, with carvings depicting an anvil, bellows and tongs, and that of a shepherd with his crook and sheep.

✚ C2

Tourist information ✉ John Harrison Memorial Hall, Roscommon ☎ 0903 26342 ◉ Mon.–Sat.10–6, Jun.–Aug.

Strokestown Park House, Garden and Irish Famine Museum ✉ Strokestown, on N5 (Dublin – Castlebar road) ☎ 078 33013; fax 078 33712 ◉ Daily 10:30–5:30, mid-Mar.–Oct. 🍴 Restaurant 💵 $$$

WESTPORT

With an octagonal center and lime trees lining both sides of the river, Clew Bay at its feet and a wealth of grand Georgian buildings, Westport is one of western Ireland's most charming market towns and is designated a Heritage Town of Ireland. The Thursday morning market at the Octagon brings the farmers into town, and there is a frenzy of buying and selling

An attractive 18th-century corner of Westport

clothes, produce and novelties. It's even more lively when the annual arts festival takes place in late September with live music, visual arts, theater and lots more.

Westport's main sight is Westport House, a lovely old Georgian mansion set in fine parkland near the quay. It dates back to 1731, but sits on the grounds of an earlier O'Malley castle, the dungeons of which are now visited by children who are happily "terrified" by horrors installed for their entertainment. Lord and Lady Altamont are in residence here, and over the years they have turned their estate into a stylish virtual museum of Irish memorabilia and craftsmanship, with a magnificent drawing room, two dining rooms, a long gallery and grand entrance hall. Up the marble staircase, four bedrooms hold such treasures as state robes and coronets and 200-year-old Chinese wallpaper. On the grounds there's an animal park, rides and amusements – including a log flume ride – and boating and fishing on the lake and river.

Between Louisburgh and Westport, Clew Bay opens before you as the road passes through stony, barren hillsides and touches the bay at several points. The 16th-century pirate queen Grace O'Malley *(Granuaile)* roamed these waters freely, darting in and out of the bay to

attack merchant ships who sailed coastal waters. When summoned to London by Queen Elizabeth I in 1575, she refused to bow in submission, proudly proclaiming herself "Queen of Clew Bay." The square tower near the harbor on Clare Island was her refuge and stronghold, and splendid views of Clew Bay and the mountains of Connemara and Mayo undoubtedly explain her deep love of the island, which also holds a 15th-century abbey and an ancient promontory fort on its southern cliffs. Regular mailboat sailings from Roonagh Pier (4 miles west of Louisburgh) carry present-day visitors to Clare Island year-round.

Five miles west of Westport, Croagh Patrick, Ireland's holy mountain, rises to a height of 2,510 feet. St. Patrick is believed to have fasted on the mountaintop for 40 days. Each year modern-day pilgrims climb the stony paths in their bare feet on the last Sunday in July for a four o'clock morning Mass at its top.

🕂 A2

Tourist information ✉ James Street ☎ 098 25711; fax 098 26709 🕓 Daily 9–6:45, Jul.–Aug.; Mon.– Sat.–9–5:45, rest of year (Sat. 9–12:45, Nov.–Feb.) **Westport House** ✉ Westport ☎ 098 25430 or 098 27766; fax 098 25206 🕓 Daily 11:30–5:30, Jul.–Aug.; Mon.–Fri. 1:30–5:30, Jun.; daily 2–5, Sep.; Sat.–Mon. 2–5, May 🍴 Tearoom 💲 $$$

DRIVE: ACHILL ISLAND AND COUNTY MAYO

Duration: 2 days

The ghost of pirate queen Grace O'Malley will follow you on this 207-mile tour that travels to Achill Island, Ireland's most scenic island and home to one of O'Malley's many strongholds.

Starting from Westport's tourist office on The Mall, take the N59 north for 8 miles to Newport.

Picturesque little Newport, which dates from the 17th century, faces Clew Bay and is sheltered by mountains. Its neo-Romanesque Catholic church was built in 1914 and features a superb stained-glass window of the Last Judgment designed by Harry Clarke.

Four miles west, Rockfleet Castle, sometimes called Carrigahowley Castle, is another of Grace O'Malley's strongholds, where the indomitable pirate queen came to live permanently after her second husband died in 1583.

Follow the N59 west to Mulrany, then the R319 to Achill Island, 28 miles.

Connected to the mainland by a bridge, Achill

Island is the largest of Ireland's islands. Only 15 miles long and 12 miles wide, the island is a scenic mix of soaring cliffs, golden beaches, heathery boglands and tiny villages. Fishing for shark and other big-game fish is excellent, and you'll find boats and guides for hire. The Atlantic Drive is spectacular, climbing from gently rolling mountain foothills, past stretches of sandy beaches, and through charming villages with excellent views of the sea, Clew Bay and the mainland. With a sheer drop on the seaward side, it will keep your heart in your throat most of the way. Yet, it's easy to see why Grace O'Malley fell in love with Achill's unspoiled wildness and profound peacefulness. Beside her Kildownet Castle are the ruins of a small 12th-century church. At the center of holiday activities is Keel, which has a fine sandy beach and a small harbor with fishing and sightseeing boats for rent. Viewed from a boat, the sea-carved rocks below the Menawn cliffs at the eastern end of the beach take on fanciful shapes. At Doogort, nestled at the foot of Slievemore, the fascinating Seal Caves cut far into the cliffs of Slievemore.

Take the R319 back to Mulrany, then turn north on the N59 for the drive to Crossmolina, passing through Ballycroy

Connacht

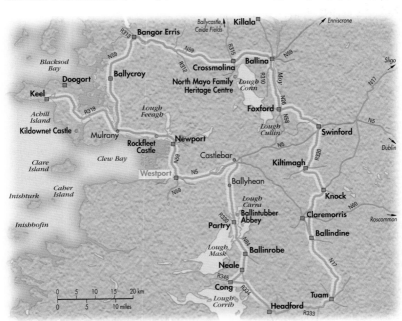

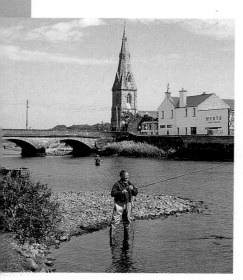

Fishing in the River Moy at Ballina

and Bangor Erris (where the N59 turns sharply east).

At Crossmolina, on the shores of Lough Conn, you'll find the huge genealogical data bank of the North Mayo Family Heritage Centre. Anyone with County Mayo family connections can track down their ancestors by searching through church registers, wills, leases and even school rollbooks. The Heritage Centre displays a collection of farm implements (including the unique *gowl-gob* spade) and household items from rural life of long ago.

Northward via the R315 to Ballycastle is Céide Fields. More than 5,000 years old, it's the oldest enclosed farm system in the world revealed virtually intact underneath the bogs. The 12-square-mile site holds relics of Stone Age rural life and includes stone walls that surrounded the ancient community and megalithic tombs. A 20-minute presentation in the visitor center sets the mood for a guided tour of the site.

Continue on the N59 to Ballina.

Founded in 1730 on the River Moy, Ballina is County Mayo's largest town. An important fishing center, it celebrates its week-long festival each July. Beside the 1892 Cathedral of St. Muiredach with its fine stained-glass window, are the ruins of an Augustinian abbey built about 1427. Eight miles north of Ballina via the R314 is Killala, which has a wealth of antiquities inluding one of the finest round towers in the country. On the east side of Killala Bay is the pleasant 3-mile beach resort of Enniscrone (N59 northeast then turn left onto the R297), whose most noted attractions are bath houses that specialize in curative submersions in hot, seaweed-enriched soakings.

Take the N57/N26 south to Foxford.

Foxford is famous for its woolen mills set up by a forward-looking nun in 1892 as a means of providing work for the many unemployed in the area. Since then, it has grown into one of the country's leading mills, producing world-renowned blankets, tweeds and rugs. View the visitor center's multimedia presentation of the mill's history, then go on the industrial tour.

Continue on the N57/N26 through Foxford on to Swinford. Follow the R320 south to Kiltimagh, then turn southeast on the R323 for 5 miles to reach Knock.

The little church in the village of Knock has become a shrine, for it was here in 1879 that an apparition of Our Lady was seen at the Church of St. John the Baptist. Now officially designated a Marian Shrine, the magnificent basilica built on the grounds has welcomed visitors from around the world, including Pope John Paul II and Mother Teresa of Calcutta. More than 1.5 million pilgrims visit the shrine annually to attend one of the seven daily Masses. The 32 pillars in the ambulatory were contributed by all counties in the country and the four medieval-style windows represent the four provinces of Ireland. On the south side of the basilica, the Knock Folk Museum portrays life in rural Ireland at the end of the 19th century.

Take the N17 south to Tuam.

A thriving commercial and agricultural center under James I's charter of 1613, Tuam was altered to include a diamond-shaped town "square" on which all roads converged. Tuam claims Ireland's first industrial museum, the Mill Museum – an operational corn mill with mill wheel and other industrial exhibits. St. Mary's Cathedral, founded in 1130 and rebuilt in the 19th century, is a fine example of Gothic-revival architecture and incorporates a 12th-century chancel with magnificent windows. The town's well-adorned but incomplete 12th-century high cross stands in its grounds.

Above: Interior of the 20th-century giant
hexagonal church at Knock
Inset: Knock's modern basilica

Leave Tuam on the N17 southwest. After
3 miles, turn west on the R333 for 9 miles
to reach Headford. Take the R334
northwest for just over 6 miles, then turn
left to Cong via the R346.

The little town of Cong was the setting for the
popular 1950s film "The Quiet Man." That,
however, is the least of its claims to fame.
More notable are the ruins of the Royal
Abbey of Cong and the impressive Ashford
Castle (see page 43).

From Cong take the R345 northeast to
rejoin the R334 and turn left to reach
Ballinrobe. Follow the N84 to Castlebar.

The little town of Partry lies between Cong
and Castlebar, 4 miles north of which you will
find the restored Ballintubber Abbey. This is
the only church in the English-speaking world
with a history of uninterrupted services since
the seventh century. What makes this all the
more remarkable is that Catholic Mass has
been celebrated within its walls since 1216
despite years of religious suppression, two
burnings and the assault of Cromwellian
troops. During these times, supplicants
sometimes had to kneel before the altar in
secret, and under open skies when there
was no roof.

Take the N60 road southwest, back
to Westport.

North Mayo Family Heritage Centre ✉ Enniscoe,
Castlehill, Ballina, about 2 miles south of Crossmolina
(off R315) on Lough Conn ☎ 096 31809; fax 096 31885
🕐 Mon.–Fri. 9–6, mid-Apr. to mid-Sep. (weekends
2–6); Mon.–Fri. 9–4, rest of year 🏛 Museum: $$;
genealogical center: free

Céide Fields ✉ About 22 miles west of Ballina, 5
miles northwest of Ballycastle on the R314 ☎ 096
43325; fax 096 43261 🕐 Daily 10–6, Jun.–Sep.; 10–5,
mid-Mar.–May and Oct.; 10–5, Nov. 🏛 $$

Foxford Woollen Mills ✉ St. Joseph's Place,
Foxford. The mills are about 20 miles north of
Castlebar en route to Ballina ☎ 094 56756; fax 094
56794 🕐 Mon.–Sat. 10–6, Sun. 2–6 🍴 Restaurant
🏛 $$ ℹ Shop, art gallery, tourist office and
exchange bureau

Knock Shrine and Knock Folk Museum ✉ Knock
☎ 094 88100; fax 094 88295 🕐 Basilica: daily 24
hours; museum: daily 10–6, May–Oct. 🏛 Basilica:
free; museum: $$

Ballintubber Abbey ✉ Claremorris, on N84 Cong to
Castlebar road ☎ 094 30934; fax 094 30018
🕐 Daily 9 a.m.–midnight 🏛 Free (donations are
always welcome)

LEINSTER

"THE gentle landscape of Leinster is one of green fields, rolling hills laced with eye-pleasing valleys and deserted beaches, framed by the soft slopes of the Wicklow Mountains."

The mighty headland of the Howth peninsula, north of Dublin Bay

LEINSTER

entered the world stage as a major cosmopolitan capital city.

The 12 counties that make up the Leinster region – Carlow, Dublin, Kildare, Kilkenny, Laois, Longford, Louth, Meath, Offaly, Westmeath, Wexford and Wicklow – have collectively borne witness to most of the complex historical events that have shaped modern-day Ireland. And at its center is Dublin, which has now

Long before Norsemen arrived in AD 840 to found Dubh-Linn (Black Pool) on the banks of the Liffey as an important trading port, prehistoric and pre-Christian settlers set up whole communities along glacial folds that edged ancient lakes. Over the centuries, lakes became bogland and nature brushed rolling hills and miles of tilled fields with all of Ireland's famed "forty shades of green" as they merged softly into the marshy browns of the bogs. The resultant landscape is pockmarked

with the remains of ancient burial sites, religious buildings, castles and other tangible records of each wave of early invaders who stayed on to become inhabitants. It was, in fact, from the iron-bladed spears *(laighens)* of invading Celts that Leinster took its name.

Leinster might well be called the "Royal Province" of Ireland. It has been a seat of power from the days of prehistoric clans who constructed the great burial mound at Newgrange to the high kings of Ireland who held court on the Hill of Tara, and from the days of Celtic, Viking and Norman conquerors to appointees of English kings and queens.

In such a setting, it is little wonder that a legacy of myths and legends endure to this day, legends that blend magically with this region's long factual history, and that have been passed from generation to generation by bardic poets and storytelling *seanashai*. Tales still abound of gods, goddesses and the heroic deeds of Finn MacCool (see page 199) and his valiant band of Fianna warriors, as well as the military and romantic exploits of the high kings.

It was just northeast of Dublin at Clontarf that the Vikings were finally

Leinster

Looking across from Lacken to the Wicklow Mountains

The remains of the old monastery of Clonmacno is beside the River Shannon in County Offaly

defeated in 1014 by Brian Ború, some say the greatest of Ireland's high kings. Englishman Oliver Cromwell arrived in 1649 and proceeded to cut a swath of slaughter from Dublin to Drogheda that claimed thousands of men, women and children as victims. And the effects of William of Orange's overwhelming victory at the 1690 Battle of the Boyne, which so profoundly changed the course of Irish history, are echoed in headlines of today.

Set amid County Wicklow's most beautiful mountain scenery, Glendalough and its twin lakes reflect the tranquility of its ecclesiastical past. To the south of The Pale's fortifications, County Wexford already bore the scars of Viking occupation when Cromwell's rampaging forces passed this way. The arrival of Normans in 1169 and the disastrous uprising of 1798 also left their imprint on that beleaguered county. Normans gravitated

Kildare's own Curragh track. Counties Louth and Meath still wear the mantle of royalty, from the little town of Kells, birthplace of the magnificent eighth-century *Book of Kells,* to the stirring Hill of Tara, to Mellifont Abbey (Ireland's first Cistercian monastery, founded in 1142), to Newgrange's enigmatic burial mound that predates the Egyptian pyramids and Britain's Stonehenge.

Away from the coast, vestiges remain of Athlone's military might when it guarded County Westmeath's lake-dotted landscape and Ireland's most important waterway, the River Shannon. Neighboring County Longford has nurtured writer Oliver Goldsmith and several other literary figures. Clonmacnois on the banks of the Shannon in County Offaly is still an impressive place of pilgrimage for thousands of visitors who come to glimpse the splendor of its ecclesiastical heyday, when its monastic community (founded in 548) presided over one of Europe's most important centers of learning. These remains are remarkably well-preserved.

The flatness of Ireland's great central plain is broken only by the Slieve Bloom Mountains in the northwest of County Laois.

While Leinster is a repository of history, it is also acknowledged to be Ireland's most progressive and rapidly changing region. In the last decade, Dublin has grown by leaps and bounds, not only in size and as a primary tourism destination, but as an important European financial center and leading commercial port. Its problems of traffic and housing spring from the swiftness of its growth and a pace of life that belies its easy-going, gentle landscape, which serves as a backdrop to the thousands of residents who commute daily from surrounding Leinster counties to the capital city.

to the lush countryside of counties Carlow and Kilkenny, founding a town that for a time outdid Dublin as an administrative center and appropriating the most scenic locations for their distinctive castles.

Legend has it that County Kildare's Hill of Allen hosted Finn MacCool and his followers during winter months. Today it is the international set who flock year-round to its horse stud farms, which consistently turn out winners on international racetracks as well as

DUBLIN

Dublin might rightly be called the birthplace of the celebrated Celtic Tiger that has brought such prosperity to Ireland in an amazingly brief period. On an international front, Ireland has attracted investments from leading industrial, commercial and financial firms, with a concentration in and around Dublin that has swelled the capital city's numbers to roughly one-third of the country's population of 3.8 million.

As fast-moving as Dublin's growth and social change have been, the city has managed to hold onto and value the treasures of its past. Side by side with its modern developments, Dublin still reflects the blemishes and beauty spots left by its colorful history. Over the centuries, the ancient city has been called many things. Baile Atha Cliath (Town of the Ford of the Hurdles) is its Irish name (a wicker bridge – the hurdles – once spanned the river).

Norsemen called it Dubh-Linn (Dark Pool) when they founded the present city on the banks of the Liffey in 840.

By any name, Dublin is one of Europe's loveliest capital cities, with proud old Georgian buildings (a style that harks back to the early 1700s to the mid-1800s, during the reigns of Kings George I to IV), elegantly groomed squares of greenery (Fitzwilliam, Parnell, Merrion), and acres of shaded leisure space (St. Stephen's Green and the Phoenix Park). Its heart beats to the rhythm of the Liffey, and its horizons extend to craggy Howth Head to the north, around the softly curving shores of Dublin Bay, to the slopes of the Dublin Mountains to the south.

Little remains of medieval Dublin, but it's easy to trace its outlines and see how the modern city has grown around it. On the south bank of the Liffey, you'll see Christ Church Cathedral's square tower – almost the exact center of the original city. To the east, Grattan Bridge stands near the "black pool" that

The elegant cast-iron arches of the Ha'penny Bridge crossing the Liffey north of Temple Bar

marked its eastern boundary and served as a Viking trading port. Little Ship Street follows the course of the Poddle river (now underground), once a city boundary on the river's south bank, and the quays along the north bank marked another outpost of the original city.

There were few substantial changes in Dublin until the magnificent Georgian buildings began to appear in the 18th century. The Victorian age arrived in the mid-1800s, leaving traces in railway stations, banks, pubs, markets and hospitals. From 1916 to 1922

Dublin was scarred by the ravages of uprising, although careful rebuilding and restoration have erased most of the scar tissue.

In the 1960s came the first "office revolution," when, in a fit of progressive zeal, the grand old city came close to demolishing many of her finest legacies. Citizens halted this destruction at an early stage, so you may walk through both past and modern structures.

The Liffey, which flows from west to east, divides the mile-long city center into "northside" (to Parnell Square at

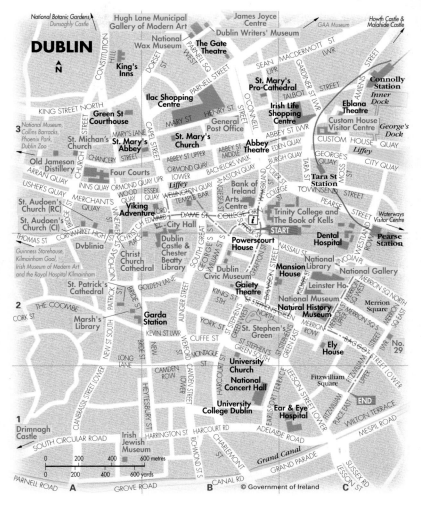

© Government of Ireland

the northern end of O'Connell Street) and "southside" (to Stephen's Green at Grafton Street's southern end). Of the Liffey's 15 bridges, O'Connell Bridge is the primary link between north and south. North of the river, O'Connell Street is an extension of the bridge and the location of landmarks like the historic General Post Office, statues of Parnell, Father Matthew and Daniel O'Connell, as well as a leading hotel, Clery's (one of Dublin's oldest department stores) and a jumble of fast-food eateries. Once the center of social life in the city, O'Connell Street had deteriorated badly over the years, but it has now undergone a massive cleanup and redevelopment plan to restore its charms. It is still advisable, however, to exercise big-city caution when walking there after dark.

To the south of O'Connell Bridge, Westmoreland Street extends for only one block before becoming College Green, a broad intersection fronting on the entrance to Trinity College. College Green then quickly becomes Grafton Street, Dublin's most fashionable shopping street. It is reserved for pedestrian traffic only and features good (and some not-so-good) street entertainment. At the southern end of Grafton Street is the cool, green oasis of beautiful St. Stephen's Green, a peaceful refuge from city streets.

The Liberties (so named in medieval times because its residents were exempt from the long arm of the law) is one of Dublin's oldest neighborhoods. It has bred some of the city's most colorful and strongly independent characters, as well as a distinctive, easily recognized accent. Its boundaries lie west of Upper Kevin Street beginning at The Coombe, its main thoroughfare (named for the valley or *coomb* of the River Poddle), and run west to somewhat indeterminate borders. Nearby are such important historic landmarks as St. Patrick's Cathedral, Christ Church

Theater and the Performing Arts

The Abbey Theatre in Lower Abbey Street is home to the national repertory company, born in 1903 when Augusta Lady Gregory, W. B. Yeats and J. M. Synge determined to perform Irish plays with Irish casts. The theater has provided a voice for such passionate writers as J. M. Synge and Sean O'Casey, even though this has sometimes rattled ultra-conservative Irish audiences. The original Abbey was quite small. When it burned in 1951, it was 15 years before its modern, functional replacement was completed.

The National Concert Hall is an intimate venue for presentations that range from jazz and folk music to classical concerts by the National Symphony Orchestra, the Irish Chamber Orchestra and a host of visiting international luminaries. On a much larger scale, The Point Depot is well equipped to host leading international rock stars, classical ballet companies and full-scale musical stage shows.

The Gaiety Theatre on South King Street is the venue for the two-performance seasons of the Opera Ireland repertory company, and international opera companies sometimes perform at The Point Depot as well.

🛈 You can pick up most concert and theater tickets at Dublin Tourism Ticketline (Desk 5) in the tourism center on Suffolk Street

O'Connell Street, taking traffic and shoppers from O'Connell Bridge to north Dublin

Cathedral and Dublin's oldest pub, the Brazen Head (see page 78), which witnessed much United Irishmen activity in the 18th century.

You will find some of the best examples of Dublin's famed Georgian architecture, a legacy of 18th-century residents, clustered around Merrion and Fitzwilliam squares and adjacent streets. Doorways whose fanlights are embellished with ornate wrought-iron decorations, cast-iron foot scrapers, doorway lamps, knockers and railings give each red-brick townhouse its own distinction. South of the Grand Canal, only a short walk from the city center, Ballsbridge is Dublin's most upscale residential section and the setting for several posh hotels and restaurants. So many embassies, including that of the United States, are located in this area that it has been dubbed by locals as "Embassy Row."

Temple Bar, Dublin's newest center of popular culture and entertainment, is the result of a massively funded and carefully planned development of a city-center section where narrow lanes

and alleys had become glaring examples of neglect and urban decay. Named for the river walkway (once known as a "bar") of Sir William Temple, whose family owned much of this site from 1554 to 1628, this area is bordered by Essex, Wellington and Aston quays to the north, Lord Edward Street and Dame Street to the south, Westmoreland Street to the east and Fishamble Street to the west. With its narrow lanes recobbled and ancient buildings restored, Temple Bar is Dublin's 21st-century bohemia. Its eclectic collection of street entertainment, avant-garde boutiques, art galleries, trendy pubs and trendier restaurants gives this area a vibrant, youthful air. The development of Temple Bar is ongoing at Cow's Lane.

"Dubs" ("jackeens" in the vernacular) are a breed, or rather, several breeds apart, with an increasingly cosmopolitan population mix. True Dubs will tell you, however, that unless you're born and bred in the city, you remain a *culchie* (country person) no matter how long you make the city your home. Arrogant? Not really – the tags are applied with good humor and more than a dollop of sharp wit, is often directed at themselves as to those other "blow-ins." Proud? Without doubt. Dubliners are happily convinced their city is not only the centerpiece of Leinster, but of Ireland and the universe as well.

Still, anything even remotely connected with reverence – including their own claims to their beloved city – is simply nonexistent in their makeup. Take, for example, when the Dubs christened a fountain – whose reclining female figure was meant to represent Anna Livia, Joyce's poetic name for the Liffey river – "The Floozie in the Jacuzzi." Or the wonderfully realistic figures of two housewife shoppers at the north end of the Ha'penny Bridge tagged "Hags with the Bags." Or the statue of Sweet Molly Malone at Nassau and Grafton

streets, now universally known as "The Tart with the Cart." Any new statue or monument erected by the city fathers is certain to fall prey to this brand of Dublin wit.

It's sometimes hard to hear Irish music as it pours from the irrepressible Irish spirit finding its voice in its own environment. With a very few exceptions, that's something you almost always have to stumble onto when the music and song are totally unplanned. In Dublin, however, that spontaneous spirit in all its passionate glory is alive and well at the headquarters of Culturlann na hÉireann in Monkstown. There's traditional entertainment here most nights of the week, but to hear some of the best musicians, go on Friday or Saturday. Fiddlers fiddle, pipers pipe, whistle players whistle, dancers take to the floor, and singers lift their fine Irish voices in informal sessions.

Excursions

If time is at a premium, the quickest way to see major attractions is by organized bus tours. Any of the Dublin Tourism centers can furnish details of what's offered during your visit and make tour bookings.

The two-hour, 45-minute open-top bus (covered double-deck bus on rainy days) tour is a delightful way to view the highlights of Dublin's major sightseeing attractions. The tour is a photographer's dream and includes Trinity College, the Guinness Brewery, St. Patrick's and Christ Church cathedrals, elegant Georgian squares, historic Phoenix Park and other points of interest. With the all-day ticket for Dublin Bus Hop-On, Hop-Off tour, you can stay aboard for the one-hour, 20-minute tour of 16 stops at major attractions, or you may elect to leave the bus at a stop of special interest and catch a later bus to complete the tour. Buses operate frequently, so you won't have a long wait for ongoing segments of the tour.

Dublin Bus also operates a three-hour Coast and Castle tour that visits the 12th-century Malahide Castle along a scenic coastal drive to the lovely fishing village of Howth, and on to Howth Head for spectacular views of Dublin Bay. A three-hour, 45-minute South Coast Tour takes you through scenery sometimes called Dublin's Riviera. The route includes Dun Laoghaire's yacht-filled harbor, Joyce's Tower at Sandycove, Killiney Bay, Bray and Greystones before turning inland to visit Avoca Handweavers at Kilmacanogue.

Leinster

Cabaret in Dublin is served up with distinctly Irish seasonings: *Danny Boy* and *The Rose of Tralee* are favorites of the audiences. You'll find an Irish comic telling Irish jokes, pretty, fresh-faced colleens dancing, singing and playing the harp, an Irish tenor or baritone, and youngsters stepping a lively jig or reel. It's Irish entertainment on the light side. No purists, these – but they're loads of fun and the performances are usually well above average. Most are held in hotels, and you can opt for

dinner and the show or come for the show alone. The most popular cabarets are those at the Burlington Hotel, and Jurys Hotel in Ballsbridge, which has been running almost 35 years.

For many Dubliners, the best possible start and finish to a Dublin evening is a visit to their favorite pub. With "Spoiled for Choice" (see page 78) as a guide to pubs, you can opt for your own "local" during your stay or embark on a pub crawl for an entertaining sampling.

ESSENTIAL INFORMATION

 TOURIST INFORMATION
• Dublin Tourism ✉ Suffolk Street ☎ 01 605 7700 🕒 Mon.–Sat. 9–5:30, Sun 10:30–3 (Jul. and Aug. only)
•Dublin Airport ☎ 01 844 5387 🕒 Daily 8–10 p.m.
• Ferry Terminal, Dun Laoghaire ☎ 01 284 6361 🕒 Mon.–Sat. 10–6
• Baggot Street Bridge walk-in center only 🕒 Mon.–Fri. 9:30–5
• The Square, Tallaght walk-in ce~nter only 🕒 Mon.–Sat. 9:30–noon and 12:30–5
ℹ A Dublin Tourism's money-saving SuperSaver Card can cut charges to seven major attractions. The Dublin Tourism website is a useful source of information for many aspects of your visit: www.visitdublin.com.

 URBAN TRANSPORTATION
Dublin Bus services all parts of the city and outlying areas, making it easy to search out accommodations beyond the city center. The main bus station, "Busáras" is on Amiens Street. Buses marked "An Lar" will be headed for the city center. Buses run from 7 a.m. (10 a.m. on Sunday) to 11:30 p.m. There is limited Nitelink bus service on Thursdays, Fridays and Saturdays, but confirm with Dublin Bus (see below) before traveling For detailed information, call Dublin Bus ✉ 59 Upper O'Connell Street ☎ 01 873 4222.
The electric train suburban service that runs from Malahide to Greystones at some 30 stations en route. Called the Dublin Area Rapid Transit (DART), the service is fast, silent and convenient, since departures are every five minutes during peak

hours, every 15 minutes other times. Service begins at 6:30 a.m. and ends at about 11:30 p.m. Some 19 feeder bus lines link up with the rail system. Timetables can be obtained at most of these stations. For information, contact DART, Pearse Street Station, Dublin 2 ☎ 01 703 3504.
Take at least one taxi ride as Dublin taxi drivers are the most knowledgeable and entertaining in the world. They cannot be hailed from the street, but may be summoned by telephone, and they operate from stands at all bus and rail stations. They're listed in the telephone directory under "Taxi-cab ranks." Rates are set by law, and all taxis are metered, with a small extra charge for each additional passenger and each piece of luggage. There's also a small additional charge between the hours of 8 p.m. and 8 a.m.
Driving is best avoided. Public transportation is efficient and frequent. Parking can be difficult. Remember, once you reach the city center, most places are going to be within easy walking distance.
Dublin's two ferry terminals are Dun Laoghaire Ferryport (☎ 01 661 0511) and Dublin Ferryport (☎ 01 874 3293), with bus and taxi service meeting ferries at both.

 AIRPORT INFORMATION
Dublin International Airport is 7.5 miles north of the city center. The Airlink bus goes to and from the airport from Busáras, the central bus station on Store Street north of the Liffey. An alternative is the Aircoach, which makes several stops in the city. Taxis are readily available at the airport.

CLIMATE – Average highs and lows

	JAN.	FEB.	MAR.	APR.	MAY	JUN.	JUL.	AUG.	SEP.	OCT.	NOV.	DEC.
	8°C	8°C	10°C	12°C	14°C	17°C	19°C	19°C	17°C	14°C	10°C	8°C
	46°F	46°F	50°F	54°F	57°F	63°F	66°F	66°F	63°F	57°F	50°F	46°F
	3°C	3°C	4°C	5°C	7°C	10°C	11°C	12°C	10°C	8°C	5°C	4°C
	37°F	38°F	39°F	41°F	45°F	50°F	52°F	54°F	50°F	46°F	41°F	39°F

A figure in the Chester Beatty Oriental collection

DUBLIN SIGHTS

Key to symbols

➕ map coordinates refer to the Dublin map on page 65; sights below are highlighted in yellow on the map
✉ address or location ☎ telephone number
🕐 opening times 🍴 restaurant on site or nearby
🚌 nearest bus or railroad station 🖐 admission charge: $$$ more than €6, $$ €4 to €6, $ less than €4
ℹ information

BANK OF IRELAND

This magnificent building was built in 1729 as the seat of the Irish Parliament. When the Act of Union was passed in 1800, Henry Grattan (whose statue stands across the way), although quite ill, rose to bid an eloquent farewell to the independent parliament. The building was acquired by the bank on the condition that the lower house be demolished to avoid any possible coup d'etat, but the House of Lords chamber, resplendent with 18th-century tapestries, a 1788 crystal chandelier, impressive silver gilt mace and lots of Irish oak woodwork, is worth a visit.

➕ B3 ✉ College Green ☎ 01 677 6801 🕐 Mon.–Fri. 10–4 🚌 All city center (An Lar) buses 🖐 Free ℹ House of Lords tours on Tue. (except public holidays) at 10:30, 11:30 and 1:45

BANK OF IRELAND ARTS CENTRE

Originally designed by Francis Johnson in 1811, the building is now the home to the Bank of Ireland Arts Centre and provides a worthwhile platform for the living arts and has a lively program of cultural and artistic events. The Story of Banking, a permanent exhibition held in the old bank armory, depicts the effects that the Bank of Ireland has had on Ireland's social and economic life during the past 200 years.

➕ B3 ✉ Foster Place ☎ 01 671 2261 🕐 Tue.–Fri. 10–4 🚌 All city center (An Lar) buses 🖐 $

CHESTER BEATTY LIBRARY AND GALLERY OF ORIENTAL ART

There are more than 22,000 cultural items in this extraordinary collection left to the Irish nation by American-Irish engineer Sir Alfred Chester Beatty (1875–1968) in 1956. Biblical materials include papyri dating from the second to fourth centuries, and the Islamic collection contains more than 270 copies of the Koran. Rare books, illuminated manuscripts and miniature paintings originate from an impressive range of ethnic groups.

➕ B2 ✉ Clock Tower, Dublin Castle ☎ 01 407 0750; fax 01 407 0760 🕐 Mon.–Fri. 10–5, Sat. 11–5, Sun. 1–5, closed Mon., Oct.–Apr. 🚌 54A (from Burgh Quay), 50, 51B, 77A, 123 (from Eden Quay) 🖐 Free

CHRIST CHURCH CATHEDRAL

Christ Church Cathedral dates back to 1038 when King Sitric erected a wooden structure, which was replaced with stone following the Norman invasion in 1169. Anglo-Norman leader Strongbow lies here, with a memorial in the cathedral nave. King Richard II came in 1394 to knight four Irish kings after they pledged allegiance to the British Crown. James II prayed here in 1689 before the Battle of the Boyne, and King Billy came back to offer thanks for his victory in that battle. The south transept, the oldest part of the upper church (1180), contains many

The Georgian Custom House is considered Dublin's finest piece of architecture

examples of late Norman and early Gothic architecture, and there are fine 16th- to 19th-century sculptures. You'll find statues of English kings, medieval carvings and oddities such as a mummified cat and rat, thought to have become trapped during a chase through organ pipes. Linked to the cathedral by a covered stone bridge is Synod Hall, which holds the "Dvblinia" exhibition (see page 74).

✚ A3 ✉ Christchurch Place ☎ 01 677 8099; fax 01 679 8991 🕓 Daily 10–5:30; closed Dec. 26 🚌 78A (Aston Quay) or 50, 51B, 123 (Eden Quay) 🏛 Donation ✚ Prayers for peace in Ireland noon Mon. to Fri.; Eucharist and sermon 11 a.m. every Sun.; call for times of Evensong and other services

CUSTOM HOUSE VISITOR CENTRE

After dark, floodlights that illuminate the gracious 1791 Customs House provide one of Dublin's most impressive nighttime sights. It was little more than a burned-out shell after the 1921 troubles, but after complete restoration, most of the interior architectural survivors of the fire can now be seen in the dome or clocktower area. There is a museum devoted to its famous architect, James Gandon, as well as a history of the building and its functions during its 200-year history.

✚ C3 ✉ Custom House Quay ☎ 01 888 2538; fax 01 888 2407 🕓 Mon.–Fri. 10–12:30, Sat.–Sun. 2–5, mid-Mar.–Nov.; Wed.–Fri. 10–12:30, Sun. 2–5, rest of year 🏛 $ ✚ 5-minute walk from O'Connell Bridge

DRIMNAGH CASTLE

Surrounded by a flooded moat, this is Ireland's last surviving medieval castle. Restored to their original style, its great hall, undercroft and battlement tower with a lookout post create a real feeling for that long-gone time in history. The 17th-century formal garden features box hedges, yew trees and an *allee* (shaded walkway) of hornbean trees.

✚ A1 ✉ Long Mile Road, Drimnagh ☎ 01 450 2530; fax 01 450 8927 🕓 Wed., Sat. and Sun. noon–5, Apr.–Oct.; Sun. 2–5, Wed. noon–5, rest of year 🚌 50, 56A, 77, 77A, (from Eden Quay) 🏛 $$

DUBLIN CASTLE

Dublin Castle is built on the site of an earlier Danish fortress. The only remaining portions of the original castle (built between 1208 and 1220) are a bit of a curtain wall and two towers. You can get a pretty good idea of the original outline from the upper castle yard (dubbed "The Devil's Half Acre" by Dubliners when this was the nerve center for repressive British

The Record Tower at Dublin Castle, one of the few remaining parts of the original building

rule for centuries). British viceroys resided in the opulent state apartments (now restored to their former elegance). It was from here that the prisoner James Connolly, patriot leader of the 1916 uprising, was taken by stretcher to Kilmainham Gaol to be executed.

Sumptuous furnishings, huge Waterford crystal chandeliers, tapestries, hand-tufted Donegal carpets mirroring the ceiling plasterwork and Robert Adam fireplaces abound, revealing the palatial lifestyle led by the viceroys. One of the most impressive rooms, St. Patrick's Hall, is cluttered with banners and coats of arms beneath an ornately painted ceiling and is now used for the inauguration of Ireland's presidents. The throne room contains a massive throne believed to have been brought to Dublin by William of Orange after his victory at Boyne.

Other points of interest are the Church of the Most Holy Trinity (formerly the Chapel Royal), the 13th-century Record Tower and the memorial outside the main gate honoring those Irish killed here during Easter Week of 1916, which stands on the spot where heads of Irish kings once were displayed

publicly on high spikes. In addition to the complex of courts, state apartments and government offices, it also houses the Chester Beatty Library (see page 70). 🚩 B2 ✉ Dame Street ☎ 01 677 7129; fax 01 679 7831 🕐 Mon.–Fri. 10–5, Sat.–Sun. 2–5 🚌 54A (from Burgh Quay), 50, 51B, 56A, 77A, 123 (from Eden Quay) 💷 $$ 🚹 Apartments may be closed for functions

DUBLIN CITY HALL

One of Dublin's finest neoclassical buildings, which dates from 1779, contains a multimedia exhibition tracing the evolution of the city from 1170 to the present day. The story is told through displays of civic regalia, including the Great City Sword and other treasures, with computer interactives, archive films, models and costumes. 🚩 B3 ✉ Cork Hill ☎ 01 672 2204; fax 01 672 2620 🕐 Mon.–Sat. 10–5:15, Sun. 2–5 🍴 Coffee shop 🚌 54A (from Burgh Quay), 50, 51B, 56A, 77A, 123 💷 $$

DUBLIN CIVIC MUSEUM

For a better understanding of Dublin and its people, take time to browse through

Next door, the Irish Writers' Centre nurtures contemporary writers by providing meeting and work space.
✚ B3 ✉ 18 Parnell Square North ☎ 01 872 2077; fax 01 872 2231 🕐 Mon.–Fri. 10–5, Sat. 10–5, Sun. 11–5, Jun.–Aug.; Mon.–Sat. 10–5, Sun. 11–5, rest of year
🍽 Restaurant and coffee shop 🚌 10, 11, 13, 16A, 19A; 10-minute walk from DART Connolly Station 💷 $$
ℹ The bookshop has an extensive stock of Irish titles and a mail-order service

DUBLIN ZOO AND THE PHOENIX PARK

Established in 1830, Dublin Zoo encompasses 60 acres on the grounds of the Phoenix Park. The zoo is especially noted for breeding lions and other large cats, having bred the first lion cubs in captivity in 1857. Its fame also rests on the picturesque landscaping and gardens surrounding two natural lakes (alive with pelicans, flamingos and scores of ornamental ducks and geese) and its spacious outdoor enclosures. Monkey islands in the "World of Primates," the antics of polar bears in "Fringes of the Arctic" and lions, jaguars and snow leopards in the "World of Cats" are among the most popular attractions. Youngsters will delight in the small Children's Pets Zoo.

Beautiful Phoenix Park, with its main entrance on Parkgate Street, is always referred to by Dubliners as "The" Phoenix Park. It is Europe's largest enclosed city park, and within its 1,652 acres are the residences of Ireland's president as well as that of the American ambassador. In addition to the Dublin Zoo, the lofty trees shade all manner of humans during daylight hours and a free-roaming herd of deer after dark. Pedestrian walkways lace the naturalistically landscaped grounds, where ornamental gardens are joined by plantings of indigenous shrubs and trees. The 205-foot obelisk, which is one of Dublin's best loved landmarks, was erected in 1817 and commemorates the Duke of Wellington, a Dublin native. The beautiful Papal Cross marks Pope John Paul II's 1979 visit to Dublin.
✚ A3 ✉ Phoenix Park ☎ 01 677 1425; fax 01 677 1660 🕐 Mon.–Sat. 9:30–6, Sun. 10:30–6, Mar.–Oct.;

Dublin's Civic Museum. Exhibits trace the city's development on many levels since Viking times to the present. In addition to the permanent collections covering Streets and Buildings, Traders, Industry, Transport, Political History and Views of Dublin, visiting exhibits are displayed from time to time.
✚ B2 ✉ 58 William Street South ☎ 01 679 4260; fax 01 677 5954 🕐 Tue.–Sat. 10–6, Sun. 11–2 🚌 10, 11, 13 (from O'Connell Street) 💷 Free

DUBLIN WRITERS' MUSEUM

Ireland's wealth of internationally recognized literary talent (including four Nobel prize winners) is celebrated in this superbly restored Georgian house that holds books, letters, portraits and personal belongings for the likes of Shaw, Wilde, Yeats, Swift, Joyce, Beckett and Behan. There are examples of magnificent stucco in this late 18th-century building, especially in the first-floor rooms. The colonnaded main salon, now the Gallery of Writers, has busts and paintings of famous names, a decorative ceiling and boisterous freizes. Children's literature is allotted its own room, and there are frequent visiting exhibitions and readings.

Making friends at Dublin Zoo

Mon.–Sat. 9:30–5, Sun 10:30–5, rest of year
🍴 Several eateries 🚌 10 (from O'Connell Street),
25, 26 (from Middle Abbey Street) 🎟 $$$
ℹ Play area, pet care area, discovery center

DUNSOGHLY CASTLE

Dating from the 15th century, this ruined castle has been designated a National Monument. The original oak roof beams are still intact as is the square tower with its rectangular turrets, a climb to the top offers terrific views.
➕ A3 ✉ 3 miles north of Finglas on N2

DVBLINIA

If you cross the elegant footbridge from Christ Church Cathedral you'll walk into a medieval setting that re-creates Dublin life from the time the Anglo-Normans arrived in 1170. It is housed in a beautifully preserved old building, the former Synod Hall. An audio headset guides you on a "Journey Through Time" among lifesize reconstructions of scenes from those long-ago times. Merchants' stalls in the "All the Fun of the Fayre" section spill over with imported and domestic wares such as medicines, clothes, foods and spices, bringing a real-life atmosphere to the street.

➕ B2 ✉ Synod Hall, St. Michael's Hill, Christ Church ☎ 01 679 4611; fax 01 679 7116 🕐 Daily 10–5, Apr.–Sep.; Mon.–Sat. 11–4, rest of year; closed Dec. 24–26 🚌 50, 51B (from Eden Quay), 78A, 123 (from Aston Quay) 🎟 $$

FOUR COURTS

The Chancery, King's Bench, Exchequer and Common Pleas are the four courts for which James Gandon designed this unique building in 1785. Political turmoil delayed its opening to 1796, and it was finally completed in 1802. Scars can still be seen on portico columns as a result of a heavy bombardment in 1922 during Ireland's civil war when anti-treaty forces occupied the building. A massive explosion destroyed irreplaceable historical records and left the building a burned-out shell. Beautifully restored, this massive Georgian edifice confronting the Liffey now functions as originally planned. The courts radiate from a circular central hall, the most interesting scenes are at lunchtime when you can witness bewigged lawyers fraternizing with their clients.
➕ A3 ✉ Inns Quay ☎ 01 886 6000 🕐 Mon.–Fri. 10:30–4:30; closed Aug.–Oct. 🚌 Any city center bus (An Lar) to O'Connell Street 🎟 Free ℹ Court sittings Mon.–Fri. 11–1 and 2–4

During special events, the entire city enters into the festive spirit. You should check with the Irish Tourist Board about specific dates during your visit. Advance inner-city accommodations reservations are vital, and prices may become a little inflated.

St. Patrick's Festival

For generations, celebrations of Ireland's patron saint were confined to March 17, but since 1996 Dublin's festival has been running over a four-day period. A theme is selected each year, and with more than 5,000 performers (including U.S. marching bands), it has grown into Ireland's largest annual celebration. The undisputed highlight is the Festival Parade, but each day is filled with street events that include a Monster Ceilí in St. Stephen's Green, carnival events along the quays, fun fairs, magic, comedy and puppet performances, and mini-parades and festivities wind up with spectacular fireworks.

🅘 For full details on future festivals, contact St. Patrick's Festival, St. Stephen's Green House, Earlsfort Terrace, Dublin 2, or visit their website at www.stpatricksday.ie

Bloomsday

For many visitors, Bloomsday, which commemorates the June 16, 1904 setting of James Joyce's *Ulysses* is reason enough to come to Dublin. At least a week before June 16 each year, Joyce scholars – as well as just plain fans – are busily attending readings, lectures and dramatic performances. The day itself, however, is anything but a serious, head-scratching analysis of the book: streets are thronged with people in period costumes reenacting

Laughter and music in the Dublin streets

DUBLIN SPECIALS

events recounted in the classic tale. Pubs visited by the novel's central character Leopold Bloom go all out with special meals and readings. And there's a general air of revelry as Dubliners celebrate turn-of-the-19th-century life in their beloved city and accord the writer a celebrity that eluded him during his lifetime.

Kerrygold Dublin Horse Show

This is the social highlight of the year. For a week in August, the showgrounds of the Dublin Royal Society are packed with sophisticated international visitors who mingle happily with Irish horse-lovers. In some of the finest jumping enclosures in the world, virtually nonstop jumping competitions are a backdrop for auctions that net enormous sales figures for handsome horses with impeccable pedigrees. The Aga Khan Trophy competition is Friday's main event. And on Saturday, the International Grand Prix of Ireland ends the week. Festivities include army band concerts, a Ladies' Day fashion competition, floral displays and arts and crafts exhibits.

Dublin Theatre Festival

October's first two weeks are devoted to the Dublin Theatre Festival, which fills every theater in the city, as well as university campuses and community halls with a series of first nights of innovative Irish drama and major overseas theater and dance companies. The festival has provided a lively platform for Irish playwrights, many new plays are performed and theatergoers have a rare opportunity to meet actors and directors in the Festival Club.

Bronze statue of the dying Cuchulain, in the central hall of the General Post Office

GAA MUSEUM

The Gaelic Athletic Association is Ireland's largest sporting organization. This museum, at the home of Ireland's national games of hurling and football, explores an integral part of Irish life and heritage. Touch-screen technology and interactives bring the games to life.

✚ Off map ✉ New Stand, Croke Park ☎ 01 855 8176; fax 01 855 8104 ⏰ Daily 9:30–5, May–Sep.; Tue.–Sat. 10–5, Sun. noon–5, rest of year 🚌 3, 11, 11A, 16, 16A, 123 ♿ $$

GENERAL POST OFFICE

The imposing General Post Office with its Ionic portico and fluted pillars was built in 1814. In 1916 its classical entrance provided a dramatic platform from which Padraic Pearse hoisted the Irish tricolor for the first time and proclaimed to his fellow Irish citizens and the world at large that Ireland would from that date on claim its independence (see page 22). After intense shelling, the building was set afire and its interior gutted. Now completely restored, its central hall holds a statue of Ireland's ancient mythical warrior hero, Cuchulain, a memorial to the men who fought here. On the marble base is inscribed Pearse's proclamation.

✚ B3 ✉ O'Connell Street ☎ 0705 7000 ⏰ Mon.–Sat. 8–8, Sun. 10:30–6:30 🚌 Any city center (An Lar) bus ♿ Free

GUINNESS STOREHOUSE

The sprawling Guinness Brewery, set on 60 acres south of the Liffey, is the largest brewery in Europe. From its home,

Guinness exports more beer than any other company in the world. The rich, dark stout it has produced since 1759 is truly the "wine of Ireland." As you enter the Storehouse, an escalator whisks you to the heart of the building into what is described as a large glass pint. Within the structure you journey through the production process of a pint of Guinness. Old machinery is utilized to present entertaining displays and audiovisuals give an insight into the history, manufacturing and advertising of Dublin's famous product. You end your visit in the rooftop bar, which has excellent views over the city, to sample a free glass of the "black stuff."

➕ A2 ✉ St. James's Gate ☎ 01 404 4800 🕐 Daily 9:30–5 🚌 51B, 78A (from Aston Quay), 123 (from O'Connell Street) 🍴 Café, bar 💷 $$$ 🅿 Free parking

Contempory art in the Hugh Lane gallery

HUGH LANE MUNICIPAL GALLERY OF MODERN ART

Occupying one of Dublin's finest Georgian mansions, the Hugh Lane Municipal Gallery of Modern Art acquired its present quarters as a permanent home for Sir Hugh Lane's art collection, which was donated to the gallery in 1908. There's an extensive collection of 20th-century Irish art, French Impressionists Manet, Monet, Renoir and Degas, and ever-changing temporary exhibitions of pieces by international contemporary artists. Look for the Jack Yeats portrait of Maud Gonne, who so capitivated his poet brother William.

➕ B3 ✉ Charlemont House, Parnell Square North ☎ 01 874 1903; fax 01 872 2182 🕐 Tue.–Thu. 9:30–6, Fri.–Sat. 9:30–5, Sun. 11–5 🍴 Café 🚌 10, 11, 13A, 16A 💷 Free 🅱 Free concerts and lectures on Sun.

IRISH JEWISH MUSEUM

Irish and Jewish documents, photographs and relics of Jews in Ireland for the past 500 years fill this museum, which is set in a former synagogue. Belfast-born and Dublin-educated Chaim Herzog opened the museum in 1985 when he was president of Israel.

➕ A1 ✉ 3–4 Walworth Road, off Victoria Street, South Circular Road ☎ 01 290 1857 🕐 Tue., Thu. and Sun. 11–3, May–Sep.; Sun. 10:30–2:30, rest of year 🚌 15A, 15B, 47, 47B 💷 Free (donations welcome)

IRISH MUSEUM OF MODERN ART AND THE ROYAL HOSPITAL KILMAINHAM

Built in 1684 as a home for retired soldiers, the Royal Hospital in Kilmainham is one of Ireland's finest 17th-century buildings, with a stylish formal facade and elegant courtyard. These days it houses the Museum of Modern Art, which includes more than 1,200 woodcuts, etchings and engravings by Irish and international artists, such as French Impressionists Manet, Degas and Renoir, and masters Rembrandt, Hogarth and Goya.

➕ A2 ✉ Royal Hospital, Military Road, Kilmainham ☎ 01 612 9900; fax 01 612 9999 🕐 Tue.–Sat. 10–5:30, Sun. noon–5:30 🍴 Coffee shop 🚌 51B, 68, 69, 78A, 206 💷 Free 🅱 Tours Wed. and Fri. 2:30, Sun. noon

Leinster

There are more than 1,000 pubs in Dublin, each with its own personality, each specializing in conversation, music or "the best pulled pint in Dublin" (a hotly debated accolade throughout the city's pubs). Those listed here are among the most interesting, but don't confine yourself to these – drop into the nearest establishment anytime you're overcome with a terrible thirst, and you'll likely go home raving about your own favorites. Non-drinkers will be pleased to know that, as centers of sociability, Irish pubs are quite happy to serve soda (minerals) as well as the hard stuff. It's the *craic* (an Irish word that sums up conversation and the ambience of an evening) that matters most and is a national art. Pub hours are from 10:30 a.m. to 11:30 p.m. in summer, to 11 p.m. in winter, extended hours on Thursday, Friday and Saturday.

Dubliners in its 130 years of dispensing drink. Mirrored partitions along the bar and high ceilings add to the setting and provide drinking "snugs" (enclosed nooks). Journalists, politicians, artists, architects and just plain people often fill bars to overflowing, and there's never a letup in the flow of lively and stimulating conversation.

SPOILED FOR CHOICE

The Brazen Head
The southside is pub country. The Brazen Head, the oldest drinking place in Ireland, may have been licensed by Charles II in 1666, but it drew its name from a beautiful redhead who couldn't contain her curiosity during a civil disturbance, stuck her head out of a window, and promptly lost it to an English sword. The entrance is tucked away at the back of a courtyard down an arched alleyway on the west side of Bridge Street. It's dimly lit inside with low ceilings, brass lanterns and uneven wooden floors. Patriots Robert Emmet, Wolfe Tone and Daniel O'Connell often came here to drink.

Doheny and Nesbitt
This is the place for people-watching. Doheny and Nesbitt, 5 Lower Baggot Street, has earned a special place in the affections of

The Stag's Head
Another long-standing favorite of Dubliners is the Stag's Head, tucked away in Dame Court. Getting there is a bit complicated, but worth the effort. The Stag's Head has been here since 1770, wearing its age with grace, its stained-glass windows and skylights, gleaming wood and mounted stag's head reflecting the soft patina of time. Regulars, from executive types to shop clerks, gather here and mingle happily with tourists. Along with its "best-pulled pint" credentials, the Stag's Head also serves an excellent pub lunch from 12:30 to 3:30 p.m.

Mulligan's
This is as much a conversation pub today as it was when it was favored by James Joyce and other Dublin notables. Mulligan's on Poolbeg Street has been a Dublin institution since 1782, and the 19th-century gas lights are among its original trappings.

Davy Byrnes
For James Joyce fans, Davy Byrnes, 21 Duke Street, still draws those who come looking for the "moral pub" described in *Ulysses*. True, the 1890s wall murals are still here, but the atmosphere these days is likely to be more that of a modern-day cocktail lounge than what Leopold Bloom encountered, with orders for mixed drinks outnumbering calls for the pint.

McDaids

Brendan Behan staked out a spot for himself, his pint and his typewriter in McDaids, 3 Harry Street, a dark, high-ceilinged pub that became his second home. Literary luminaries such as Patrick Kavanagh and Flann O'Brien also drank here, and many current wordsmiths followed suit. Who knows, in such an ambience, they may become the great writers of the future.

The Old Stand

Patronized by what sometimes seems to be at least half of Ireland's rugby team, as well as other athletes, The Old Stand at 37 Exchequer Street is, not surprisingly, a center for sports conversation. All those sports figures mingle with a mixed clientele. A favorite lunch and after-work drinking spot for office workers.

Ryan's

Northside pubs are traditional and popular with locals. Ryan's, 28 Parkgate Street, is a real gem. Located in the Phoenix Park area, it has been in the Ryan family since 1920. Ryan's is worth a visit just for the decor: superb antique mirrors, four brass lamp fittings mounted on the bar counter and a magnificent old oak and mahogany central bar with a unique double-faced mechanical clock and partitions of ornate, beveled-mirrored dividers. Heads of state and celebrities from the movie and theater worlds regularly mingle with natives to enjoy the great atmosphere.

Kavanagh's

Adjacent to what was once the main gate to Glasnevan Cemetery, Kavanagh's, 1 Prospect Square, is now run by its eighth-generation Kavanagh proprietor. The pub has been here for over a century-and-a-half and during that time has accumulated an inexhaustible fund of stories about gravediggers who would bang stones against the pub's wall and then wait for drinks to be passed through an opening and placed on their waiting shovels.

Kavanagh's remains today, as it has always been, a plain, unadorned working-man's pub, with sawdust on the floor, worn wooden booths and cubbyholes, and a dart game or two.

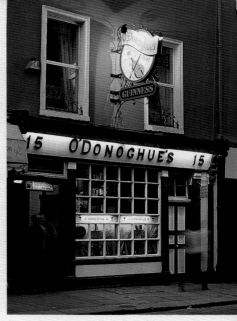

Share in the gossip and hospitality of the city pubs

Pubs with Music

In recent years, there has been an expansion of the kind of music performed in pubs, from traditional to jazz, blues, country, rock and even Cajun. You can check in local newspapers if you're in search of a musical evening. Oliver St. John Gogarty in Temple Bar is considered one of the city's best music pubs and features traditional Irish music nightly most of the year, which can go on well into the early hours.

You won't find a better ballad club in all of Ireland than the Abbey Tavern out in Howth, 9 miles north of Dublin. The bar and restaurant is low-ceilinged, candlelit and has a fire glowing on cool nights, making it an informal, cozy place to eat. Shows in the big hall run through a host of ballads you've heard, then go on to some you'll never hear anywhere except on Irish soil. You can opt for a dinner and show package, or go for the show only. It is essential to reserve ahead. There's a good bus and train service out to Howth. O'Donoghue's, 15 Merrion Row, is a magnet for young and not-so-young musicians who flock here bearing guitars, uilleann pipes, bones and spoons and just about any musical instrument they have to hand. Music is spontaneous and lively and although it's always packed to the gills, it remains a popular gathering place.

Exhibits at Kilmainham Gaol evoke the bleak reality of a term of imprisonment

JAMES JOYCE CENTRE

Of all the literati to grace the Dublin scene during the 20th century, James Joyce has undoubtedly earned the greatest reputation, so it is fitting that this lovely 18th-century Georgian house is devoted to the writer and his work. Take time to browse in the extensive library and gaze the portraits of those featured in the master's work. You can see the original doorway rescued from the now demolished No. 7 Eccles Street, the imagined residence of the "Ulysses" hero, Leopold Bloom. The center is also a starting point for an hour-long walking tour of the Joycean sites.

➕ B3 ✉ 35 North Great George Street ☎ 01 878 8547 🕐 Mon.–Sat. 9:30–5, Sun. 12:30–5 🍴 Café 🚌 3. 10, 11, 13, 16, 19 💷 $$

KILMAINHAM GAOL

In the years between its opening in 1796 and its closure in 1924, Kilmainham Gaol has held political leaders of rebellions in 1798, 1803, 1848, 1867 and 1916. President Eamon de Valera was confined within its walls in 1916 and again in 1923 and was its final prisoner. Though the cells hold no prisoners these days, corridors evoke a strong sense of patriots held here such as Robert Emmet, Charles Parnell, volunteers involved in the Easter Week Rebellion of 1916, and James Connolly and the 14 people executed with him in May 1916. As a musuem documenting the Irish struggle for independence, a visit to Kilmainham Gaol is a profoundly moving experience not easily forgotten.

➕ A2 ✉ Inchicore Road, Kilmainham ☎ 01 453 5984; fax 01 453 2037 🕐 Daily 9:30–4:45, Apr.–Sep.; Mon.–Sat. 9:30–4, Sun. 10–4:45, rest of year 🚌 68, 69, 78A, 206 💷 $$

LEINSTER HOUSE

Since 1925, this 1745 mansion has been the home of Ireland's Parliament (Oireachtas na hÉireann), which is composed of the Dáil (the lower house) and the Seanad (the senate). Look for the memorial on Leinster Lawn that commemorates Arthur Griffith, Kevin O'Higgins and Michael Collins, all among the founders of the Republic of Ireland. Leinster House is flanked by the National Gallery on one side, the Natural History Museum on the other.

➕ C2 ✉ Kildare Street ☎ 01 618 3000 🕐 Check for visiting hours when Parliament is not in session; otherwise, admittance is only as an invited guest of a member of Parliament 🚌 Any city center (An Lar) bus

Georgian Leinster House, Ireland's parliament building

MARSH'S LIBRARY

Jonathan Swift and James Joyce are among Dubliners who have made great use of the 25,000-volume literary collections housed in Marsh's Library, the first public library in Ireland. Built beside St. Patrick's Cathedral in 1701 by Archbishop Narcissus Marsh, its beautiful interior remains unchanged since it opened, with dark oak bookcases and unique wire cages in which readers were locked when perusing rare books. Some books were actually chained to the shelves. The four collections cover a wide range of subjects (theology, ancient history, music, law, travel and medicine) and include about 300 manuscripts, including *The Lives of the Irish Saints*, which dates to 1400.

➕ A2 ✉ St. Patrick's Close ☎ 01 454 3511 🕐 Mon. and Wed.–Fri. 10–12:45 and 2–5, Sat. 10:30–12:45 🚌 50, 54A, 56A (from Eden Quay) 💷 $$

NATIONAL GALLERY

In his youth, George Bernard Shaw spent many inspirational hours in the National Gallery and expressed his appreciation and gratitude by bequeathing royalties from his plays for its upkeep. Its doors first opened in 1864 with only 125

paintings, a collection that has grown to include 2,500. There's a major collection of works by Irish artists, and European masters such as Rubens, Rembrandt, Monet and Degas are well represented.

A fascinating collection of Irish portraits lines the grand staircase, culminating in the fiery Countess Markiewicz, a contemporary of W. B. Yeats (see page 89) who was furious at being pardoned for her part in the Easter 1916 Uprising. Representing works up to the 19th century, the gallery has excellent computer facilities for obtaining information about its paintings. The Millennium Wing, opened in 2002, houses a center for the study of Irish art, temporary exhibition galleries and an archive dedicated to Jack B. Yeats.

➕ C2 ✉ Merrion Square West ☎ 01 661 5133 🕐 Mon.–Sat. 10–5:30, Thu. 10–8:30, Sun. 2–5; closed Good Friday and Dec. 24–26 🍽 Restaurant 🚌 Any city center (An Lar) bus 💷 Free ℹ Guided tours Sat. at 3 and Sun. at 2:15, 3 and 4

NATIONAL LIBRARY OF IRELAND

Those with an interest in Irish studies or tracing Irish ancestry will find the National Library an invaluable resource. Opened in 1890, it now holds thousands

The imposing granite facade of the National
Museum of Ireland, Collins Barracks

of volumes, many of them first editions,
and works of Irish writers. James Joyce
fans will recognize the library as the
Chapter Nine setting in Ulysses.

➕ C2 ✉ Kildare Street ☎ 01 603 0200 🕐 Hours
vary, call to confirm; closed Nov. 🚌 Any city center
(An Lar) bus 💷 Free

NATIONAL MUSEUM OF IRELAND

Opened in 1890, the National Museum of
Ireland's collections include artifacts
spanning the centuries from 2000 BC to
the 20th century. The archeological
section has relics from the Iron Age to the
15th century. Prehistoric and Viking
Ireland, Ireland's Gold and Ancient Egypt
collections breathe life into each era. The
Road to Independence is a study of
Ireland from 1916 to 1921.

➕ C2 ✉ Kildare Street ☎ 01 677 7444
🕐 Tue.–Sat. 10–5, Sun. 2–5 🍴 Café 🚌 Any city
center (An Lar) bus 💷 Free

NATIONAL MUSEUM OF IRELAND, COLLINS BARRACKS

Collins Barracks, which occupy 18 acres
north of the Liffey, are the oldest military

barracks in Europe, built in 1701. When
the National Museum purchased the
large, rather austere building in 1994, its
decorative arts, weapons, furniture,
costumes, silver, ceramics and glassware
collections were moved from their
Kildare Street home and installed in these
more spacious rooms. The radical
Protestant barrister Wolfe Tone, who set
up the United Irishmen in Belfast, was
held prisoner here, and his pocketbook
from that time is among the wealth of
items on display.

➕ Off the map ✉ Benburb Street ☎ 01 677 7444
🕐 Tue.–Sat. 10–5, Sun. 2–5 🍴 Café 🚌 25, 25A, 66,
67, 79, 90 💷 Free ℹ Audiovisual room and
community and education room

NATIONAL WAX MUSEUM

Wax replicas of every Irish hero or
heroine you've ever heard of fill this
terrific fantasy land. The Hall of
Megastars is populated by celebrities such
as Madonna and Dublin's own U2.
There's a lifesize depiction of Da Vinci's
Last Supper and a Chamber of Horrors
for the stout of heart. The World of
Fairytale and Fantasy will entertain
the younger set.

➕ B2 ✉ Granby Row, Parnell Square ☎ 01 872
6340 🕐 Mon.–Sat. 10–5:30, Sun. noon–5:30 🚌 11,
13A, 16A, 22, 22A (from Westmoreland Street) 💷 $$$

NUMBER TWENTY-NINE

So perfectly has this four-story townhouse
been restored to its late 18th-century
comfort and elegance that you may feel
you're an invited guest of the middle-class
family who occupied it back then. From
top to bottom, every item is authentic to
the period, whether genuine antique or a
meticulous reproduction by Irish artisans.
The living rooms are the epitome of
respectability, and the upper-floor
bedrooms, especially the nursery – where
you can admire an enormous doll's house
–, exude charm.

➕ C2 ✉ Lower Fitzwilliam Street (entrance on
corner of Upper Mount Street) ☎ 01 702 6165; fax 01
702 7796 🕐 Tue.–Sat. 10–5, Sun. 2–5; closed Dec.
11–25 🍴 Tearoom 🚌 7, 8, 10, 45 (from city center)
💷 $$

OLD JAMESON DISTILLERY

Back in the sixth century, *uisce beatha* (pronounced "ish-ke ba-ha") which translates to "the water of life," was the name first given to Ireland's unique blended whiskey. Later, it was anglicized to "fuisce" before eventually evolving into "whiskey."

The Jameson Distillery, housed in an old warehouse that once used to mature whiskey, features an audiovisual history of the making of Irish whiskey, a museum that includes a copper-pot still, distillery model and other implements of the trade. With any luck, you'll be chosen as one of four tasters to try various brands. Luck or no luck, everyone gets a sample in the Ball of Malt bar. A reminder: when you bend an elbow, don't forget to turn to your neighbor and raise your glass in the traditional Irish toast, *slainte* (pronounced "slawn-che") – it means "good health."

Interior of a grand bedroom in the museum of Number Twenty-Nine

➕ A3 ✉ Bow Street, Smithfield ☎ 01 807 2355; fax 01 807 2369 ⏰ Daily 9:30–6; closed Good Friday and Dec. 25 🍴 Café 🚌 67, 67A, 68, 69, 79, 90 💷 $$

ST. AUDOEN'S CHURCH OF IRELAND AND ROMAN CATHOLIC CHURCH

The Celtic Church of St. Columcille stood on this site before the Normans replaced it in 1190, dedicating it to St. Ouen (eventually corrupted to its present spelling). The three bells in its tower are reputed to be the oldest in Ireland (1423), and there's an early (before 1309) Christian gravestone known as the "Lucky Stone," which supposedly possesses strange powers. Take note of the 1190 west doorway and the 13th-century nave. The churchyard park is bordered by a section of the old city walls, and steps lead down to St. Audoen's Arch, the only surviving gateway of the old city.

The Roman Catholic church next door is considerably younger, dating from 1847, and considerably more intact than its neighbor. Its fine interior is accessible by a side door. The two giant clam shells, brought to Dublin from a Pacific Ocean voyage, are now used as holy water containers.

➕ A3 ✉ Cornmarket (off High Street) ☎ 01 677 0088 ⏰ Daily 9:30–5:30, Jun.–Sep. 🚌 21A, 78A, 78B 💷 $

ST. MICHAN'S CHURCH

St. Michan's Church dates to the 17th century, but its square tower is that of a 1095 Danish church that stood on this site. Through some strange process not fully understood, elements from the soil and the air in the crypt combine to perfectly preserve bodies that have lain here for centuries. Mummified bodies, which include those of a 15th-century nun and the Sheare Brothers (patriots executed for treason during the 1798 rebellion) can be viewed through a small hatch. Their co-conspirator in that rebellion, Robert Emmet, was comforted by St. Michan's rector in his last hours, and his remains are reputed to be buried in the churchyard.

➕ A3 ✉ Church Street ☎ 01 872 4154 ⏰ Mon.–Fri. 10–12:30 and 2–4:30, Mar.–Oct.; 12:30–3:30, Nov.–Feb.; Sat. 10–12:45 all year 🚌 34 💷 $$

ST. PATRICK'S CATHEDRAL

St. Patrick is said to have baptized Christians on this site, and there's been a

Leinster

The Anglo-Normans founded Dublin's parish church of St. Audoen's

church here since AD 450. The present building, the largest church in the country, replaced the earlier structure in 1191. From 1320 to 1520, this was Ireland's first university, and in the 17th century Englishman Oliver Cromwell's troops used it as a stable. Huguenots worshiped here from 1666 to 1816, and reminders of its long history meet your eye on all sides, from Celtic gravestones to centuries-old Irish regimental banners to memorials for some of Ireland's most famous citizens, including Carolan, last practitioner of the Irish bardic tradition. The tomb of the cathedral's best-known dean (1713 to 1745), Jonathan Swift (author of *Gulliver's Travels* and a plethora of satiric essays), is in the south aisle near that of his beloved "Stella." Christians of all denominations are welcome at all church services.

🚩 A2 ✉ St. Patrick's Close ☎ 01 453 9472; fax 01 454 6374 🕓 Mon.–Sat. 9–6, Mar.–Oct.; 9–5, rest of year 🚌 50, 54A, 56A (from Eden Quay) 💷 $$

ST. STEPHEN'S GREEN

Since 1690 St. Stephen's Green, at the foot of Grafton Street, has been preserved as a bucolic respite from the hustle and bustle of city streets. It is beautifully landscaped with mature plantings, an artificial lake and a network of pathways winding through its colorful flower beds. There are numerous statues and busts of famous Irish men and women, including James Joyce, Robert Emmet, Wolfe Tone and Sir Arthur Guinness. The park is also surrounded by some of the finest buildings in Dublin dating back to the city's Georgian prime. They include the fashionable Shelbourne Hotel with statues of Nubian princesses and their ankle-fettered slaves decorating the front, and the neo-Byzantine interior of the Roman Catholic University Church. Dublin office and shop workers often head for the Green for a picnic lunch, and visitors also gravitate to its peaceful tranquility in the very heart of the city.

🚩 B2 🕓 Mon.–Sat. 8–dusk, Sun. 10–dusk 🚌 Any city center (An Lar) bus

TRINITY COLLEGE AND THE BOOK OF KELLS

Trinity College was founded by Queen Elizabeth I in 1592 on a 40-acre site in the heart of the city, ostensibly "to civilize Ireland with both learning and the Protestant religion." Catholics were allowed entry – and free education – provided they converted. The roll of honor is impressive: Edmund Burke, Jonathan Swift, Oliver Goldsmith, Bram Stoker, Wolfe Tone, William Congreve, J. M. Synge, Samuel Beckett have all passed through these hallowed portals.

Walk through its gates and you're in a world of cobbled squares and red-brick buildings from the early 1700s called the Rubrics, the college's oldest surviving structures. The lofty vaulted Long Room – where the ghosts of many literati stalk – and Colonnades Gallery in the Old Library hold some of Ireland's most important antiquities, including the magnificently illustrated ninth-century *Book of Kells*. The richness of color and design throughout this four-volume, handwritten, Latin transcript of the four gospels is absolutely stunning. "The Book of Kells, Turning Darkness into Light" is a major exhibition, and you'll find the "The Dublin Experience," a

Old Library Hall, Trinity College

dramatic 45-minute multimedia presentation that traces the city's history, is a great way to begin your Dublin stay, and one that will make each day here more meaningful. Also on view are the ancient books of Durrow and Armagh.

Since 1801 Trinity College has had the right under copyright law to claim a free copy of all British and Irish publications and now houses nearly 3 million volumes in eight buildings. Even on a selection basis, nearly half a mile of new shelving is needed each year to keep up with the recent publications, which are now housed off-site.

✚ B3 ✉ College Green ☎ 01 608 2320
🕐 Old Library: Mon.–Sat. 9:30–5, Sun. 9:30–4:30 (Sun. noon–4:30, Oct.–May); closed 10 days over Christmas and New Year 🚌 Any city center (An Lar) bus
💷 Campus: free; Old Library: $$$
Dublin Experience ✉ Davis Theatre, Arts Building, Trinity College 🕐 Daily 10–5, late May–Sep. 💷 $$

Leinster

WALK: SOUTH OF THE LIFFEY

Refer to route marked on city map on page 65.

Dublin is a small, vibrant city that's a delight to explore on foot. From broad O'Connell Street on the northside to the leafy green spaces of St. Stephen's Green on the southside and the tiny lanes of Temple Bar, you can soak up the atmosphere of a city steeped in history, yet firmly in step with today and looking forward to tomorrow. Pick up the Heritage Trails Guide from the tourist office, which examines this route in addition to musical, literary and other special-interest walks. Allow about three hours.

Begin at the tourist office on Suffolk Street, turn left onto Andrews Street, then down Trinity Street to Dame Street. Cross Dame Street to the Central Bank Plaza and Cope Street into Crown Alley (behind the bank) to reach Temple Bar.

Chances are that something will be going on in Temple Bar. Allow time to wander the maze of tiny 18th-century cobbled streets that only a few years ago were lined with ancient, dilapidated warehouses. Urban renewal has brought an amazing cultural vibrancy to this area, with street entertainment that includes jazz, ethnic and rock concerts, street theater, art exhibits and The Ark, an arts center and theater for children. Look for the Temple Bar Art Gallery and Studios and some of Dublin's most interesting shops, quirky boutiques and equally interesting restaurants, cafés and pubs (see page 67). Crown Alley takes you to Temple Bar Square (site of many open-air entertainments and sidewalk artists) and Merchants Arch, through which you will see the rejuvenated, cream-colored Ha'penny Bridge (see page 64), which exacted a half-penny toll from pedestrians from 1816 to 1919.

Take Temple Bar Street to Parliament Street, turn left and walk to the City Hall.

The Corinthian-style City Hall was built between 1769 and 1777 as the Royal Exchange, and it is now the venue for meetings of Dublin City Council. Its

impressive entrance rotunda displays statues of Daniel O'Connell and other Irish leaders, and the corporation's coat of arms and motto are represented in the floor mosaic. During the 1780s, this was a meeting point for volunteer rallies, and during the 1798 rebellion it was used by government troops as barracks and torture chambers. The roadway outside City Hall was once the entrance to the medieval city through the Dame Gate.

Turn left up Cork Hill (between City Hall and Newcomen's Bank) and walk to the Upper Castle Yard gate.

Dublin Castle really doesn't look much like a castle these days. That's because of drastic 18th-century renovations that left intact only a few of the original towers (1204) and no trace of the curtain wall's massive towers, drawbridge or portcullis. Surviving today are the record tower and the Bermingham tower (from the 14th century). Dubliners will point out with a wry smile that Van Nost's statue of justice atop the upper castle yard gate was placed with its back to the city's citizens (see page 71). The elegant state apartments are open to the public, as are 10th-century Viking defenses, which were exposed by renovation work in 1990, and the impressive Chester Beatty Library and Gallery of Oriental Art (see page 70).

Walk east to Dame Street, continue east on Dame Street to meet College Green.

The Bank of Ireland, a magnificent Georgian structure, only became a bank in 1800 after the Irish Parliament legislated its own death when it passed the detested Act of Union. The elegant former House of Lords is open to the public during banking hours (see page 70). Opposite the bank is Trinity College (see page 84) and you'll find the beautifully decorated *Book of Kells* in the Colonnades. While Catholics were barred from attending Trinity College unless they obtained special dispensation until 1966, women (non-Catholics, of course) were admitted as early as 1903. On the corner of Grafton Street, the Provost's House is a superb Georgian mansion.

From College Green, walk south on Grafton Street, a pedestrian avenue lined with fashionable shops. The lovely bronze statue near the corner of Nassau and Grafton streets depicts Molly Malone

Powerscourt – a maze of fascinating shops, market stalls, cafés and restaurants

of "the Dublin's Fair City" song. The figure has been irreverently (but affectionately) dubbed the "Tart With the Cart." Turn right at Johnson's Court, a narrow lane, and proceed to Powerscourt Town House shopping center.

Set in a 1774 townhouse built by Lord Powerscourt, this shopping center is a far cry from its modern counterparts. Both the house itself and the courtyard have been only slightly modified to accommodate a wide variety of small shops and also several restaurants.

Return to Grafton Street and walk south.
At the foot of Grafton Street, St. Stephen's Green is a beautifully landscaped oasis of greenery and calm in the heart of the city and is a favorite sunning and lunching spot for Dubliners. Once known as "Beaux Walk," the north side of the Green now houses some of Dublin's most prestigious private clubs (see page 66).

Turn left on St. Stephen's Green North, then left onto Dawson Street for Mansion House.

In January 1919 the first assembly of Dáil Éireann (the Irish Parliament) met in this beautiful 1710 mansion, now the official residence of the Lord Mayor of Dublin. It is used mainly for receptions and exhibitions and is not open to the public.

Return to St. Stephen's Green North and turn left onto Kildare Street. Leinster House (see page 80) is on your right. From the north end of Kildare Street, turn right onto Nassau Street, which becomes Leinster Street, then Clare Street before reaching Merrion Square.

Take a look at the blue plaques on many of the Georgian houses that line this square, one of Dublin's finest. They commemorate notable former residents such as W. B. Yeats and Daniel O'Connell.

Continue south along the west side of the square, which becomes Merrion Street, then turn left into Lower Baggot Street. Turn right onto Fitzwilliam Street and on your right is Fitzwilliam Square.

A pocket of well-preserved Georgian architecture, this square, although among the city's smallest, is worth browsing to appreciate elegant fanlights above front doors, elaborate iron bootscrapers and other ingenious details such as glass recesses for lamps. The studio of one of Ireland's most famous artists, Jack B. Yeats, was in No. 18.

Leinster

There must be something in the air in Ireland that nurtures great writers! For such a small country, Ireland has contributed an inordinate number of articulate, sharp-witted writers who have used the well-turned phrase to produce a wealth of words both timeless and universal. Dublin has been home to many of the country's best writers, and while some of the landmarks they left behind have disappeared and others have changed, the following sights will surely bring you closer to that rich literary legacy, as will a visit to The Writer's Museum on Parnell Square.

James Joyce portrait by Jacque Emile Blanche
©ADAGP, Paris and DACS, London 2002

DUBLIN'S LITERARY GREATS

Samuel Beckett Born in Cooldrinagh in Foxrock, Dublin in 1906, Samuel Beckett had a brilliant academic background. He moved to Paris and turned to writing novels and short stories before moving into works for the stage. His most memorable play is undoubtedly *Waiting for Godot*, quickly followed by such bleakly horrifying comedies as *End Game*. A prolific poet, novelist and playwright, Beckett produced a body of work considered to be perhaps the greatest influence on mid-century European drama. He died in Paris in 1989.

Brendan Behan With youthful years spent at 14 Russell Street, Brendan Behan was born in Dublin in 1923. He became involved with the IRA by the age of 15 and was sentenced to jail for 14 years in 1942. He was released in a 1946 amnesty and set about chronicling his prison experiences in plays like *The Quare Fellow* and *The Hostage* in a bluntly honest, irreverent style that often angered fellow Dubliners. He died in 1964 and was laid to rest in Glasnevin Cemetery. No doubt his spirit still roams

the city streets and bends a ghostly elbow in McDaid's pub, one of his favorites, still reveling in the vagaries of life in Dublin today.

Elizabeth Bowen Born in Dublin at 15 Herbert Place off Lower Baggot Street in 1900, Elizabeth Bowen studied and lived abroad for much of her life, although her ironic wit enlivens novels, short stories and essays, many of them based on Irish life. Novels such as *Friends and Relations*, *The Heat of the Day* and *The Death of the Heart* mark her as a master of modern literature. She died in London in 1973.

James Joyce The house at 41 Brighton Square West, Rathgar was the birth place of James Joyce in 1882. From his self-imposed exile he mapped the face of his native city in unremitting detail. A museum devoted to Joyce memorabilia now occupies the Martello Tower in Sandymount, where he lived for a time in 1904 with Oliver St. John Gogarty. The tourist board has prepared a "Ulysses Map of Dublin," but the meanderings of Joyce's character Leopold Bloom can be traced from the book as unerringly as if Joyce had written a guidebook to the city rather than his *Ulysses* masterpiece. Bloomsday is celebrated every June 16 (see page 75). The James Joyce Centre at 35 North Great George's Street has a library and book and coffee shop.

Thomas Moore In 1779 at 12 Aungier Street, Thomas Moore was born and acquired much of his higher learning at Trinity College. Although opinions differed widely during his lifetime as to whether songs from his *Irish Melodies* were truly Irish or merely "stage-Irish," many are still popular today with the Irish and visitors alike. He died in England in 1852, having suffered mental illness for several years.

Iris Murdoch Born in Dublin to an Anglo-Irish family in 1919, Iris Murdoch wrote a series of distinguished and highly successful intellectual novels. Several deal brilliantly with conflicting loyalties of families such as her own, most notably *The Red and the Green*, published in 1965 and set in the turbulent 1916-23 period of Irish life. She died in England in 1999 after a long illness.

Sean O'Casey A product of Dublin's northside slums, Sean O'Casey was born in 1884. Self-educated, he was deeply involved with the labor movement and worked closely with James Connoly in the Irish Citizens Army. His first play to be accepted by the Abbey Theatre was *The Shadow of a Gunman*, a highly controversial work that caused consternation among ultra-conservative audiences. Later, *The Plough and the Stars* was to cause the most dramatic row in Ireland for years. When the Abbey refused to produce *The Silver Tassie*, O'Casey left Ireland and remained abroad until his death in 1964.

Cornelius Ryan You'll know Cornelius Ryan, who was born in 1920 at 33 Heytesburn Street (off the South Circular Road), for his outstanding World War II novels *The Longest Day* and *A Bridge Too Far*. He died in Washington, D.C. shortly before the latter was published in 1976, after a long battle with cancer.

George Bernard Shaw Best remembered as the dramatist whose prolific output includes *St. Joan*, *Man and Superman* and a wealth of other plays, George Bernard Shaw was born at 33 Synge Street in 1856. He continued to write plays, political treatises and autobiographical sketches right until his death in 1950. His birthplace has been restored to the way it was when Shaw lived here and is open to the public.

Abraham Stoker Although Abraham (Bram) Stoker, born in 1847 at 15 Marino Crescent in Clontarf, wrote a dozen novels, his literary immortality is assured by his masterpiece *Dracula*. Quite possibly, it is the most reprinted, translated, filmed, serialized and drawn-in-comic-strips novel of all time, and has moved into the world's folklore. Stoker died in 1912.

Jonathan Swift The house at 7 Hoey's Court, where Jonathan Swift was born in 1667, stood very near St. Patrick's Cathedral, his last resting place after some 32 years as the cathedral's most famous dean. Trinity College (see page 84), where Swift studied, also echoes with memories of the great irreligious satirist, poet and novelist who penned such masterpieces as *Gulliver's Travels*, and his relationships with "Stella" and "Vanessa" are debated even today. He died in 1745, leaving funds to found St. Patrick's Hospital for Imbeciles, the first institution if this kind in Ireland. His body of work reflects a compelling mixture of compassion and rage at mankind's behavior.

Oscar Wilde Born at 21 Westland Row in 1856, many critics consider Oscar Wilde's finest work to be *The Ballad of Reading Gaol* (an account of his years in prison on a charge of homosexuality). His brilliance in challenging conventional thinking and espousing sometimes bizarre new ideas shines through such other works as *The Importance of Being Earnest* and his gripping novel *The Picture of Dorian Gray*. He died penniless in Paris in 1900.

W. B. Yeats The birthplace of W. B. Yeats (1865) was 5 Sandymount Avenue, and from 1928 to 1932 he resided at 42 Fitzwilliam Square. Aside from his poetry and *The Celtic Twilight* about "romantic Ireland," one of Yeats' most important contributions to Irish culture was his involvement in the founding of Dublin's Abbey Theatre (see page 66). He was often seen in Toner's pub on Lower Baggot Street in Dublin. Yeats died in Paris in 1939, but at the end of World War II his remains were returned to Ireland for burial at Drumcliffe near his beloved Thoor Ballylee (see page 46) where his more esoteric writings were produced.

REGIONAL SIGHTS

Key to symbols

✚ map coordinates refer to the region map on page 60; sights below are highlighted in yellow on the map

✉ address or location   ☎ telephone number

◉ opening times   🍴 restaurant on site or nearby

🚉 nearest bus or railroad station   💵 admission charge: $$$ more than €6, $$ €4 to €6, $ less than €4

ℹ information

ATHLONE AND THE SHANNON

Straddling the River Shannon, the historic town of Athlone is a premier center for cruising in the heart of Ireland. The river marks a change in character between the two halves of the town, with narrow streets of old buildings grouped around the castle on the west bank and 19th- and 20th-century developments on the east. Athlone has always been an important crossing on the Shannon (*Áth Luain* means the Ford of Luan), and Athlone Castle, dating from 1210, was a powerful defense of this strategic ford of the river.

During Oliver Cromwell's rampage through Ireland, the castle was the focus of seiges of the town in 1690 and 1691. At the end of the 18th-century, the ruined walls were heavily reconstructed when there was a threat of a Napoleonic invasion. An audiovisual presentation in the visitor center details the seige history, and there are exhibits on the castle, the town and the power resources of the Shannon. The Museum of the Old Athlone Society includes medieval gravestones and mementos of the great Athlone-born tenor, John McCormack; his birthplace is marked by a bronze plaque in The Bawn, a narrow lane off Mardyke Street.

South of Athlone along the river is one of Ireland's holiest sites, Clonmacnois, where St. Ciaran founded a monastery in 548. It was plundered by Irish chieftains, Vikings and Anglo-Normans, and it finally gave in to its attackers when Cromwell's forces desecrated it beyond restoration. Today you'll find among its ruins a cathedral, eight churches, two round towers, the remains of a castle, more than 200 monumental slabs and three sculptured high crosses. There are guided tours during the summer months, an excellent presentation at the visitor center and an informative 5-mile rail tour of the Blackwater raised bog.

East of Athlone on the N6 road is Locke's Distillery. Established in 1757, Locke's was one of the first licensed distilleries in the world and operated for nearly 200 years before it closed in 1957. Restored as a museum, it uses the original machinery to demonstrate whiskey-making techniques.

The River Shannon is the longest river in the Ireland. Rising in a humble pool in County Cavan, it carves a ponderous course to Limerick through the brimming flood plains and water meadows of several counties straddling the Leinster-Connacht border. At first the landscape around the river appears monontonous – a shallow saucer of endless unremarkable arable and pasture land broken by lakes, rivers and canals – there are few memorable vistas.

The smallish watery counties forming the geographical heart of Ireland are often portrayed as places to get through on the way to somewhere more interesting. Busy, dreary main roads blast through on radial routes from Dublin to the west coast of counties Mayo and Galway and facilities for visitors are limited compared with popular western or southeastern spots. However, these lakeland counties offer a less stereotyped picture of Ireland.

The Shannon is not only an important navigable waterway, but also a popular recreational base for fishing and boating activities, scenic interest and wildlife habitats. Visitors are welcomed with true Irish hospitality, with no pressure to buy sweaters or shamrock table linen!

✚ A3

Tourist information ✉ Athlone Castle, St. Peter's Square ☎ 0902 94630 ◉ Daily 9:30–5:30, Jun.–Sep.; Mon.–Sat. Apr., May, Oct.

Athlone Castle ✉ St. Peter's Square ☎ 0902 72107 ◉ Mon.–Sat. 10–4:30, Sun. noon–5, May–Sep. 💵 $$

Clonmacnoise and Bog Tour ✉ 4 miles north of Shannonbridge on R357, Co. Offaly ☎ 0905 74195

Boats moored at the harbor in Dalkey

🕐 Daily 9–9, mid-Mar. to mid-Sep; 10–6 mid-Sep–Oct.; 10–5:30, rest of year 🍴 Tearoom 🤚 $$
Locke's Distillery ✉ Kilbeggan, Co. Westmeath
☎ 0506 32134; fax 0506 32201 🕐 Daily 9–6,
Apr.–Oct.; 10–4, rest of year 🍴 Restaurant 🤚 $$

AVOCA

Avoca, a pretty hamlet of neat white cottages in a wooded setting, is the home of Avoca Handweavers, Ireland's oldest hand-weaving mill dating from 1723, whose weaves, colors and patterns have won worldwide acclaim. The Avonmore and Avonbeg rivers combine to become the Avoca River, here inspiring 19th-century poet Thomas Moore's tribute to its tranquility *Meeting of the Waters*. A path leads down to the river bank and a clearing, which holds a bust of the poet; the tree stump on which he sat while composing his famous lines is marked with a plaque.

Just 4 miles north toward Rathdrum in one of County Wicklow's most beautifully forested areas is Avondale House. Charles Stewart Parnell, a heroic and tragic figure among Ireland's most prominent nationalist leaders, was born and lived much of his life in this 1777 mansion. Much of his patriotic fervor undoubtedly came from his mother, an American with strong anti-British leanings. His political career was crowned by land reforms achieved by his leadership of the Land League. His popularity, however, was dealt a death blow when he was named correspondent in a divorce action against his long-time mistress Katherine (Kitty) O'Shea, from which he never recovered politically. There's a small museum filled with mementos of his life (1846–91) and an interesting gift shop. A walk in the adjacent forest park provides a restful interlude.
➕ C2
Tourist information ✉ Fitzwilliam Square, Wicklow
☎ 0404 69117; fax 0404 69118 🕐 Mon.–Sat. 9–6,
Jun.–Sep.; Mon.–Fri., rest of year
Avondale House and Forest Park ✉ 1 mile south of
Rathdrum ☎ 0404 46111; fax 0404 46111 🕐 Daily
11–5, mid-Mar.–Oct. 🍴 Restaurant 🤚 $$

DALKEY

Originally a fishing village at the southern end of Dublin Bay, Dalkey is one of the Leinster coast's most charming spots. In recent years it has become a stylish address for several stars. Nothing new, really – George Bernard Shaw lived for a time in a cottage on Dalkey Hill, and writers Flann O'Brien and Hugh Leonard (still a resident) have called it home.

Leinster

Off the coast from Collemore Harbour, 22-acre Dalkey Island is inhabited these days only by a few wild goats, but there is evidence that people lived here as early as the fourth century BC. It's a wonderful get-away-from-it-all spot, and even better if you bring a picnic. During summer the Heritage Centre can arrange for local boat owners to take you to the island and come back for you at a prearranged time. The Heritage Centre is located in restored Dalkey Castle, and its exceptionally helpful staff can steer you to other points of interest in the area and arrange guided tours with advance notice.

Killiney Bay has been likened to the Bay of Naples, and it is best viewed from Victoria Park, which is only a short walk from Dalkey along the Vico Road. A beautiful public beach leads to Killiney Hill and Victoria Park. Panoramic views of the bay add to the tranquility of the park's open green spaces interspersed with rocky outcroppings, which are perfect for hiking up for an even better view.

➕ C3

Tourist information ✉ Dublin Tourism, Suffolk Street ☎ 01 605 7700 🕐 Mon.–Sat., 9–5:30, Sun. 10:30–3 (Jul.–Aug.)

Dalkey Castle and Heritage Centre ✉ Castle Street, Dalkey ☎ 01 285 8366; fax 01 284 3141 🕐 Mon.–Fri. 9:30–5, Sat.–Sun. 11–5, Apr.–Oct.; Sat.–Sun 11–5, rest of year 🚌 8, DART Dalkey Station 🎟 Free

DROGHEDA

Drogheda stands at the lowest bridging point of the River Boyne, just a few miles from the site of the famous Battle of the Boyne in 1690. Something of the historic medieval town can still be seen in the hilly streets, though little remains of the old town walls. To the west of Drogheda lies the Boyne Valley, and while it is filled to overflowing with historical landmarks, none is more significant than this stretch along the Louth and Meath border. It was here that William of Orange ("King Billy") defeated James II, changing the course of Irish history dramatically.

The Boyne Valley is strewn with some of Ireland's most important archeological monuments, more than 40 in all, and the visitor center in Donore unfolds their story before you set off to explore this remarkable landscape. It is also the required starting point from which to tour the two most impressive megalithic tombs, Newgrange and Knowth. The visitor center operates a minibus service to and from these wonders. The numbers for each tour are strictly limited, but the experience is well worth the wait.

Newgrange was probably built by the first settlers who came to Ireland from the European continent more than 5,000 years ago. This makes it possibly 1,000 years older than Stonehenge. We know almost nothing about them or what the ornamental spirals and other decorations at this massive burial mound symbolize. We don't even know for whom the structure was built, whether holy men, chieftains or kings. What we do know is that they were skilled builders, for the corbeled roof above the burial chamber has kept out the dampness of 40 centuries, the 62-foot-long passage still serves quite well as an entry to the 19-foot-high chamber, and the stone at its entrance remains an enduring testament to prehistoric craftsmanship. This amazing 36-foot mound includes 200,000 tons of stone and a six-ton capstone. Stones as large as 16 tons each came from as far away as County Wicklow.

Archeologists are constantly carrying out research at Newgrange in an effort to unravel such mysteries as the reason a roof box above the doorway is so placed that the sun's rays reach the burial chamber only at 8:58 a.m. on the shortest day of the year, and then for exactly 17 minutes!

At busy times you will have to arrive early in the day to ensure admission to Newgrange. Archeological work continues in the Boyne Valley, which means that some sites may be closed. About a mile northwest of Newgrange, Knowth is still under excavation. Here there are two passage tombs, with another 17 smaller tombs in the immediate vicinity. Like Newgrange's artwork, the enigmatic passage tomb artwork at Knowth is some of the finest in Europe.

Directly west of Newgrange is a traditional 333-acre farm growing barley, wheat and other grains. The cows, bulls,

The mid-18th-century Church of St. Peter, Drogheda

heifers, goats, pigs, ponies, Hampshire Downs sheep (the ones with a "teddy-bear coat"), rabbits, dogs and chickens are the main attraction. One of the farmers will lead you through this thriving menagerie, with a running commentary on just how the farm works.

🕂 C4

Tourist information ✉ Drogheda Bus Station, Donore Road ☎ 041 983 7070 🕓 Mon.–Sat. 9:30–5:30, Sun. noon–4:30, May–Sep.

Boyne Valley Visitor Centre ✉ Donore, Co. Meath (for directions see drive on page 95) ☎ 041 988 0300; fax 041 980 3071 🕓 Daily 9–7 Jun.–mid-Sep.; 9–6:30, May and mid-Sep.–Oct.; 9:30–5:30, Mar.–Apr. and Oct.; 9:30–5, rest of year. Last tour for Knowth and Newgrange departs 1.5 hours before closing time 🎫 Newgrange/Knowth: $$$; visitor centre: $

Newgrange Farm ✉ Located at Slane village, 7 miles from Drogheda on N51 ☎ 041 982 4119; fax 041 982 4119 🕓 Daily 10–5, Easter–Aug. 🍴 Coffee Shop 🎫 $$

DRIVE: BOYNE VALLEY

Duration: 1–2 days

This historic 84-mile drive through Ireland's past passes through pleasant countryside rich in megalithic and early-Christian monuments.

> *Starting from the tourist office at Drogheda, take the N1 for Belfast. After 5 miles turn left, following signposts for Boyne Drive, Monasterboice. After half a mile, turn left again.*

Monasterboice was once a large monastic community. Pick your way between ancient and modern graves to see two of the finest high crosses in the country. These free-standing carvings in stone were of a quality unparalleled anywhere in Europe at the time they were erected, and yet the very high round tower is a reminder that these remarkable works of art were created in the midst of Viking plunder. The West Cross stands close to the round tower, while the 17-foot-high Cross of Muiredach – so called because of the inscription on the base, which says, "A prayer for Muiredach by whom this cross was made" – is smaller and more perfect in appearance. The messages on these crosses follow coherent themes of God's grace to man and the parallels between Old and New Testaments. On Muiredach's Cross, look for the stories of Adam and Eve, Cain and Abel, the Last Judgment and the crucifixion of Christ.

An event of religious significance of more recent times was the visit of Pope John Paul II in 1979, and the point where he celebrated Mass is marked on the main Belfast to Dublin road.

> *Continue past Monasterboice. After a mile, turn right for Mellifont. After a mile, turn left on the Drogheda road, R168, and after another mile, turn right for Mellifont.*

To walk in the footsteps of monks who

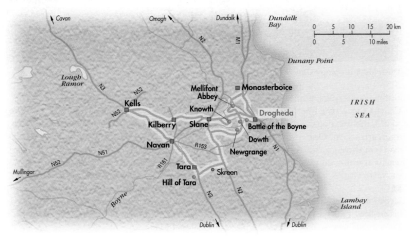

The vast passage tomb at Newgrange is faced with sparkling quartzite

founded Mellifont Abbey here on the banks of the Mattock river in 1142 is to drink in the peacefulness of a setting that invites meditation. The chapter house and ruins of the cloister still remain from the structures built in the 13th century, but the foundations alone are left of the original building. An octagonal lavabo once equipped with water jets and basins is the most interesting structure.

Return to the crossroads and turn right. After 2 miles turn right. Go straight over the crossroads, following the signpost to King William's Glen. After 1 mile turn right on to the N51, then 2.5 miles farther on, turn left and follow signs for Newgrange (see page 92).

Irish architecture may have begun in the Boyne Valley in 3000 BC. People who had only stone and wood for tools created the most impressive monuments of their kind in Western Europe. Little is known of these people or of those interred in these prehistoric tombs, but excavations have shown that they cultivated crops and cleared areas of forest.

The mound at Newgrange, constructed with water-rolled pebbles, is retained by a curb of great stone blocks lying end to end, topped by white quartz and granite boulders. The passage is lined with huge stones, and the central cross-shaped chamber is roofed with a vault untouched in 5,000 years. Standing around the mound is an incomplete circle of stones.

At Dowth, a larger passage tomb has two chambers, while Knowth has two passage tombs surrounded by 18 smaller ones. Knowth was used from the Stone Age, and in the early Christian era was a seat of the high kings of Ireland. The significance of the Boyne Valley tombs is that here artwork combines with the engineering feats of the passage tombs of Ireland. Spirals, lozenges, zigzags, sunbursts – figures cut in stone with stone implements – decorate the monuments.

Return by minor roads to the N51 and turn left for Slane.

Slane occupies an attractive curve on the River Boyne and is overlooked by the Hill of Slane, where St. Patrick is said to have announced Christianity's arrival in Ireland. Legend or fact, the summit of Slane Hill would certainly have been ideal for that purpose, looking down as it does on sweeping views of the Boyne Valley. From the

One of Kells' four high crosses

over the fertile plains of Meath and beyond. From the time that pagans worshipped here, Tara has figured in Irish history and legend. The high kings were seated here and it was the center of political and religious power before the arrival of Christianity. A *feis* (festival) at royal Tara was held at harvest or at the crowning of a king. Burial mounds here go back some 4,000 years, and there are earthworks and low walls of earth dating from the Iron Age. All else of Tara's regal trappings must be left to your imagination as you view this low hillside and feel the mystical presence of pagan priests and ancient royalty. A presentation in the visitor center will give you a fuller understanding of the importance of this place.

Five chariot roads led here from all parts of Ireland. The *rath* of the synods is an elaborate earthwork. The mound of the hostages, a Stone Age passage tomb that stands inside the royal enclosure, is an Iron Age hill fort and encloses the royal seat, a ring fort. On Cormac's House is the stone of destiny, said to be the inauguration stone of the kings. Also here are the banquet hall, the enclosure of King Laoghaire, the sloping trenches and *grainne's* enclosure. A statue of St. Patrick recalls his profound influence, but it was the coming of Christianity that led to the eventual decline of Tara.

Return to the N3 and turn right. After 2 miles turn left, following signs to Skreen Church and Cross, go straight over two sets of crossroads and follow a narrow, uneven road for 4.5 miles, then turn left toward Drogheda. After 1 mile turn left toward Slane on the N2 and follow the marked route for the Battle of the Boyne site.

It does not take a great effort of the imagination to picture the field of battle in 1690, when the armies of William of Orange and James II met in a conflict that was significant for Ireland, Britain and Europe. A huge orange and green sign beside the deep waters of the Boyne marks the main site of the conflict, while helpful signs along the way show where the opposing armies camped, where battle was joined and where the river was crossed. The route passes along the Boyne Navigation Canal, once a link in Ireland's waterways system.

Take the N51 back to Drogheda.

viewpoint on the hill, the pleasant village of Slane can be seen running steeply down to the banks of the river. Just to the east is the cottage of the poet Francis Ledwidge, who died during World War I.

Slane Castle on the banks of the Boyne river is the home of the Mount Charles family. Badly damaged by fire in 1991, the castle is not open to the public, but the magnificent amphitheater in front of the house is used regularly as a stage for spectacular rock concerts.

Take the N51 for Navan, and after 1 mile turn right on the R163 for Kells.

In the sixth century, St. Colmcille founded a monastic settlement on this site. Kells, or Ceanannus Mór, became one of the great religious centers of Western Europe. This is where Ireland's most celebrated illuminated medieval manuscript, the famous *Book of Kells*, was written, now on view in the library at Trinity College, Dublin (see page 84). Facsimiles of the book are on display in the Kells Heritage Centre. St. Columba's Church at the top of Market Street was built on the original site. It is by far the most impressive building in the town. Four high crosses and a round tower are in the grounds.

Take the N3 (via Navan) for Dublin, and after 6 miles turn right at the signpost for Tara.

The Hill of Tara commands majestic views

DUN LAOGHAIRE

This is a place to promenade along the extensive harbor piers, past the villas on the front or through the parks. Savor the Victorian features of the place that was called Kingstown from the visit of George IV in 1821 until the establishment of the Irish Free State. When the granite piers were completed in 1859, the harbor was the biggest artificial haven in the world. Ships and ferries to England use the port and it is home to several yacht clubs, of which the Royal St. George and the Royal Irish are the oldest. The town also boasts Ireland's National Maritime Museum, housed in the Mariners' Church.

Built during the Napoleonic Wars in the early 19th century, the Martello Tower, which was home briefly in 1904 for James Joyce and Oliver St. John Gogarty, is now a museum displaying Joyce's personal letters, manuscripts, books, photographs, walking stick, waistcoat and other personal possessions. Lectures and poetry readings are held here, and there are marvelous sea views from the parapet. The Martello Tower and the nearby "Forty-foot" gentlemen's bathing place are vividly described in James Joyce's novel *Ulysses*.

An old stone jetty on the tranquil lakes of Glendalough

➕ C3

Tourist information ✉ Ferry Building, Dun Laoghaire ☎ 066 979 2083 🕐 Mon.–Sat. 9–5

James Joyce Tower and Museum ✉ Sandycove ☎ 01 280 9265 or 01 872 2077 🕐 Mon.–Sat. 10–1 and 2–5, Sun. 2–6, Apr.–Oct. 🚌 8 (from Burgh Quay, Dublin), DART Sandycove Station 💷 $$

GLENDALOUGH

Glendalough, the glen of two loughs, is the loveliest and most historic of all its Wicklow rivals. Two beautiful loughs lie deep in a valley of granite escarpments and rocky outcrops. On its green slopes are the gentle contours of native trees, on its ridges the jagged outline of pines. Add to this picturesque scene a soaring round tower and ruined stone churches in the valley, and you have a combination which makes Glendalough one of the most beautiful and historic places in Ireland. St. Kevin found solitude and spiritual peace in this place of exquisite natural beauty, and he lived a hermit's existence here for many years. Further up the valley is St. Kevin's Bed, a precarious rocky ledge high on a cliff-face (only safely accessible by boat) where the saint used to sleep. When he died at an advanced age in 617, he left behind a great school that had grown up around his teachings and had gained respect throughout the Western world as an institution of higher learning.

Throughout this mystical glen, ruins trace the history of his time here and the turbulent centuries since. The main group of ruins are just east of the Lower Lake. Among the most interesting are the Church of the Rock (Tempall na Skellig) and St. Kevin's Bed (a tiny hollowed-out hole) to the east of the oratory and about 30 feet above the lake. There are several stone churches, numerous crosses and a round tower. All in all, this is a place to linger, with an excellent choice of routes for keen walkers.

➕ C2

Glendalough Visitor Centre ✉ 7 miles east of Wicklow town ☎ 404 45325; fax 404 45626 🕐 Daily 9:30–6, mid-Mar. to mid-Oct.; 9:30–5, rest of year 🚌 Scheduled bus service from Dublin daily (check with tourist information (☎ 01 605 7700) for times of departure) 💷 $$

Leinster

HOWTH

The pretty village of Howth sits at the
northern end of Dublin Bay's curve, and
Howth Castle crowns a steep hill, with
splendid views of the bay and village.
While the castle is not open to the public,
visitors are welcome to walk the pathways
of its renowned 30-acre garden, which has
been maturing since 1875. The gardens
are open year-round, but it is in May and
June that more than 2,000 varieties of
rhododendron are at their most colorful.
The Transport Museum on the castle
grounds holds a small collection of horse-
drawn trams and buses, as well as other
public and military forms of transport. A
growing suburb of Dublin, this fishing
village still has a busy harbor.
✚ C3

Tourist information ✉ Mains Court, Swords ☎ 0184
00077 🕐 Mon.–Fri. 9–5
Howth Castle Gardens and Transport Museum ☎ 01
848 0831 🕐 Castle gardens: daily dawn–dusk;
museum: daily 10–5, Jun.–Aug.; Sat.–Sun. 2–5, rest of
year 🚌 31, DART Howth Station 🎟 Museum: $

KILKENNY

Kilkenny is a fascinating sightseeing
town. Its narrow, winding streets and
well-preserved structures make it perhaps
the most perfect example of a medieval
town in Ireland today. Its Irish name is
Cill Chainnigh, or St. Canice's Church. A
little monastery established here by the
good saint in the sixth century on the
grounds of the present St. Canice's
Cathedral, whose round tower dates back
to the original settlement. But it was the

The rocky promontory of Howth Head

Leinster

The 150-foot Long Gallery in Kilkenny Castle – decorated with carved oak beams

Normans and later the Anglo-Normans who built up the dignified town as a trading center that enjoyed the protection of royalty until the mid-14th century.

It was in 1366 that the infamous Statutes of Kilkenny forbade any mingling of Anglo-Normans with the native Irish. By the time Englishman Oliver Cromwell arrived in 1650, the city's population was demoralized, making it easy for him to seize the town, slaughter many residents and banish others to Connaght and confiscate their property. Both Kilkenny Castle and the lovely St. Canice's Cathedral, built in the 13th century, were badly treated by Cromwell. Now beautifully restored, the cathedral is a repository for many fine medieval monuments, including 13th-century carvings and colorful stained-glass windows. You can climb its ninth-century round tower in good weather for clear views over the town. The impressive Kilkenny Castle (the seat of the Butler family) was also restored and continued to be used as a residence until 1935. In 1967 the Marquess of Ormonde gave it to the people of Kilkenny, who turned it over to the state two years later. Rich in artworks – there are miles of oil portraits – and elegant furnishings, it is open for tours conducted by guides well-versed in stories

of the people who lived here. Ask about "Black Tom," then get set to hear some rather outrageous tales.

Walking Kilkenny streets is a delight – don't miss Kyteler's Inn, a pub and restaurant on St. Kieran Street. It's the former residence of Dame Alice Kyteler who escaped a fiery death when convicted of witchcraft in 1324. Also be sure to visit the Rothe House on Parliament Street, a typical middle-class Tudor home, and the Tholsel, Kilkenny's city hall, which was erected in 1761 as a tollhouse and market.

Seven miles from Kilkenny is Dunmore Cave, a series of underground caves whose records date back to the ninth-century Irish triads.

➕ B2

Tourist information ✉ Shee Alms House, Rose Inn Street ☎ 056 51500 🕐 Mon.–Sat. 9–7, Sun 11–1 and 2–5, Jul.–Aug.; Mon.–Sat. 9–6, Sun. 11–1 and 2–5, Apr.–May, Sep.; Mon.–Sat 9–5, rest of year

St. Canice's Cathedral ✉ Irishtown ☎ 056 64971 🕐 Mon.–Sat. 9–1 and 2–6, Sun. 2–6, Easter–Oct.; Mon.–Sat. 10–1 and 2–4, rest of year 🎟 $

Kilkenny Castle ✉ The Parade ☎ 056 21450 🕐 Daily 10–7, Jun. to Sep.; 10:30–5, Apr.–May; Tue.–Sun. 11–12:45 and 2–5, rest of year 🎟 $$

Dunmore Cave ✉ Ballyfoyle, 7 miles from Kilkenny ☎ 056 67726 or 056 51500 🕐 Daily 9:30–7:30, mid-Jun. to mid-Sep.; 10–5, mid-Mar. to mid-Jun. and mid-Sep.–Oct.; (guided tours only) 🎟 $

Leinster

DRIVE: WITCHES AND CASTLES

Duration: 1–2 days

Norman castles, ecclesiastical ruins and tales of medieval witches haunt Kilkenny, the starting point for this 201-mile drive. Kildare's horse country appeals to followers of the sport of kings, and beautiful gardens near Portlaoise have universal appeal. Celtic kings and St. Patrick draw you on to Cashel.

From the tourist office in Kilkenny, take the R700 southeast for 11 miles to Thomastown.

This prosperous little market town on the banks of the River Nore is named after Thomas FitzAnthony Walsh, seneschal of Leinster, who built a castle and walled the town in the early 13th century. Among its interesting and ancient ruins are the remains of the 13th-century church where there are fragments of a high cross and some badly weathered effigies. Three miles away, the Kilfane church ruins have an impressive medieval stone effigy of a crusader in full armor. Grennan Castle, 1.5 miles to the southwest, is now in ruins. The most impressive remains of ancient buildings in the town are those of a large church dating from the 13th century.

Jerpoint Cistercian Abbey, 2 miles southwest of Thomastown on the N9, is one of Ireland's finest monastic ruins. Founded in the 12th century, it was dissolved and its lands given to the Ormonde family in 1540. The extensive remains are awe-inspiring, with the original Romanesque pillars, a fine chancel and the most decorative cloister arcade of any Irish church. The detailed secular and religious carved figures are an accurate portrayal of the armor and clothing of 15th- and 16th-century Ireland. A visitor center provides information on the abbey's long history. Jerpoint Abbey dates back to 1158, and the riverside ruins of the Benedictine and later Cistercian monastery contain many monuments and sculptures of saints and knights from medieval times.

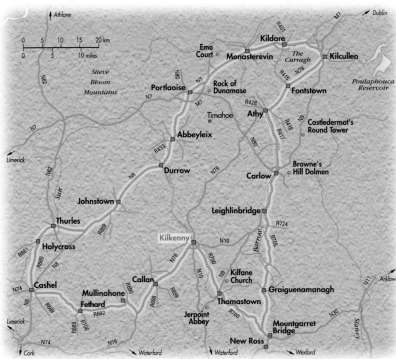

Brimming with character and winding roads, the old town of New Ross sits along the River Barrow

Here you'll find a 15th-century tower and cloister, and a small visitor center with picnic grounds.

Mount Juliet, signposted from the town center, was once one of Ireland's largest private estates, covering 1,411 acres of woodlands, pastures and landscaped lawns. Now a luxury hotel, the grounds provide an exceptionally beautiful drive off the main roads, and its public rooms are open to everyone.

Take the R700 southeast for 14 miles to Mountgarret Bridge, where it joins the N30 for the short drive to New Ross.

There is much evidence of medieval origins in the narrow streets of New Ross, which was built on a steep hill overlooking the River Barrow. The town invites exploration on foot, as many of the streets are stepped and inaccessible to vehicles. The long bridge in the town center connects New Ross to County Kilkenny. The original bridge was built around 1200 and the town was soon walled. In 1643, it held off a siege by the Duke of Ormonde, but fell to Englishman Oliver Cromwell just six years later. It was captured

and then lost by insurgents in 1798, leaving the town in flames and many of its inhabitants slain.

The Tholsel (Town Hall) had to be rebuilt in 1806 when the original 18th-century structure fell victim to subsidence. It has a fine clock tower and holds the maces of Kings Edward III and Charles II and ancient volumes of the minutes of the old town corporation. The 1798 memorial at the Tholsel depicts a "croppy boy," typical of the insurgents who assaulted the town.

Head north on the N30, turn left on the R700, then right after a short distance on the R705 for 23 miles to join the N9 at Leighlinbridge for the 7-mile drive into Carlow.

The village of Graiguenamanagh (the Granary of the Monks), between New Ross and Carlow, was once a place of great ecclesiastical importance. Occupying the site was the Abbey of Duiske, built between 1207 and 1240. It was suppressed in 1536, but determined monks stayed on for many years afterward before abandoning the extensive settlement. By 1774 it stood in ruins and the tower collapsed. A large part of the church was roofed in 1813 and Catholic services were resumed. In the 1970s, a group of dedicated locals undertook a major restoration, and today the completely restored abbey serves as the parish church.

The county town of Ireland's second smallest county, Carlow was an Anglo-Norman stronghold, strategically placed on the border of the English "Pale," a protected area around Dublin and its environs. The 640 insurgents who fell here during their 1798 attack on the town are remembered by a fine Celtic cross.

The west wall and the two flanking towers of 13th-century Carlow Castle can be seen near the bridge across the Barrow. This Norman castle was destroyed not by Cromwell, who captured it in 1650, but by one Dr. Middleton in 1814. In his zeal to convert it into an asylum, he tried to reduce the thickness of the walls with explosives, rendering it no more than a dangerous shell, most of which had to be demolished. The ruins of the castle, a stronghold of the earls of Thomond are near the Barrow Bridge.

The Cathedral of the Assumption on Tullow Street is a fine Gothic-style building erected between 1828 and 1833. Of special interest are its 151-foot lantern tower and the marble monument of the 19th-century political writer Bishop Doyle by the sculptor John Hogan. On College Street, next to the tourist information, a state-of-the-art museum is being built. It's due to open in 2003.

Two miles east of Carlow on the L7, Browne's Hill Dolmen is thought to be Europe's largest, with a 100-ton capstone. Its exact purpose is a matter of speculation, but many believe the megalithic structure marks the burial place of an ancient local king.

Follow the R417 north to Athy. Turn northeast on the N78 for Kilcullen, then northwest on the R413 to its junction with the N7, which takes you west to Kildare.

En route to Kildare, stop in Athy to view the Dominican church, a striking example of modern architecture. Inside are George Campbell's outstanding *Stations of the Cross*. To the southeast of Athy, Castledermot's ecclesiastical ruins are a round tower, two high crosses and the remains of a Franciscan friary church.

In the heart of Ireland's horse-breeding and training country, the market town of Kildare's sits on the edge of the vast Curragh plain, and the National Stud, Ireland's most famous breeding ground, is nearby. Stroll around here and you'll understand why Irish horses are so prized around the world. You can visit the 288 stalls and watch horses being groomed and exercised. The history of the horse from prehistoric times to the present day is represented in the Horse Museum. The Japanese garden, whose design symbolizes the lifespan of man, took four years to lay out (1906–10) and today is considered Europe's finest Oriental garden (see page 106).

East of town, horse racing has reigned supreme for centuries at the Curragh, where all the Irish Classics are run. The Curragh Camp, handed over to the Irish army in 1922, has been an important military station for a century. Here you can see the famous 1920 armored car "Slievenamon" in which Michael Collins was traveling when the fatal ambush of 1922 took place.

The Hill of Allen, legendary home of Irish folk hero Finn MacCool (see page 199) and the site of three royal residences in ancient Leinster, is northeast of town and is crowned by a 19th-century battlemented stone tower.

Take the N7 southeast to reach Portlaoise.

Set at the junction of the Dublin to Limerick and Dublin to Cork main roads, Portlaoise is also the site of Ireland's national prison. Four miles east of town, the Rock of Dunamase rises 200 feet above the plain, with the ruined 12th-century castle of Dermot MacMurrough, one-time king of Leinster.

Emo Court, 8 miles northeast of Portlaoise off the N7, is probably the premier attraction of County Laois. "Magnificent" is the only word for this neoclassical mansion designed in 1790 by the celebrated architect James Gandon, designer of the Custom House and several other Dublin landmark buildings. The grand house is open to the public and the landscape of woodland and lake is undergoing careful restoration. The formal gardens and extensive parkland are famous for their statuary, an avenue of giant sequoia trees and sweeping lawns dotted with neatly clipped yew trees, all providing a perfect foil for this fascinating 18th-century mansion. If you enjoy walking, the impressive lake and woodland areas are a real treat. Access to the house is by guided tour only.

To the west of town, the many roads crossing the Slieve Bloom Mountains offer scenic drives.

Take the N8 for 9 miles south to Abbeyleix.

This attractive town has tree-lined streets, neat town houses and a fountain in the square. It is noted for the de Vesci Demesne, known as Abbeyleix House. The great house, which dates to 1773, is not open to the public, but the splendid grounds are. They include formal terrace gardens to the west of the house, a "wild garden" called the Paradise Garden, which is carpeted with bluebells in spring, and an American garden with magnolia trees. There is also a magnificent avenue of lime trees. The Heritage House in Abbeyleix is a fine example of Gothic architecture built in 1884 and designed to be a focus for visitors to this historic town. Interactive multimedia displays tell the story of Abbeyleix and the surrounding area.

Take the N8 southwest to the N75 turnoff to Thurles.

In ancient times, the O'Fogartys fortified this site on the River Suir, and although the Norman Strongbow's army was soundly defeated here in 1174, Anglo-Normans returned later to build a castle that would protect the crossing. Today it is a busy, well-laid-out marketing center for the surrounding agricultural area. It is also the cathedral town of the archdiocese of Cashel and Emly.

Take the R660 south for 13 miles to reach Cashel.

Cashel is a prosperous town catering well for the tourist and is best known for the Rock of Cashel (see page 129). Look above the ground floor of the shop opposite city hall to see the battlements and gargoyles of what was 15th-century Quirke's Castle, named after a family who lived there in the 19th century. At the southwest end of Main Street, the ornamental fountain is in memory of Dean Kinane and his efforts in bringing a much-needed extension of the railway to Cashel in 1904.

Take the R692 southeast to Fethard.

Fethard was an important Anglo-Norman settlement in medieval times. Remnants of the old town walls and their flanking towers

Fine monastic ruins at Jerpoint Abbey

can still be seen. In the town center, there are keeps of three 15th-century castles, including that of Fethard Castle. Well-preserved remains of a priory contain several 16th- and 17th-century tombs. More than 1,000 exhibits of rural life in this area are on display at the Folk, Farm and Transport Museum.

Take the R692 northeast to Mullinahone. Turn right for Callan, then turn north on the N76 for the 11-mile drive back to Kilkenny.

Jerpoint Abbey ✉ Thomastown, Co. Kilkenny ☎ 056 24623 ⏰ Daily 10–5, Mar.–May and Oct.; 9:30–6:30, Jun.–Sep.; 10–4, Nov. 🍴 $$

The National Stud ✉ Tully, Kildare, Co. Kildare (off Dublin to Limerick road, N7) ☎ 045 21617 ⏰ Daily 9–5, mid-Feb. to mid-Nov. 🍴 Restaurant 🍴 $$$

Emo Court ✉ Emo, Co. Laois (6 miles northeast of Portlaois) ☎ 0502 26573 ⏰ Tue.–Sun. 10:30–5, mid-Jun. to mid-Sep.; gardens: daily dawn–dusk 🍴 $$

The Heritage House ✉ Abbeyleix, Co. Laois ☎ 0502 31653; fax 0502 30059 ⏰ Mon.–Sat. 10–6, Sun, 1–6, May–Sep. 🍴 $$

Fethard Folk Farm and Transport Museum ✉ Cashel Road, Fethard ☎ 0502 31516 ⏰ Sun.11:30–5 🍴 $

Leinster

MALAHIDE

The speed at which Malahide is growing as a favored residential suburb of Dublin has not robbed it of its old-fashioned seaside atmosphere, and its popularity is enhanced by its many quality restaurants. There is a good beach to the east of the town, and an even better one farther along the coast at Portmarnock. There are two historic buildings on the way to Portmarnock – a martello tower, built in the early 1800s as a provision against Napoleonic invasion, and Robswall's Castle, a tower house to which a Victorian house has been added.

Malahide's most famous relic of history is its castle, one of the major showpieces of the Dublin area. Its core is medieval and, in spite of considerable changes from the intervening centuries, it still appears from the outside as a product of the Middle Ages. Malahide Castle is the stately residence that was occupied until 1973 by the descendants of Lord Talbot de Malahide, its founder in 1185. One of the many historic happenings within its walls occurred in 1690 when some 14 Talbot cousins sat down to breakfast together one morning before leaving to fight for King James in the Battle of the Boyne, a battle in which all met their death.

Set in a 268-acre demesne whose formal gardens alone are worth a visit, the castle still retains traces of the original moat. Inside there is magnificent oak paneling and plasterwork, fine Irish period furniture and many paintings, including a rich collection of portraits of historical Irish figures on loan from the National Gallery in Dublin (see page 81). These are strikingly displayed in the great 17th-century dining hall.

A separate building holds the Fry Model Railway Museum, the first of its

Malahide Castle to the north of Dublin city houses much of Dublin's National Portrait Collection

kind in Ireland. On display are more than 300 handmade model trains, trams and railroad artifacts left by the late Cyril Fry, an enthusiastic railway engineer.

Farther north of Malahide is Newbridge House, another magnificent desmesne of 350 acres, and dating from 1737, this mansion has one of the finest Georgian interiors in the country. Its great red drawing room is just as it was when the Cobbe family was in residence here, giving you a perfect picture of how wealthy families entertained. To see how the downstairs house staff and the estate-workers kept the wheels turning, visit the kitchen and laundry, as well as the coach house, dairy, carpenter's shop and blacksmith's forge, all equipped with 19th-century implements. Within the grounds there's a 29-acre traditional farm, complete with farm animals.

✠ C3

Tourist information ✉ Dublin Tourism, Suffolk Street ☎ 01 605 7700 ⏰ Mon.–Sat. 9–5:30, Sun. 10:30–3, Jul.–Aug.

The huge frontage of Russborough House displays heraldic lions

Malahide Castle and Fry Model Railway Museum
✉ Malahide ☎ Castle: 01 846 2184; railway: 01 846 3779 ⏰ Castle: Mon.–Sat. 10–5, Sun. 11–6, Apr.–Oct.; Mon.–Fri. 10–5, Sat.–Sun. 2–5, rest of year
🍴 Restaurant 🚌 42 (from Beresford Place), DART Connolly Station to Malahide 💷 $$$

Newbridge House and Traditional Farm
✉ Donabate (12 miles north of Dublin on Belfast road) ☎ 01 843 6534 ⏰ Tue.–Sat. 10–1 and 2–5, Sun. 2–6, Apr.–Sep.; Sat.–Sun. 2–5, rest of year
🍴 Coffee shop 🚌 33B (from Eden Quay) 💷 $$

RUSSBOROUGH HOUSE

One of the most imposing of Ireland's Great Houses, Russborough was built by architect Richard Castle for Joseph Leeson, later Earl of Milltown. It was built from granite and in the Palladian style. Construction began in 1741 and took 10 years to complete. Its interior features fine stucco ceilings, marble fireplaces, inlaid floors, mahogany staircase and displays of silver, bronze, porcelain and antique furnishings. The rhododendron garden is open in spring.

✠ C3

✉ Blessington, Co. Wicklow (about 2 miles south of Blessington) ☎ 045 865 239; fax 045 865 054
⏰ Daily 10:30–5:30, May.–Sep.; Sun. only 10:30–5:30, Apr. and Oct. 🍴 Restaurant 💷 $$

A LONG TRADITION
OF SPECTACULAR GARDENS

Leinster is one of Ireland's most fertile regions. County Wicklow, in fact, bills itself as "The Garden of Ireland." Their annual Garden Festival from late May to mid-July proves the point (information available from Wicklow Tourist Information, Wicklow town).

The gardens listed here are only a few of those you will want to visit, and *"Gardens and Garden Centres,"* a useful illustrated guide to Leinster gardens outside the Dublin area, is available from the Midlands-East Regional Tourism Authority.

Celbridge Abbey Gardens

It was for Jonathan Swift, that Esther Van Homrigh (immortalized as "Vanessa" by the writer) planted these grounds around her father's late-17th-century home. The grounds, situated on the Liffey river, are nothing short of magnificent. Their care and development are looked after by the Order of St. John of God, which provides training and employment for adults with learning difficulties and creates a historical, cultural and environmental space for the public. There's an ancient bridge overlooking Vanessa's Bower, which is thought to be the oldest bridge on the Liffey, and theme walks feature the Swiftian and Grattan walks (Henry Grattan, the great Irish parliamentarian, was a frequent visitor here). The house is not open to the public, but guided tours are available.

Japanese Gardens and St. Fiachra's Garden

On the grounds of the Irish National Stud (see page 102), the breathtakingly beautiful Japanese Gardens' underlying theme of the "Life of Man" depicts human progression from the cradle to the grave and beyond. Japanese lanterns, small brooks crossed by Japanese-style bridges and other Oriental touches make this garden (four years in the planning, 1906–10) unique in Ireland. It has won international accolades.

To celebrate the millennium, St. Fiachra's Garden was planted in 1999 around a natural setting of wetland, woodland, rocks, lakes and islands. The visitor center, with coffee shop, wine bar and craft shop is in the Japanese style, and there are picnic grounds.

Mount Usher Gardens

Mount Usher Gardens rank among the leading – and loveliest – horticultural centers in Ireland. Its 20 acres of flowers, trees, shrubs and lawns lie in the sheltered Vartry river valley, and although it is not a true botanical garden, its plants come from many parts of the globe. Spindle trees from China, North American sweet gum and swamp cypress, the New Zealand ti tree, African broom and Burmese juniper are among those represented in a magnificent setting of superb landscaping. There's a spacious tea room at the entrance, as well as a shopping courtyard.

National Botanic Gardens

Since 1795 the National Botanic Gardens have fostered the native Irish affinity for all growing things. Their 50 acres (once home to poet Thomas Tickell) hold a variety of garden groupings, from decorative plantings to vegetable, herbal, scientific and medicinal plants to economic plants and exotic species from around the globe. There are fascinating tropical greenhouses and a small orchid room. Dedicated gardeners will delight in the wealth of botanical information, and even those who have never had dirt under their fingernails will find this a place of beauty and tranquility.

Powerscourt Gardens

Powerscourt Gardens were designed and laid out between 1745 and 1767. Perched on high ground with a view of Great Sugarloaf Mountain, magnificent Japanese and Italian gardens slope downward and are dotted with statuary and ornamental lakes. The 1,000-acre

The Italian and Japanese gardens at Powerscourt are renowned for their beauty

demesne, which straddles the River Dargle, holds rare shrubs, massive rhododendrons and a deer park. Powerscourt House, an impressive 18th-century mansion built on the site of an earlier castle, was gutted by fire in 1974, and a restored section now holds an audiovisual history, shops and restaurant.

St. Anne's Park Rose Garden

St. Anne's Park Rose Garden is one of the prettiest in Dublin, with climbers, floribunda, hybrid tea and old garden roses in profusion. In April and May, daffodils are in full bloom. Much loved by Dubliners, this lovely oasis of beauty is a horticultural bonus to city visitors.

Tullynally Castle Gardens

The 30-acre pleasure grounds and walled gardens on the grounds of the massive Gothic revival Tullynally Castle date from the early 1800s. In addition to the two ornamental lakes and a grotto, there's a Chinese garden with pagoda and a Tibetan garden of waterfalls and streams. A note of fantasy is struck by fanciful sculptures that a local artist created using roots and trees. A magnificent avenue of 200-year-old Irish yew trees lead to the romantic walled gardens. Guided tours of the castle are also available.

Celbridge Abbey Gardens ✉ Clane Road, Celbridge, Co. Kildare ☎ 01 627 5508; fax 01 627 9192 🕐 Mon.–Sat. 10–6, Sun. noon–6 🚌 67, 67A (from Middle Abbey Street, Dublin) 👜 $$

Japanese Gardens and St. Fiachra's Garden ✉ Tully, Co. Kildare (Irish National Stud signposted from Kildare Town) ☎ 045 521 617; fax 045 522 964 🕐 Daily 9:30–6, mid-Feb. to mid-Nov. 👜 $$$

Mount Usher Gardens ✉ Ashford, Co. Wicklow ☎ 0404 40205 or 0404 40116; fax 0404 40205 🕐 Daily 10:30–6, mid-Mar.–Oct. 👜 $$

National Botanic Gardens ✉ Glasnevin Hill Road, Glasnevin, Dublin ☎ 01 837 4388 🕐 Mon.–Sat. 9–6, Sun. 11–6, Jun.–Aug.; Mon.–Sat. 10–4, Sun. 11–4:30, rest of year 🚌 13A, 19, 134 👜 Free

Powerscourt Gardens ✉ Enniskerry, Co. Wicklow ☎ 01 204 6000; fax 01 204 6900 🕐 Daily 9:30–5.30; varies in winter months 👜 $$$

St. Anne's Park Rose Garden ✉ Mount Prospect Avenue, Clontarf, Dublin ☎ 01 833 1859; fax 01 833 8763 🕐 Daily dawn–dusk 🚌 30, 44A 👜 Free

Tullynally Castle Gardens ✉ Castlepollard, Co. Westmeath ☎ 044 61159; fax 044 61856 🕐 Gardens: daily 2–6, May–Aug.; castle: mid-Jun.–Jul. 🍴 Coffee shop 👜 Castle and gardens: $$ For further information contact:

ℹ Midlands-East Regional Tourism Authority ✉ Dublin Road, Mullingar, Co. Westmeath ☎ 044 48761; fax 044 40413

ℹ Wicklow Tourist Information ☎ 0404 69117; fax 0404 69118 🕐 Mon.–Sat. 9–6, Jun.–Sep.; Mon.–Fri., rest of year

Wexford's church spire towers over this Viking town lying beside the River Slaney

WEXFORD

As the safest haven close to the south-eastern point of Ireland, Wexford has always been a natural landing place for travelers from Wales, Cornwall in England, and France, and it was the first Irish settlement to fall to the invading Normans in 1169. But these were not the first invaders – the Vikings settled here in the ninth or 10th century and gave the town its name.

Wexford exudes an air of the past, its central streets still adhering to the medieval plan, and the quays, not so busy now as they once were, reflecting a long maritime heritage. Fragments of the medieval town walls survive, at the northern edge of town near the rail and bus station, the Westgate Tower is the only surviving gateway of five in the old town walls, and it is fairly well preserved.

Nearby, Selskar Abbey stands on the site of an ancient pagan temple dedicated to Odin, and later a Viking church. King Henry II came here in 1172 to do penance for his murder of the devout Thomas à Becket.

Go by the wide intersection known as the Bull Ring at the north end of Wexford's Main Street and spend a few minutes reflecting on the bravery of the pikemen who are portrayed by the bronze statue there. Until Oliver Cromwell visited his wrath on the town in 1649, a great high cross stood here, and when Cromwell destroyed it, he slew some 300 people who knelt in prayer before it. While bull-baiting was once the main attraction here, there is now an open-air market every Friday and Saturday.

On Wexford's Crescent Quay, take a look at the Commodore John Barry (1745–1803) statue, and if you pass through Ballysampson, Tagoat (10 miles from Wexford), tip your hat to his birthplace. Homage is due to this seafaring Irishman, as he is credited with founding the U.S. Navy after being appointed by George Washington in 1797.

Take a drive down the Hook peninsula through historic and quaint old villages. The ruins of the Knights Templars foundation still stand at Templetown; Hook lighthouse, built over seven centuries ago, is the oldest in Europe. Near Fethard-on-Sea, the Normans first landed in Ireland. At Ballyhack, catch the car-ferry over to Passage East on the County Waterford side for 10 minutes on the water to see these shores as they were seen by Viking and Norman invaders.

Just 3 miles west of Wexford, overlooking the River Slaney, Irish National Heritage Park is a marvelous 35-acre park holding reconstructions of a

campsite, farmstead and portal dolmen from the Stone Age (7000–2000 BC) and a cist burial and stone circle from the Bronze Age (2000–500 BC). You can also view an ogham stone, ringfort and *souterrain*, (an early Christian monastery), corn-drying kiln, horizontal water mill, Viking boathouse and an artificial island habitat known as a *crannog*, all from the Celtic and early Christian ages (500 BC to AD 1169). Also here are a Norman *motte* and bailey, the first Norman fortification in Ireland, and a round tower from the early Norman period (1169–1280). There's also a nature walk of real beauty, and an excellent craft and book shop.

In 1858, when Patrick Kennedy left Dunganstown (near New Ross, see drive page 100) for America, it was to escape the ravages of a devastating famine. He left behind a five-room thatched home set among stone farm buildings. A little more than a century later, his great-grandson, John Fitzgerald Kennedy, held the office of president of the United States and returned to visit his ancestral home.

The John F. Kennedy Park and Arboretum is the tribute paid to the president by the Irish government and United States citizens of Irish origin. It was officially opened by President Eamon de Valera in 1968 and covers 623 acres, of which more than 300 are set aside as the arboretum. Already there are more than

4,500 species of shrubs, and the number is expected to reach 6,000 in a few years.

In the Forest Garden, there are trees from all five continents. There are lovely shaded walks throughout the park, with shelters and convenient resting spots. If you follow the signposts to the top of Slieve Coillte, you'll be rewarded by a marvelous panorama of south Wexford and the splendid estuary of the Barrow, Nore and Suir rivers. Be sure to stop by the Forest Garden's reception center and see the explanatory display fashioned in beaten copper.

Bird watchers should visit the reserve adjacent to Wexford Harbour, where over 240 species of birds and more than a third of the world's Greenland white-fronted geese winter. There is an informative visitor center and observation tower.

➕ C1

Tourist information ✉ Crescent Quay ☎ 053 23111 ⏰ Daily 9–6, Jul.–Aug.; Mon.–Sat. 9–6, Apr.–Jun. and Sep.–Oct.; Mon.–Fri. 9:30–5:30, rest of year

Irish National Heritage Park ✉ Ferrycarrig (3 miles outside town) ☎ 053 2733; fax 053 20911 ⏰ Daily 9:30–6:30 🍴 Restaurant 💲 $$

John F. Kennedy Arboretum ✉ Dunganstown, Co. Wexford (about 6 miles from New Ross) ☎ 051 388 171; fax 051 388 172 ⏰ Daily 10–8, May–Aug.; 10–6:30, Apr. and Sep.; 10–5 , rest of year 💲 $$

Wexford Wildfowl Reserve ✉ North Slob (3 miles east of Wexford town) ☎ 053 23129 ⏰ Daily 9–6, mid-Apr.–Sep.; 10–5, rest of year 💲 Free

MUNSTER

Munster

" **D** *UBBED 'a most populous and plentiful country' by the poet Edmund Spenser in 1596, Munster's six counties are as inviting and beguiling today. *"**

Mountain views between Kenmare and Glengarriff

Munster

MUNSTER

Munster's six counties – Clare, Cork, Kerry, Limerick, Tipperary and Waterford – straddle the southern part of Ireland, which is a sort of mini Ireland. Outstanding examples of scenic, archeological, historical and cultural charms that make this country so special are liberally scattered across the face of Munster, a virtual grab-bag of sightseeing riches. Here you'll find the world-famous lakes of Killarney, Blarney's magical stone and Waterford's exquisite crystal. You'll also find the country's sunniest and driest climate in east Munster, the wettest in the west.

The dramatic coastline changes from wide, sandy beaches to steep, surf-fringed cliffs that soar above secluded coves and small fishing village harbors to deep-water commercial ports and craggy peninsulas. Mizen Head is Ireland's southernmost point, crowned by a lighthouse whose summit perch overlooks striking cliffscapes. The bustling port cities of Cork, Limerick and Waterford encircle the coast, with reminders of their legends and history happily rubbing elbows with the sounds and sights of an astonishingly progressive present.

Inland mountain chains march across Munster, vibrant in spring with deep hues of rhododendrons, softened in the fall by more subtle shades of heather. To the east, the Comeragh and Knockmealdown ranges give way to the midland Galtees, Slieve Felims and Silvermines. Some of the earliest traces of the Stone Age inhabitants are found

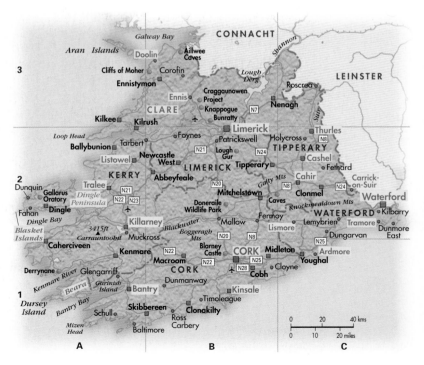

Garinish Point harbor against the backdrop of Beara Peninsula

in Blackwater Valley. Ireland's highest peak, 3,400-foot high Carrantouhill is the star of Kerry's Macgillycuddy's Reeks, while the gentler slopes of the Slieve Mish range form the backbone of the Dingle Peninsula, "the last parish before America." Ireland's famed "forty shades of green" create a glorious patchwork quilt of fertile stone-walled fields and Tipperary's Golden Vale plain. Sprinkled in this rural scene are small, thriving market towns.

Amid all these scenic splendors, ancient ringforts, dolmens, cairns and other archeological relics bring to life a prehistoric landscape. Monasteries, massive castles and round towers trace Christian, Viking and Norman invasions over long centuries.

If cultural and artistic activities are high on your priority list, traditional Irish music is featured in many city pubs. You may find your most memorable evenings happen when that same music spontaneously breaks out in the most unlikely rural settings. Munster's cities arrange year-round programs of opera, first-rate jazz and musical and theatrical productions. Its

art galleries rank with the best in Europe. The Irish have an inborn flair for drama, and several local drama groups present surprisingly professional productions. Count yourself lucky if you run across a night of theater featuring an amateur troupe – when the last curtain falls, the cast often adjourns to the nearest pub along with members of the audience. It's great fun.

It's also great fun to show up for at least one day's racing at the three-day "meets" held at racetracks in Clonmel, Tramore, Mallow, Killarney and Limerick, where the atmosphere is not unlike that of old-time county fairs in the United States. For more energetic outdoor enthusiasts, excellent facilities for almost every sport, from golf to river (coarse fishing) and deep-sea fishing are never far away. County Kerry's Dingle Peninsula and Ring in County Waterford are important *Gaeltacht* (pronounced "Gwale-tuct") areas, where Irish is the thriving, everyday language.

In short, Munster is a shining example of modern Ireland flourishing on the enduring foundation of its past.

Munster

CORK

Ireland's second largest city (with a population of 136,000) is cosmopolitan and friendly. Its charter dates to 1185, by which time Cork already had a rich and colorful past.

St. Finbar arrived in 650 to found a monastery on the small swampy island cradled by hills to the north and south and called it Corcaigh (Marshy Place). Since then, Cork has seen Danes come storming in as plunderers in the ninth century, only to settle in as permanent residents, followed by Normans in the 12th century, who stayed on to build fortifications, great churches and abbeys. It was Englishman Oliver Cromwell who broke the pattern when he captured the city in 1649 and proceeded to impose a harsh repressive regime. Inevitably, resistance to such measures spawned a fierce sense of independence that even today underlies the Cork spirit.

These days, the bustling modern city is an important industrial and financial center, with a deep-water commercial harbor that comes right into the heart

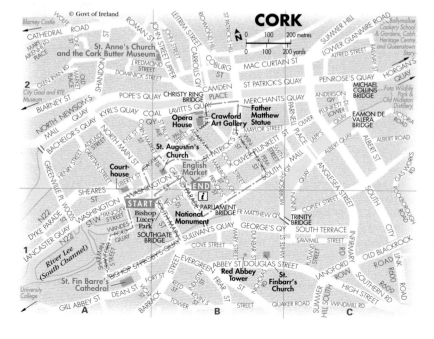

© Govt of Ireland

CORK

Cork city "buskers" making heart-stopping, foot-tapping music

of the city. A busy ferryport 10 miles to the southeast at Ringaskiddy provides a convenient passenger service to France and Britain.

The People

The citizens of Cork are a lively, cultural bunch, among Ireland's most able traders and merchants, and much attuned to the arts. "Sure, it's only an accident of geography that Dublin is the capital of Ireland" is a sentiment readily expressed by Cork natives. That enormous civic pride is firmly rooted in the city's history and an implacable abhorrence of injustice.

The natives of Cork love nothing more than to show off their city, and they are quick to welcome strangers in their unique, lilting accent (delivered at breakneck speed), which may take a little getting used to. They have also retained in their everyday speech many words and phrases which have been long disused elsewhere. So if you overhear a woman described as *mauzy*, you'll know that, heavy of hips, she's really "a fine lump of a woman." Friendly they most certainly are, and perhaps because of their mercantile bent, that friendliness often expresses itself in practical terms – just ask Corkonians for directions or advice and they'll jump at the chance to be helpful.

Cork Cuisine

A leading Irish food critic based in Dublin recently wrote, "There are considerably more good restaurants per head of population in Cork than we can even dream of in the capital." In truth, you can name almost any ethnic cuisine, and you'll find it offered in at least one of those eateries. Menus run the gamut, from traditional boiled bacon and cabbage to gourmet Continental dishes. Unique to this city and dear to the hearts of many natives is *drisheen*, not unlike the black pudding you'll encounter throughout the

Munster

country. Cork is also home to the Beamish brewery, which has been dispensing stout since 1792.

Finding Your Way Around

Cork's compact city center sits on an island ringed by the two-prong Lee river, crossed by no less than 16 bridges – a bit confusing when you suddenly encounter another channel of the river you thought you had just left behind. Vessels actually sailed up Patrick Street as late as 1760 (it was paved over in 1791), and in 1780 there was a canal down the center of the Grand Parade. The river cuts across the city from east to west and is bounded by hills on the north and south.

The major points of reference in the city center are St. Patrick's Street (just call it Patrick Street) and the Grand Parade. Other main arteries are Washington Street (which becomes Western Road as it runs past University College and heads out toward Killarney); South Mall, from which you turn onto Mary Street to reach Douglas Road en route to the airport; and MacCurtain Street, a busy one-way thoroughfare just across St. Patrick's Bridge that leads to both the main Cobh to Youghal to Waterford road and Cork to Dublin motorway. St. Patrick's Hill, at the foot of Patrick Street, is breathtakingly steep, its stepped sidewalk leading to a sweeping view of the city and harbor from the Montenotte section.

ESSENTIAL INFORMATION

TOURIST INFORMATION
• Cork Kerry Regional Tourism Authority ⊠ Aras Fáilte (Tourist House), Grand Parade ☎ 021 425 5100; fax 021 425 5199; www.info@corkkerrytourism.ie ⊕ Mon.–Sun. 9–7, Jul.–Aug.; Mon.–Sat. 9:15–5:30, rest of year.
• There is also a freephone information service in the arrivals terminal of Cork Airport.

URBAN TRANSPORTATION
Double-decker buses cover the city, with 14 routes running north to south. Hours are 7 a.m. to 11 p.m. Monday through Saturday, less frequently on Sunday. Most buses can be boarded on Patrick Street. A short walk from Patrick Street, the Parnell Place Bus Station (☎ 021 450 8188) offers frequent service to the airport and such nearby points as Blarney, Cobh, Kinsale and Crosshaven as well as major destinations around the country. They also conduct scenic tours from Cork to Blarney, Macroom and Killarney.
From late May until late September, an open-air double-decker bus will get you to such Cork highlights as the Cork City Gaol, City Library, St. Finbarr's Cathedral, Crawford Municipal Art Gallery, Triskel Arts Centre, English Market, Cork Opera House, Custom House and the Courthouse. Stay on the bus for the entire 70 minutes of the tour or opt to get off at an attraction and rejoin the tour on the next bus. You can buy a ticket, which is good for the day, at the tourist office or from the driver on the tour bus at one of its stops. Bus Eireann ☎ 021 450 8188.
Cork is well served by taxis, with major stands along St. Patrick's Street, the South Mall and many hotels. For taxi pickup elsewhere, call Cork Taxi Co-op ☎ 021 427 2222.
Cork Railway Station, Lower Glanmire Road (☎ 021 450 6766), about a five-minute walk from the city center, provides service to Cobh, Dublin, Mallow, Milstreet, Killarney and Tralee.

AIRPORT INFORMATION
Located only 4 miles from the city center Cork Airport (☎ 021 431 3131), is reached via the Kinsale road and provides service to national and international destinations. There is a hourly bus service from the main airport entrance to Cork city bus station. A taxi journey will take less time and costs around €9.

CLIMATE – Average highs and lows

JAN.	FEB.	MAR.	APR.	MAY	JUN.	JUL.	AUG.	SEP.	OCT.	NOV.	DEC.
8°C	8°C	9°C	12°C	14°C	16°C	16°C	18°C	16°C	13°C	10°C	8°C
46°F	46°F	48°F	54°F	57°F	61°F	61°F	64°F	61°F	55°F	50°F	46°F
4°C	4°C	4°C	5°C	8°C	10°C	12°C	12°C	11°C	8°C	5°C	4°C
39°F	39°F	39°F	41°F	46°F	50°F	54°F	54°F	52°F	46°F	41°F	39°C

Blarney Castle, home to the famous Blarney stone

CORK SIGHTS

Key to symbols

✚ map coordinates refer to the Cork map on page 114; sights below are highlighted in yellow on the map

✉ address or location ☎ telephone number
🕐 opening times 🍴 restaurant on site or nearby
🚌 nearest bus or railroad station 💶 admission charge: $$$ more than €6, $$ €4 to €6, $ less than €4
ℹ information

BALLYMALLOE COOKERY SCHOOL AND GARDENS

Food expert Darina Allen has brought international fame to the very best of Irish cuisine by fostering the proper use of seasonal native produce. The outstanding herb garden holds the largest collection of culinary and medicinal plants in Ireland, as well as fruit and vegetable gardens. Just for fun, wander through the Celtic maze. The Garden Café practices what the school preaches in its lunch and dinner menus, and the adjoining shop stocks quality cookware.

✚ C2 ✉ Shanagarry, East Cork, on N25 at Castlemartyr, between Youghal and Cork ☎ 021 464 6785 or 464 6422; fax 021 464 6909 🕐 Gardens: daily 11–6, Apr.–Sep., guided tours by appointment; café and shop: daily Easter–Oct. 💶 Gardens: $$

BLARNEY CASTLE

There's a lovely sense of tranquility about the grounds and ruins of this historic castle – and a sense of magic about its stone that bestows the gift of eloquence on anyone who climbs its 120 steep steps to lean backward from the battlements and bestow a kiss on it. The legend of its powers rose from Queen Elizabeth I's frustration in dealing with Irish chieftain Cormac MacCarthy, Lord of Blarney, and his smiling flattery that veiled wiliness with eloquence. Her declaration, "This is nothing but blarney – what he says, he never means!" added a new word to the English language and may have given rise to the legend of the "gift of eloquence" associated with the stone. But it was Father Prout who in the 1830s, may have also bestowed magic on the stone when he wrote, "There is a stone there That whoever kisses Oh! He never misses To grow eloquent" Be that as it may, by the time you've gone through all the necessary exertions, you'll have earned a silver tongue! The Rock Close in the castle gardens is said to have been much favored by ancient Druids.

A short stroll from the castle you'll find Blarney Woollen Mills, one of Ireland's oldest, turning out fine wools and cloths since 1741. These days, the large premises hold a vast collection of Irish crafts, and there's a lovely traditional-style pub.

➕ A2 ✉ Blarney (4 miles northwest of Cork city on N617, signposted from Cork city at Patrick Street Bridge) ☎ 021 438 5252 🕐 Mon.–Sat. 9–dusk, Sun. 9:30–5:30; closed Dec. 24–25 🍴 Blair's Inn (see page 206) 🚍 Buses and coach tours from Parnell Street Bus Station, Cork 💷 $$

Blarney Woollen Mills (retail shop) ✉ Blarney ☎ 021 438 5280 🕐 Daily 9–8, until 6 at weekends, mid-May to mid.-Oct.; 9–6, rest of year

CITY GAOL AND RADIO TELEFÍS ÉIREANN MUSEUM

This infamous building housed many a patriotic rebel in the late 1800s and early 1900s. Their grim prison existence is re-created vividly by lifesize figures, the cells in which they lived and fascinating exhibits. On a happier note, in the former governor's house, the Radio Telefís Éireann Museum collection is well worth a visit. RTE operates Ireland's four state-sponsored television channels. Located in the original studio of 1927, exhibits cover the early days of radio. Allow two hours.

➕ A2 ✉ Sunday's Well ☎ 021 430 5022 🕐 Daily 9:30–6, in summer; 10–5, rest of year 🚍 No bus service – short walk from city center 💷 Gaol: $$; museum: $$

COBH HERITAGE CENTRE – THE QUEENSTOWN STORY

There is a strong tug of ancestry for many Americans descended from the thousands of Irish families who departed Queenstown, now named Cobh (Haven), as they fled the famine in search of a better life. Sadly, many never reached those hope-filled shores because of the appalling conditions on overcrowded and ill-equipped "coffin ships." The Queenstown Story in Cobh's Victorian railroad station tells their tale in heart-wrenching detail through a moving multimedia exhibition and startlingly lifelike figures of emigrant families.

While in Cobh, take time to visit the Gothic-revival St. Colman's Cathedral, with its 47-bell carillon, rose window

above the main doorway, mosaic flooring and richly colored windows.

➕ C2 ✉ Cobh Heritage Centre, Cobh, 15 miles east of Cork city, via Waterford Road (N25) to signposted turnoff for R632 ☎ 021 481 3591; fax 021 481 3595 🕐 Daily 9:30–6 (last admission 5) 🍴 Restaurant 🚉 Frequent rail service from Cork city 💷 $$

ENGLISH MARKET (CITY MARKET)

A leftover from colonial days, this cavernous market housed in a 1786 building carries on a Cork tradition that dates from the 1600s. Wall-to-wall foodstuff stalls peddle meats, vegetables, pastries and just about anything else that shows up on Cork tables. It's terrific for eavesdropping and a unique opportunity to mingle with Cork homemakers going about their daily lives.

➕ B2 ✉ Entrances from Grand Parade, Patrick Street, Oliver Plunkett Street, and Princes Street 🕐 Mon.–Sat. 9–5:30 💷 Free

FOTA WILDLIFE PARK

More than 90 species of exotic animals including giraffes, ostriches, zebras, oryx, kangaroos and lemurs roam the park's 40 acres of open natural surroundings. More than just a zoo, the park is also heavily involved in conservation and rehabilitation of threatened species. The adjoining Fota Arboretum features trees and shrubs from China, Japan, Australia, the Himalayas and other countries around the world.

➕ C2 ✉ Fota Island, Carrigtwohill, 10 miles east of Cork city on the Cobh Road ☎ 021 481 2678 🕐 Mon.–Sat. 10–6, Sun. 11–6 (last admission 5) Apr.–Oct.; Sat.–Sun. 10–3, rest of year 🍴 Coffee shop 🚉 Frequent rail and bus service from Cork city 💷 $$$

OLD MIDLETON DISTILLERY (JAMESON HERITAGE CENTRE)

This marvelous old distillery traces the history of Irish whiskey since it was perfected by Irish monks in the 16th century, when they called it *uisce beatha*, "the water of life." There's an informative guided tour, ending with a complimentary glass of Jameson whiskey.

✚ C2 ✉ Midleton, County Cork, 12 miles east of Cork ☎ 021 461 3594; fax 021 461 3642 🕒 Daily 10–6 (tours on demand), Apr.–Oct.; 3 tours daily 11:30, 2:30 and 4, Nov.–Mar. 🍴 Restaurant 🚌 From Cork and Waterford 👆 $$

ST. FIN BARRE'S CATHEDRAL

In a location that eventually proved to be Cork city's birthplace, this magnificent Church of Ireland 1870 French Gothic cathedral is the descendant of the 650 monastery that grew into a seat of learning of international renown. Its ornate interior is notable for unique mosaics and its impressive great west window.

✚ A1 ✉ Bishop Street, three blocks past South Main Street Bridge ☎ 021 496 3387 🕒 Daily 10–5:30, Apr.–Oct.; 10–12:45 and 2–5, rest of year 👆 Free (donations welcome)

SHANDON – ST. ANNE'S CHURCH AND THE CORK BUTTER MUSEUM

St. Anne's is distinguished by its red-and-white "pepper pot" steeple, which houses its famous bells and its "four-faced liar" clock that never shows the same time on

its four faces. Climb the winding belfry stairs and your reward is to follow numbers on the bell strings that send *The Bells of St. Mary's* ringing out over the city. Nearby is the old Butter Exchange, which houses the Cork Butter Museum, an unusual subject for a museum, but well worth a visit.

✚ A2

St. Anne's Church ✉ Church Street ☎ 021 450 5906 🕒 Daily 9–6, Jun.–Sep.; 10–4, Oct.–May 🍴 Isaac's (see page 207) 🚌 2 from Merchant's Quay 👆 $$

Cork Butter Museum ✉ O'Connell Square ☎ 021 430 0600 🕒 Sun.–Fri. 10–1 and 2–5, Apr.–Sep. 🚌 2 from Merchant's Quay 👆 $$

UNIVERSITY COLLEGE CORK

The Gothic revival architecture of University College Cork buildings creates a fitting backdrop for this 11,000-strong student body that makes up an important segment of Ireland's National University. The campus grounds hold notable gardens and wooded areas, and of special interest is the Honan Chapel that features Harry Clarke stained-glass windows. Ancient Irish ogham inscriptions star in the Stone Corridor, and you can also visit the Crawford Observatory.

✚ A1 ✉ Western Road ☎ 021 490 3000 🕒 Mon.–Sat. 9–5, (tours by appointment) 🚌 5, 8 👆 Free

St. Patrick Street, Cork's main shopping thoroughfare

Munster

WALK: CORK'S MERCANTILE PAST

Refer to route marked on city map on page 115.

One of Cork's charms is that it is such a good walking city. Free of urban pressure and appealingly compact, walking is without a doubt the best way to get around the city if you want to capture its true flavor and mingle with the people who give it life. Cork constantly challenges Dublin's supremacy, refusing to play second fiddle. Allow one-and-a-half hours.

Begin at Bishop Lucey Park, across the Grand Parade from the tourist office.
Also known as City Park and named for a much-loved bishop of Cork, Bishop Lucey Park holds a section of the medieval city walls. The eight bronze swans adorning a sculptured fountain celebrate the 800th anniversary of Cork's 1185 charter.

Walk right to reach the junction of Grand Parade and South Mall, and turn left onto South Mall.
That impressive statue at the junction of the two streets commemorates Irish rebels in the 1798 and 1867 uprisings. Irishmen who perished in the two World Wars are honored by the War Memorial alongside the river, and the uncarved granite stone nearby is the Hiroshima Memorial. South Mall is a wide, tree-lined street that was once an open channel bringing ships right up to waterside cellars to unload merchandise.

Turn left on Winthrop Street.
The General Post Office on your left as you walk east on Winthrop Street was built on the site of the late 18th-century Theatre Royal, complete with busy coachyard facilities.

Continue east and turn right on St. Patrick's Street (known simply as Patrick Street).
The statue in the center of the street at the foot of Patrick Bridge depicts Father Matthew, the "Apostle of Temperance" fondly remembered in these parts for his lifelong fight against Irish alcoholism in the 1800s.

Turn left across Patrick Street into Lavitts Quay, then left at the Opera House into Emmet Place.
Despite the opera house's resemblance to a

lump of concrete, this 1960's addition to municipal culture regularly presents ballet, opera and drama productions (see page 122). By contrast, its next-door neighbor is an imposing building that houses the Crawford Art Gallery, worth a visit just for its restaurant. Built in 1724 as the Custom House when ships could unload onto what is now the sidewalk. Irish and international artists are represented in its fine collections, which include classical casts from the Vatican Galleries presented to Cork in 1818. The museum houses a collection of local landscape painting.

Turn left on Academy Street, then right on Patrick Street and look to your right for the three tiny streets described below.
The tiny lanes of French Church Street, Carey's Lane and Sts. Peter and Paul's Street became a safe haven for a colony of Huguenots who fled France in the 18th century to escape religious persecution and settled first in French Church Street. A few steps farther on, Carey's Lane was the site of a chapel in 1776, when Catholics were forbidden by law to have churches on main streets. The Huguenot graveyard is just behind the old wall on the right of the lane. Pause at the next small street on your right to feast your eyes on the elaborate stonework of the Church of Sts. Peter and Paul's, which blossomed from the original chapel in the lane and opened in 1868.

Follow Patrick Street to where it curves to the left into the Grand Parade and turn right to the junction of Cornmarket and Castle streets.
Once a lively and thriving open-air flea market, the Coal Quay (Cornmarket Street) was a vibrant part of the city's life for at least a century. It's lined with stalls presided over by shrewd, witty Irish countrywomen hawking odds and ends of every description. These days you're more likely to find second-hand clothing and furniture.

From Castle Street, turn left at North Main Street, then right on Washington Street and continue to Grattan Street, turn left, cross Clarke's Bridge, then right onto Wandesford Quay to Sharman Crawford Street and on to Bishop Street.
Built in French Gothic style and designed by William Burges, the majestic limestone St. Fin Barre's Cathedral boasts three splendid spires

St. Fin Barre's Cathedral was designed by William Burges

and a magnificent interior with angels gazing down from a starry apse. It's a true "must see" (see page 119).

Turn right along French Quay and cross the bridge to South Main Street and continue walking east, then turn right on Tobin Street.

At first glance, this narrow little street seems an unlikely setting for the arts, but the Triskel Arts Centre is alive with activity, from contemporary arts and crafts exhibitions to theatrical productions and cutting-edge films.

Continue down Tobin Street to Grand Parade and cross over to the entrance of the English Market.

Also known as the City Market (see page 118), the colorful English Market is the perfect place to end your walk, have a break, rest your feet and have a cup of tea or light meal in the balcony restaurant.

Munster

CORK'S CULTURAL SCENE

Cork city is packed with cultural activities, whether of a traditional or a contemporary nature. No matter what time of year you visit, you can count on attending a cultural event, and in most cases costs are moderate. The city has been designated City of Culture for 2005.

Cork's opera house presents plays and musical stage shows of the highest caliber, concerts by leading orchestras and musical stars, and ballet and other dance performances.

The Everyman Palace Theatre is housed in the venerable gilt-and-gingerbread Old Palace Theatre, a venue steeped in the city's theatrical history. It hosts high-quality performances of its resident company, as well as visiting troupes from around the country, Great Britain and America. There's coffee service at intermission, and audiences often mingle with actors who relax in the Theatre Bar.

Cork is the perfect place to enjoy traditional Irish music at its best, and the best of the best can be found in many of the city's numerous pubs. Ballads, jigs and reels liven the cozy atmosphere Wednesday through Saturday nights in An Bodhran, a century-and-a-half old pub frequented by university students as well as a nice mix of other age groups.

Bagpipes, bodhráns, fiddles and guitars hold forth just about every night of the week at the popular Lobby Bar featuring top traditional bands and soloists. Both pubs sometimes present contemporary music.

Check local newspapers for other pubs featuring music, traditional and contemporary. Check also for weekend discos or clubs, which change times and places frequently.

Cork holds so many special events and festivals that it sometimes seems its citizens stand ready to throw a party at the drop of a hat. Choirs and dance teams from around the world descend on Cork in late April or early May for the Cork International Choral and Folk Dance Festival, with most of the action set in the City Hall. In September the Cork Folk Festival keeps alive the deep-rooted music that is so much a part of Irish culture.

Considered by many to be the star of Cork's festivals, the Cork Jazz Festival in October attracts some of the greats of the jazz world – the city rings with lively music that pours from pubs and theaters. It is ranked among the top three jazz festivals in the world. The equally famed Cork Film Festival in late September or early October gives independent film makers a showcase for their work. It is one of Ireland's oldest and biggest film events. Established in 1956, the festival brings the best of international cinema to the Irish audience – and the visitors. It also gives Corkonians a chance to don their best bib and tucker for the many gala evenings that are so much a part of the festivities.

An Bodran
✉ 42 Oliver Plunkett Street ☎ 021 427 4544
Cork's Opera House
✉ Emmet Place
☎ 021 427 1168
The Everyman Palace Theatre
✉ 17 MacCurtain Street ☎ 021 450 1673
The Lobby Bar
✉ 1 Union Quay ☎ 021 431 1113

A somber character dressed for one of Cork's street festivals

DRIVE: ISLAND CITY, MAGIC STONE

Duration: 1–2 days

This 159-mile drive takes you from the center of Cork to Blarney to kiss the famous stone and northwest through historic towns before turning east and south for the spectacular drive across the Vee.

> *Start at Tourist House, Grand Parade, in Cork. Cross Patrick Street bridge and turn left for the signposted 6-mile drive northwest on the R617 to reach Blarney.*

The well-preserved ruins of Blarney Castle, built in 1446, draw visitors not just for their history, but also for the magical powers attributed to the famous stone embedded in its parapet wall. Kissing the magical stone involves lying on your back and hanging over an open space (see page 117). About 600 feet from the castle is the superb Scottish baronial mansion, Blarney Castle House, set amid lovely 18th-century gardens.

> *Leave Blarney on the R617. After a few miles, turn northwest on the R579 for Kanturk.*

One mile south of town, unfinished Kanturk Castle was begun in 1609 by Irish chieftain MacDonagh MacCarthy, who planned it as the largest mansion in Ireland, with a large quadrangle and four-story towers at each corner. Alarmed at its size and strength, the English Privy Council ordered work to cease, declaring that it was "much too large for a subject." The roofless, stout walls and towers have survived in remarkably good condition.

> *Drive southeast on the R576 to its junction with the N72, then turn east for 9 miles to reach Mallow.*

Set on the River Blackwater, Mallow was a popular spa town during the 18th and early 19th centuries; its lively social life prompted the famous song *The Rakes of Mallow*. The fine fortified 16th-century house replacing 12th-century Mallow Castle, which was burned in 1689 on the orders of King James II, now stands in fairly complete ruins in its own park by the river crossing. From the tourist office in Cork or Youghal, ask for the Blackwater drive map and chart that shows a wealth of historic relics.

About 9 miles north of Mallow via the N20, the little town of Buttevant saw the world's first steeplechase in 1752, run between its church steeple and the one in Doneraile. Buttevant was the model for "Mole" in Edmund Spenser's *The Faerie Queene*.

> *Take the N73 northeast for 21 miles to Mitchelstown.*

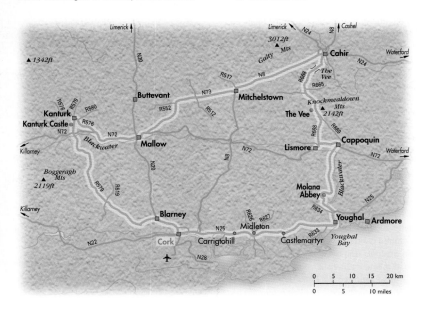

Early evening sunshine lights up the clock tower
in Youghal

road en route to Lismore.

The viewing points along this drive through a
gap in the Knockmealdown Mountains
provide spectacular panoramic views of
Killballyboy Wood, Boernagore Wood, the
Galtee Mountains, the Golden Vale of
Tipperary, Bay Lough and the Comeragh
mountain range.

**Continue south on the R668 for 8 miles
to Lismore.**

This historic little town, site of an ancient
monastic center, is beautifully located on the
Blackwater river. Its most outstanding
attractions are Lismore Castle, whose gardens
are open to the public, the Protestant cathedral
with grave slabs from the ninth and 11th
centuries, and the modern Romanesque-style
Catholic cathedral. A marvelous program in the
Heritage Centre depicts the town's history. The
center has booklets tracing the interesting town
walk and the riverside Lady Louise's Walk.

Ten miles northeast of this tidy, attractive
19th-century town via the N8, the signposted
Mitchelstown Caves are an underground
wonderland of passages and high-ceiling
limestone chambers, including the biggest
chamber in the British Isles. The Old Caves
were used as a refuge for a 16th-century Earl
of Desmond, who had a price on his head.
There are escorted tours through 2 miles of
the fantastic, netherworld.

**Follow the N8 for 18 miles northeast
to Cahir.**

Occupying a small islet in the River Suir,
Cahir Castle was built in the 13th century by
the de Berminghams and was held by the
Anglo-Norman Butlers until 1599, when the
Earl of Essex captured it after a three-day
siege. Englishman Oliver Cromwell made a
fierce show of force before the walls in 1650
and sent in surrender terms. Historians differ
as to whether the garrison accepted the terms
immediately or held out until they saw the
heavy ordnance ranged against them. They
did, however, surrender before the walls were
battered again, and the castle thus remained
in sound condition. It has been restored
almost to its original condition, and there is
an excellent audiovisual show

**Head south on the R668 through
Clogheen to begin the Vee mountain pass**

Take the N72 east for 4 miles to the bridge on the outskirts of Cappoquin and turn right on an unclassified road to a T-junction. Turn right on the road signposted Youghal that follows the Blackwater river south to the sea, then turn right on the N25 south for Youghal.
Youghal, (pronounced "yawl" meaning yew wood), is filled with mementos of its past. The picturesque harborside town was once the home of Sir Walter Raleigh, who brought the potato and the tobacco plant to Ireland, and the setting for the 1954 movie "Moby Dick." At the tourist office on the harbor, ask for their *Tourist Trail* booklet for information about the town's history and major sights, including the impressive 1776 clock tower, which now holds a museum featuring Walter Raleigh memorabilia,

remnants of the old town walls, and Myrtle Grove, the home of Sir Walter Raleigh. Harbor cruises are sometimes available, deep-sea fishing charters can be booked at the tourist office.

Eight miles east of Youghal, via a signposted turnoff from the N25, is the pretty little seaside village of Ardmore (see page 126). It has a fine group of ecclesiastical remains, including one of the most perfectly preserved round towers in Ireland. There are also bracing cliff walks along the sea's edge.

Follow the N25 west for 28 miles to return to Cork.

Tourist information ✉ Market House, Market Square, Youghal ☎ 024 92447; fax 024 20171 🕐 Daily 9–5:30, mid-Mar.–Oct.; Mon.–Fri. 9–5, rest of year

The Mitchelstown Caves are a massive pre-glacial underworld

REGIONAL SIGHTS

Key to symbols

✚ map coordinates refer to the region map on page 112; sights below are highlighted in yellow on the map

✉ address or location ☎ telephone number

🕐 opening times 🍴 restaurant on site or nearby

🚏 nearest bus or railroad station 🎟 admission charge: $$$ more than €6, $$ €4 to €6, $ less than €4

ℹ information

ARDMORE

One of the most perfectly preserved round towers in Ireland rises some 98 feet above the attractive little seaside village of Ardmore. St. Declan came from Wales to found a monastic settlement here in the fifth century, and the tower is just one of several remarkably intact remains still on view. Look for the incredibly tiny St. Declan's Oratory – legend says that the grave in one corner is that of St. Declan himself. Traces of architectural styles of the 10th to 14th centuries are visible in the ruins of the cathedral, and of special interest are a set of panels on its west gable, which holds sculptured biblical scenes such as the Adoration of the Magi, the Weighing of Souls and the Judgment of Solomon. This pretty village invites a leisurely stroll along the sandy beach.

✚ C1

Tourist information ✉ Seafronts parking lot, Ardmore

☎ 024 94444

BANTRY AND THE BEARA PENINSULA

Named for an ancient Celtic chieftan, the little town of Bantry sits at the head of 21-mile-long Bantry Bay, surrounded by hills. Twice (in 1689 and 1796) the French attempted naval invasions of Ireland from this inlet, only to be defeated by great storms and faulty communications. Between Bantry and Glengarriff, look for an "Artist's Studio" roadside sign in Ballylickey, which marks the studio of Raymond Klee, a fine, Welsh-born, award-winning artist whose remarkable paintings of the Irish landscape are popular with visitors.

Bantry House sits on the southern outskirts of town in a magnificent demesne, where beautifully landscaped lawns and gardens look out over the bay. The 1750 Georgian mansion is the ancestral home of the Earls of Bantry, and holds an impressive collection of European antiques, paintings, sculptures, tapestries and other precious items.

Within the grounds you'll find the French Armada Exhibition Centre, where you can view the remarkably preserved remains of the frigate *Surveillante*, which came to a watery end when it was scuttled, after the 1796 expedition led by Wolfe Tone and the United Irishmen came to a disastrous end, and lay buried on the sea-bed for 200 years. Extracts from Wolfe Tone's journal bring an immediacy to those long-ago events. You can visit house and exhibition center jointly or individually.

The 30-mile Beara Peninsula is a narrow, mountainous finger of land stretching out to sea between Bantry Bay and the Kenmare River. Its northwest corner falls within County Kerry, marked by the Cork – Kerry border that runs

Mizen Head Signal Station guides vessels along the rocky coastline

The classical pavilion in the Italianate gardens on Garinish Island, off Glengarriff

along the Caha mountain range. Glengarriff sits at the head of the peninsula, and a drive through its wild, sparsely populated landscape is a pleasant three- or four-hour diversion when you're traveling from Glengarriff to Kenmare or Killarney.

About a mile offshore from Glengarriff, in a sheltered inlet of Bantry Bay, is the lovely little Garinish Island, whose elaborately landscaped Italianate garden has brilliantly hued plants and flowers collected from around the world and interspersed with classical pavilions and meandering pathways. A ferry ride from Gengarriff takes you over to these splendid gardens thriving in the warming effects of the Gulf Stream. Playwright George Bernard Shaw loved the place, and parts of *St. Joan* were written here.

Gougane Barra's densely wooded mountains have been over the centuries a natural refuge for those desperately seeking religious freedom. St. Finbar chose an island in the lake at its center as the setting for his sixth-century monastery. During the Penal Laws days, when they were forbidden to celebrate Mass, Irish worshippers held services in this secluded setting. The woods are laced with lovely walkways, making this a delightful stop.

Mizen Head is Ireland's most southwestern point, and its signal station sits high above the wild Atlantic water. A breathtaking 172-foot suspension bridge soars 150 feet above crashing waves at the cliff base below. Views of the coasts are simply magnificent. The visitor center is located in the keeper's house and engine room, with audiovisuals, archives, maps and a bird and sea look out.

✚ A1

Tourist information ✉ The Square, Bantry ☎ 027 50229 🕔 Mon.–Sat. 9–7, Sun. 10–6, Apr.–Oct.

Bantry House and 1796 Bantry French Armada Exhibition Centre ✉ Bantry, (on the east side of the town) ☎ House: 027 50047; Armada Centre: 027 51796 🕔 House: daily 9–6, Mar.–Oct.; Armada Centre: daily 11–4, Mar.–mid-Oct. 🍽 O'Connor's Seafood Restaurant in Bantry (see page 206) 🎫 House: $$$; Armada Exhibition Centre: $$ (joint tickets available)

Garinish Island ✉ Glengarriff ☎ 027 63040 🕔 Mon.–Sat. 10–5, Sun. 11–5, in summer; varies rest of year 🎫 Boat to island: $$$; Island: $$

Mizen Head Signal Station Visitor Centre ✉ Mizen Head, Goleen ☎ 028 35115; fax 028 35225 🕔 Daily 10–6, Jun.–Sep.; 10:30–5, mid-Mar. to May and Oct.; 11–4, rest of year 🎫 $$

Gougane Barra National Forest Park ✉ 15 miles northeast of Bantry off R584, signposted on the Macroom to Glengarriff road ☎ 026 42837 🕔 Phone to confirm times 🎫 $$ (parking fee only)

Cahir Castle sits inside the protection of a forbidding stone curtain wall

CAHIR

Cahir, a rocky islet in the River Suir, has been the natural site of fortifications as far back as the third century. It was one of BrianBorú's homes during his reign as high king of Ireland. The present magnificent castle was built by the 13th century Normans and held by the Anglo-Norman Butlers until Queen Elizabeth I's favorite Earl of Essex captured it in 1599. Articles ending the Cromwellian wars were signed here in 1652, and title was held by Butler descendants until 1961. The state took over in 1964 and restored the castle to near-original condition and refurnished residential apartments with authentic reproductions that bring alive its centuries-old history. Guided tours are available on request. Don't miss the excellent audiovisual show, "Partly Hidden and Partly Revealed."

The town of Cahir is something of a time warp and some of its shops and houses appear little changed for decades. Keating's Draper's Shop traded in pre-decimal currency until it closed down a few years ago. Unusual for towns in the Irish Republic, there is a war memorial in the main square dedicated to the local men who joined Irish regiments and fell in World War I.

The other curiosity is the quaint Swiss Cottage that stands in pretty woodland gardens by the riverside just outside the town. Its thatched, corkscrew timbered building with eyebrow windows looks like something out of Hansel and Gretel rather than the Swiss Alps. Designed in 1810 by British architect John Nash for the Butler family, it was rescued from dereliction in 1985–89 by enthusiastic conservationists and extensively restored. The original hand-painted French wallpapers and fabrics have been faithfully copied, and it is now elegantly furnished with many period pieces.

✚ C2

Tourist information ✉ Cahir ☎ 052 41453 🕐 Mon.–Sat. 9–6, Sun. 11–5, Apr.–mid-Sep.
Cahir Castle ✉ Castle Street, Cahir, (on the east side of the town) ☎ 052 41011 🕐 Daily 9:00–7,

There is probably no truth in the legend that Ormond Castle was the birthplace of Anne Boleyn, mother of Queen Elizabeth I. Today the town is much prouder of a more recent hero, Sean Kelly, the racing cyclist who was ranked world champion for five consecutive years. Carrick rejoiced when Kelly won the 1988 *Tour de France*. A square in the town is named after him.

🕇 C2
✉ Castle Park (off Castle Street), Carrick-on-Suir
☎ 051 640787 🕒 Daily 9:30–6:30 (last admission 5:45), mid-Jun.–Sep. 🔲 $$ ⓘ Access by guided tour only

CASHEL

Undoubtedly Ireland's most majestic historical landmark, the lofty Rock of Cashel soars 300 feet above the town of Cashel and its surrounding plains. After you view the audiovisual "Strongholds of the Faith," wander among the ancient stones and ruins, climb to the top of the cathedral tower to wonder at Tipperary's Golden Vale plains, and gaze at the stone Cross of Cashel with a base that may have been a pre-Christian sacrificial altar. Ancient Celts worshipped here, and Irish kings built their palace on the sacred site. It was here that St. Patrick came in the year 450 to preach to Aengus, king of Munster, using the shamrock as a symbol of the Trinity. Aengus saw the light, and with his family accepted baptism.

Murtough O'Brien presented the Cashel of the Kings to the church in 1101, and in 1127 Cormac MacCarthaigh built the little chapel that is his namesake. It's a miniature gem of Romanesque style. In the years that followed, the fortunes of the sacred place vacillated with the fluctuations of royalty and church power. In 1748 the archbishop of the day left it abandoned and unroofed because – so the Irish say – his coach and four could not make it up the steep incline to its great west door.

No visit to the Rock of Cashel is complete without a look next door at the Brú Ború Heritage Centre. The resident Brú Ború troupe of traditional musicians and dancers perform daily during the

mid-Jun. to mid-Sep.; 9:30–5:30, mid-Mar. to mid-Jun. and mid-Sep. to mid-Oct.; 9:30–4:30, rest of year
🔲 Crock of Gold Tea Room, across the road 🔲 $$
Swiss Cottage ✉ Ardfinnan Road ☎ 052 41144
🕒 Tue.–Sun. 10–6, Apr.–Sep.; 10–1 and 2–4:30 (guided tours only), rest of year 🔲 $$

CARRICK-ON-SUIR

The town of Carrick is noteworthy for its beautiful Tudor mansion – rare amid Ireland's hundreds of fortresses and abbeys. Despite its name, Ormande Castle is completely unfortified. The original 15th-century castle fell into ruins centuries ago. Not so the adjoining Elizabethan manor house, built by the 10th Earl of Ormond ("Black Tom") to entice Queen Elizabeth I to visit. The grand edifice never did succeed in that effort, but it did survive the centuries to stand as Ireland's best example of that period. Two of the 15th-century towers are consolidated into the manor house, and the decorative plasterwork is among the best in the country.

The sense of history is intense at the Rock of Cashel

summer season, and facilities here include a craft center, a folk theater, subterranean exhibition and an information center.

Although the town tends to be overshadowed by the Rock, as one of Ireland's designated Heritage Towns, it is well worth a visit in its own right. A good place to start is the town hall's Folk Village, an attractive reconstruction of local village lifestyles. Wandering from one thatched village shop to another is a step back in time. In the informal setting, shops are interspersed with other facets of daily life, including a forge and the Penal Chapel. Cashel's ecclesiastical prominence predates the arrival of St. Patrick as changing exhibitions at the Heritage Centre portray. On permanent display is a large scale model of the town in the 1640s, and the "Royal Heirlooms and Relics of the House of McCarthy Múr" provides a glimpse into the lifestyles of ancient Gaelic royalty.

From June to September, a tram departs the center to tour the historic sites in the town. Adjoining the Georgian St. John the Baptist Cathedral and nearby 14th-century town walls, the GPA Bolton Library holds fascinating manuscript collections, some of which date to the 12th century. The complete works of Machiavelli are here, as is the Nuremberg Chronicle of 1493, works by Dante and a host of other larger-than-life figures, including part of Chaucer's *Book of Fame*, printed by Caxton.

➕ C2 **Tourist information** ✉ Town Hall, Main Street ☎ 062 61333 ⏱ Mon.–Sat. 9–6, Apr.–Jun. and Sep.; Mon.–Sat. 9–6, Sun. 11–5, Jul. and Aug.

The Rock of Cashel ✉ Cashel ☎ 062 61437 ⏱ Daily 9–7:30, mid-Jun. to mid-Sep.; 9–5:30, mid-Mar. to mid-Jun.; 9–4:30, rest of year 💲 $$

Brú Ború Heritage Centre ✉ Cashel ☎ 062 61122 ⏱ Mon.–Fr. 9–5, mid-Jun.–Sep.; theater performances Tue.–Sat. at 9 p.m., Jun.–Sep.

🍴 Restaurant 💲 Center: free; show: $$$

ℹ Ask about banquet and show evenings available in summer months

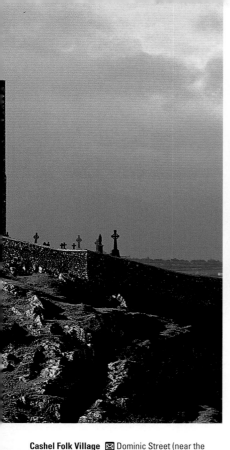

Colorful buildings line the streets of Dingle town

to this day. You may feel the very essence of Celtic magic has been distilled into the air of the Dingle Peninsula. Or perhaps it is only the soft, lyrical accents of the Gaelic, which is the everyday language here, that make it seem so.

West of town, Ventry Harbour was, according to legend, the scene of a fierce battle between "King of the World" Daire Doon and King of Ireland Finn MacCool (see page 199). Still farther west, Dunbeg Fort perches on a high promontory, one side surrounded by earthen trenches, and its 22-foot-thick wall riddled with an elaborate *souterrain* (inner passage).

From the high cliffs of Slea Head you get the most sweeping view of sheltered coves below and the Blasket Islands. The last of their tiny population was moved to the mainland in 1953, when the fishing industry failed to provide a living wage and the government gave land grants for small farm holdings on the peninsula. Visitors from Springfield, Massachusetts may feel a special bond to the people of the Blaskets, since many islanders emigrated to that city.

Boats go out from Dunquin Harbour on an intermittent basis during summer months. There are very good potteries on the peninsula: Louis Mulcahy operates a pottery studio and workshop at Clogher Beach, Ballyferriter where he trains local

Cashel Folk Village ✉ Dominic Street (near the Rock of Cashel) ☎ 062 62525 🕙 Daily 9:30–7:30, May–Oct.; 10–6, Mar.–Apr. 🎫 $$

Cashel Heritage Centre and Tram Tour ✉ Town Hall ☎ 062 62511 🕙 Daily 9:30–5:30, Jul.–Sep.; Mon.–Fri. 9:30–5:30, rest of year 🎫 Free

St. John the Baptist Cathedral and GPA Bolton Library ✉ John Street ☎ 062 61944; fax 062 62511 🕙 Tue.–Sun. 10–5:30, Mar.–Oct.; otherwise by appointment; inquire at Cashel Heritage Centre 🎫 $

Celtic Plantarum Dundrum ✉ Dundrum, Co. Tipperary (on R505, Cashel road) ☎ 062 71303 🕙 Daily 9–dusk 🎫 Free

DINGLE PENINSULA AND THE BLASKET ISLANDS

The Dingle Peninsula is the most westerly point of land in Europe, its offshore Blasket Islands the "last parish before New York." Its beginnings are shrouded in the mists of prehistory, which left its marks scattered over the face of the Slieve Mish mountains, along its coves and rocky cliffs and in the legends that persist

Munster

potters in the production of many unusual items.

Ballyferriter is also the focal point for a summer-school program that brings students to study Gaelic and live with local families who use the language in their everyday lives. Stop at the old schoolhouse in the center of the town, now the Oidhreacht Chorca Dhuibhne (Corca Dhuibhne Regional Museum). Dingle's long history is illustrated by more than 200 photographs, artifacts and text, and you'll leave with more than a nodding acquaintance with the region's beehive huts, standing stones, mysterious graves, ring forts and other relics.

One of the peninsula's most astonishing remains is Gallarus Oratory between Dunquin and Ballyferriter. It's a marvelous specimen of early Christian architecture. Built in an inverted-boat shape, it has remained completely watertight for more than a thousand years, its stones perfectly fitted without benefit of any kind of mortar. Look also for the Alphabet Stone in the churchyard of the ancient ruined Kilmalkedar church. The pillar is carved with both the Roman alphabet and ogham strokes.

In a low, sprawling building that seems to nestle into its waterside setting in Dunquin, the Blasket Centre presents the story of the Blasket Islanders in innovative displays and productions that bring to vivid life the harshness of their daily lives and the richness of their literary works. Every image inside is enhanced by the clear view of the islands through a seaward-looking wall of glass.

Dingle (its ancient Irish name is An Daingean, The Fortress) is a busy little market town that sits at the head of the Dingle Peninsula. Both town and peninsula have become a mecca for some of Ireland's most talented crafts people, and you may want to pick up at least one Irish treasure here. There's good crafts browsing at The Wood in Ceardlann Na Coille, a cluster of small cottages housing crafts workshops. You can take a bit of the Irish landscape home if you stop by the Irish Wildflowers shop, which is also a small art gallery. Across the road, silversmith Brian de Staic fashions unique

necklaces with your name inscribed in strokes of the ancient ogham language.

In recent years, Fungi the dolphin has moved in to Dingle Bay, promptly becoming the beloved pet of locals and visitors alike. He's fun to watch as he cavorts through the water, following the small boats that bring visitors out for a closer look and perhaps a swim with the playful dolphin.

To reach the northern shores of the peninsula, take the Connor Pass road from Dingle town to Castlegregory. Views from the pass and along the coastal road from Castlegregory into Tralee go from best to better with each curve in the road, an embarrassment of scenic splendors that has quickly exhausted the film supply of many camera buffs.

✚ A2
Tourist information ✉ The Quay, Dingle

Returning to pasture along the clifftop road near Dingle

☎ 066 915 1188 🕐 Daily, Mar.–Oct. ⓘ You can make reservations on one of the many boats that visit Fungi daily during summer months

Ballyferriter Pottery ✉ Ballyferriter ☎ 066 915 6229 🕐 Daily 9–8, Jul.–Aug.; 10–5:30, rest of year

The Blasket Centre ✉ Dunquin ☎ 066 915 6444 🕐 Daily 10–6 (last admission 5:15), Jul.–Aug.; 10–6, Easter–Jun. and Sep.–Oct. 🍴 Café 💲 $$

Corca Dhuibhne Regional Museum ✉ Ballyferriter ☎ 066 915 6333 🕐 Daily 10–5, Apr.–Sep.; by appointment rest of year 🍴 Coffee shop 💲 $

Irish Wildflowers shop ✉ Dingle ☎ 066 915 2200

The Wood ✉ Ceardlann Na Coille, less than a mile west of Dingle on the coast road

DOOLIN

Such is the international reputation of this tiny village set at the edge of the Atlantic (5 miles southwest of Lisdoonvarna) as a focal point for traditional Irish music, that musicians from around the world flock here to play in O'Connor's Pub. The appreciative audiences are as diverse as the musicians.

Don't be put off by Doolin's ungainly sprawl as it is an excellent base for exploring the Burren. There is a good choice of cafés and restaurants, and it's advisable to book hotels ahead during summer months. It is the closest mainland point to the Aran Islands (see page 38), and boats leave the pier daily for the 30-minute voyage to Inishmore and Inisheer islands.

✚ B3

Tourist information ✉ The Cliffs of Moher, Liscannor ☎ 065 708 1171 🕐 Daily 9:30–5:30, Apr., May, Sep. and Oct.; 9:30–7:30, Jun.–Aug.

O'Connor's Pub ✉ Doolin ☎ 065 707 4168

Trees force their way up in the limestone Burren

ENNIS AND COUNTY CLARE

Ennis is a bustling market town with many historical buildings and tiny, winding streets. Of special note is the 13th-century Franciscan friary on Abbey Street. For detailed exploration of the town, stop by the tourist office for *Ennis – A Walking Trail*, an excellent guide for an hour-and-a-half tour. County Clare's incredible history is captured in displays at the Treasures of Clare Museum, located in a former convent.

The Craggaunowen (pronounced "Crag-an-owen") Project brings a sense of reality to everyday Irish life during the Bronze Age and early Christian era. The small castle has an interesting display of medieval art objects. In the lake a short walk away is a fascinating re-creation of a crannog (a Bronze Age lake dwelling). There's a cooking site of the Iron Age, and the earthen ring fort on the grounds holds a reconstructed farm home of some 15 centuries ago. Of special interest is the glass shelter that has been constructed to house the tiny leather curragh built by Tim Severin for his

daring voyage across the Atlantic to retrace St. Brendan's legendary route of AD 700.

There's an eerie moonscape look to much of the Burren's 100-square-mile limestone area. Its rich plant life belies the overwhelming sense of remoteness at first glance. Make your first stop the Burren Display Centre to view exhibits to help you understand what you'll see or try the Burren Exposure visitors center, which provides an overview of the area and its unique landscape, history and flora. You can view elaborate audiovisual presentations. Walking all or part of the 26-mile signposted Burren Way is the best way to discover the relics of ancient civilizations, as well as the astonishing flora thriving in such an unlikely setting. Nearby, a local farmer discovered Aillwee Cave, a natural wonder, about 50 years ago. Its awesome stalactites, stalagmites, waterfall and relics of brown bears who eons ago hollowed out snug pits have made it one of the most popular visitor attractions in the Shannonside region.

The Shannon region has many ancient buildings, often carefully restored to

in tracing your roots, you will find the "Ireland West 1800-60" exhibition fascinating as it takes you through famine and emigration years.

The 5-mile stretch of the Cliffs of Moher that rise to as high as 754 feet can only be described as breathtaking. They are best viewed from O'Brien's Tower, which in Victorian days was especially built on the highest cliff to afford a good vantage point for early 19th-century tourists. Mountains as far apart as Kerry and Connemara and the Aran Islands are clearly visible in good weather. Clifftop walks are tempting, but call for extreme caution, as there is a real danger that the ground may give way. The visitor center, just off the large parking lot, has an exceptionally good selection of Irish literature and music.

⊞ B3

Tourist information ✉ Arthur's Row, Ennis ☎ 065 682 8366 ⚙ Mon.–Sat. 9:30–5:30; also Sun., Jul.–Aug.

Aillwee Cave ✉ Ballyvaughan, Ennistymon (28 miles from Ennis) ☎ 065 707 7036 ⚙ Daily 10–5.30 🍴 Café 🎟 $$$

Treasures of Clare Museum ✉ Arthur's Row, Ennis ☎ 065 682 3382 ⚙ Mon.–Sat. 9:30–5:30 🎟 $

Craggaunowen Project ✉ Quin, Co. Clare, 10 miles from Ennis, signposted from Quin, north on R469 ☎ 061 360 788 ⚙ Daily 10–6 (last admission at 5), Apr.–Oct. 🍴 Tearoom 🎟 $$$

Burren Display Centre ✉ Kilfenora, 8 miles northwest from Ennis on the Lahinch Road ☎ 065 708 8030 ⚙ Daily 9:30–6, Jul.–Aug.; 10–5, Mar.–Jun. and Sep.–Oct. 🍴 Tea shop; Vaughan's Pub in Kilfenora 🎟 $$

Burren Exposure ✉ Ballyvaughan ☎ 065 707 7277 ⚙ Sun.–Thu. 11–6, Fri.–Sat. 10–4:30 🎟 $$

Clare Heritage and Genealogical Centre ✉ Corofin, 6 miles northwest from Ennis on the Lahinch Road ☎ 065 683 7955; fax 065 683 7540 ⚙ Exhibition: Mon.–Fri. 9:30–5:30, Sat.–Sun. 10–5, May – Oct.; centre: Mon.–Fri. 9–5 🎟 $$

Cliffs of Moher ✉ On R478 near Liscannor ☎ 065 708 1565 ⚙ Tower and center: daily 9–8, Jun.–Aug.; ring to confirm times for rest of year 🍴 Tearoom 🚌 From Ennis Bus Station ☎ 65 682 4177 🎟 Free

Knappogue Castle ✉ Quin (9 miles from Ennis, signposted from Quin, south on R469) ☎ 061 368 103 ⚙ Daily 9:30–5:30 (last admission at 4:30), May–Oct. 🎟 $$

achieve full tourist potential. Besides well-known Bunratty (see page 144), there are tower houses like Knappogue Castle, which was built in 1479 and whose restoration has been faithful to that 15th-century character.

If you've been looking for a mate, Lisdoonvarna, 7 miles north of Ennistymon on road N67, is the place to be in September. That's when Europe's largest matchmaking festival imbues this little North Clare town with song, dance, storytelling, serious matchmaking and all-round gaiety. The tourist office in Ennis can fill you in on exact dates. If you're not looking for romance, Lisdoonvarna is also famous for its Victorian Spa Complex and Health Centre, where you can drink or bathe in the therapeutic mineral waters which have been dispensed here since the 18th century.

If there's any County Clare connection to the ancestors you want to trace, it is quite likely you'll find help among the thousands of family records at the Clare Heritage and Genealogical Centre. Write for a Genealogical Research Form, which details the research material available and fees involved. Even if you aren't engaged

KILLARNEY

The friendly, ebullient residents of Killarney more than offset what is a popular perception of the town as more commercial than any other town in Ireland. "Commercial," in Killarney's case, simply translates into an abundance of good accommodations, eateries and entertainment. Killarney's wealth of natural beauty can be a bit overwhelming. Not to worry – the *jarveys* (drivers of open horse-drawn vehicles), boatmen and bus-tour people have it all worked out. Their routes will take you to the high points, and although it is perfectly possible to wander around on your own, do go along for at least one of the organized tours, whether by car, boat or coach. It's great fun. The guides know and love the scenery and embellish every spot with the folklore that will make the experience even more memorable. If you're ready for a break from driving, Bus Eireann runs several good day trips to nearby locations, such as the Ring of Kerry and the Dingle Peninsula (page 131).

For a lasting memento of your visit, stop in the Frank Lewis Gallery, which specializes in landscapes of the area, portraits and sculptures by local artists.

A broad valley holds the three main lakes, with Lough Leane (the Lower Lake) closest to Killarney and separated from the Middle Lake by Muckross peninsula. It was on one of its 30 islands that dedicated monks faithfully recorded Irish history from the 11th to the 13th century in the *Annals of Innisfallen*. The Middle Lake covers 600 acres, holds four islands, and is connected to the small, narrow Upper Lake and its eight islands by a broad river called the Long Range. The lakes and streams are connected to the Atlantic by the River Laune. Their waters catch the shimmering reflections of birch, oak, mountain ash and arbutus, while hovering over all are the peaks of some of Ireland's finest mountains: Macgillycuddy's Reeks, with Carrantuohill, the country's highest mountain; the Tomies; the Mangerton range; and Torc. As a Killarney *jarvey*

once said, "Sure, 'tis a grand sight, one of God's blessings."

Killarney's boatmen are legendary for their skillful navigation of the lakes and their store of wondrous tales. Boats depart from the Ross Castle pier for two-and-a-half-hour tours, which include the Gap of Dunloe, Ross Castle, Muckross House and Gardens and Torc Waterfall. Check at the tourist office for times and reservations. You can visit these sights on the Ring of Kerry Drive (see pages 138–140).

Set on 11,500 acres of parkland and surrounded by marvelously landscaped gardens, the Victorian mansion Muckross House was built in 1843, bought by Americans in 1911, and presented as a gift to the Irish people in 1932. The first two floors are furnished in the manner of the great houses of Ireland, while its upper floors hold fascinating exhibits of maps, prints and other documents, as well as a small wildlife and bird collection. A folk museum and crafts shop bring to vivid life the Kerry country lifestyle of a time long past. The surrounding gardens feature azaleas and rhododendrons.

A strong feeling of having stepped back in time is inevitable at the Muckross Traditional Farms, where Irish farm life of years gone by continues in living exhibits – crops are sown and harvested, homemakers go about their daily chores,

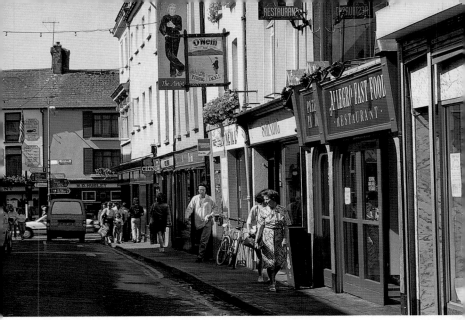

Narrow shopping street in the small, neat town of Killarney

and carpenter, blacksmith and wheelwright carry on their trades. Adults and children will delight in the authentic barnyard with its animal occupants.

The tower house and two rounded towers that join remnants of a curtain wall are all that remain of Ross Castle, a late 15th-century O'Donoghue Ross stronghold set on the shores of the Lower Lake about 2 miles from town. Your imagination will help resurrect it to its life when it was an Irish chieftain's home. Late 16th- and early 17th-furnishings are on display, and the view of lakes and islands from the top is superb.

Near Cahirciveen, Valentia Island is joined to the mainland by a causeway. Silhouetted against the horizon, 10 miles offshore, the sharply pointed Skellig Islands are home to thousands of puffins, gannets and other seabirds. It was not always a sanctuary for birds. For it was on Skellig Michael, a massive rocky hulk that rises steeply 700 feet above the sea, that a colony of sixth-century monks did the seemingly impossible when they built a retreat of stone beehive huts. For six centuries it was an impenetrable monastic refuge, abandoned in the 12th century.

Today the Skellig Islands are a 45-minute boat ride from the mainland in good weather, and you reach the ruins after a climb of no fewer than 640 steps. Your climb is rewarded with magnificent views and a sense of wonder at the stone beehive huts, that have survived all these centuries without mortar, two oratories and a church.

Begin or end your visit to the Skelligs with a stop in the Skellig Heritage Centre on Valentia Island. The imaginative stone building, framed by grassy mounds, seems to grow right out of the landscape. It is here that you can view programs and displays on the area's history. Pick up an excellent guide book from the crafts shop, and ask for ferry service information.

➕ A2

Tourist information ✉ Beech Road ☎ 064 31633; fax 064 34506 🕓 Mon.–Sat. 9:15–5:30, Oct.–Jun.; Mon.–Sat. 9–6, Sun., 10–6, Jun. and Sep.; Mon.–Sat. 9–8, Sun. 10–6, Jul. and Aug.

Muckross House ✉ Kenmare Road (N71) ☎ 064 31440; fax 064 33926 🕓 Daily 9–7, Jul.–Aug.; 9–5:30, rest of year 🍴 Tearoom in coach house 🚌 From Killarney 🎫 House and farm: $$$

Ross Castle ✉ Ross Road, off Muckross Road (N71) ☎ 064 35851 🕓 Daily 9–5:45, Jun.–Aug.; 10–6, May and Sep.; 11–6, Apr.; Tue.–Sun. 10–5, rest of year 🎫 $$

The Skellig Experience ✉ Skellig Heritage Centre, Valentia Island, 7 miles off the Ring of Kerry on R765 ☎ 066 947 6306 🕓 Daily 9:30–7, Jul.–Aug.; 10–7, Apr.–Jun. and Oct. 🍴 Café 🎫 $$

Old farm machinery and peat mound at Glenbeigh bog village

DRIVE:
RING OF KERRY

Duration: 1–2 days

The 112-mile Ring of Kerry takes top billing on this tour as you travel from one scenic wonder to the next. The route skirts the edges of the Iveragh Peninsula to Kenmare, then circles back over the mountains via Moll's Gap and Ladies' View to Killarney. Mountains, lakes, sandy beaches and offshore islands form an unforgettable panorama, and Killarney town has its own fair share of splendid lakes, antiquities and legends.

Starting at the tourist office on Beech Road in Killarney, take the N72 northwest for 13 miles to Killorglin.

Perched on hills above the River Laune, Killorglin is an ideal starting point for this drive. In mid-August, this quiet town is abuzz with the three-day Puck Fair dating from 1613 (see page 147). Pubs stay open around the clock, and every sort of street entertainment goes on non-stop. This is also a traditional gathering place for the country's traveling people, who come to engage in some hard-driving horse trading.

Turn southwest on the N70 to Glenbeigh.

On the main street of this village, look for the bog village adjoining the Red Fox Inn. Bogs have always played an important role in Ireland, and this re-creation is an authentic depiction of the lives of the peatbog communities.

Follow the N70 southwest to reach Caherciveen.

The drive along the southern banks of Dingle Bay from Glenbeigh to this small town at the foot of the Bentee Mountain is one of island-dotted coastal scenery and fields studded with prehistoric stone ring-fort ruins, with clear views of the Dingle Peninsula across the water. At Caherciveen, Valentia Island comes into view. (see page 136). There is a ferry service, and it is accessible by car via a causeway at Portmagee. The island is noted for its superb scenery of cliffs, mountains, seascapes and vivid subtropical flowers.

Drive 10 miles south on the N70 to Waterville.

Set on a strip of land that separates Ballinskelligs Bay from the island-sprinkled Lough Currane, this popular resort and fishing center is also known for its superb golf course. Mountains rise from the lake's shores, and on Church Island there are ruins of a 12th-century church that was dedicated to a sixth-century holy man, St. Fionan.

Continue south, then east on the N70 for 22 miles towards Sneem.

Just beyond Coomakista Pass on the N70, and one mile before Caherdaniel, is Derrynane House. Set in the wooded National Park, this was the birthplace of Daniel O'Connell in 1775. The house is maintained as a museum containing memorabilia on Ireland's beloved "Liberator." Most of O'Connell's political life was spent here; Caherciveen's Heritage Centre includes displays on his life.

On the drive east on the N70 from Waterville to Sneem, just east of Caherdaniel, is Castlecove where, about a mile and a half north of the road, you will see Staigue Fort, one of the country's best-preserved Iron-Age stone forts. The circular stone walls, 13 feet wide and 18 feet high, have held over the centuries without the benefit of mortar. Along their interior are several flights of stairs in near perfect condition.

Derrynane National Historic Park covers 320 acres and incorporates semitropical plants and coastal trees and shrubs, as well as fine coastal scenery. There is a well-marked nature trail, and swimming is accessible to visitors. The pretty town of Sneem, situated where the Ardsheelaun estuary joins the Kenmare River, is popular for brown trout and salmon fishing, and its fine sandy beaches provide safe swimming. George Bernard Shaw wrote part of *St. Joan* here. Sneem is also the last resting place of

Father Michael Walsh, who was a parish priest in the area for 38 years in the 1800s and was immortalized as "Father O'Flynn" in a well-known Irish ballad. Two miles to the south in Parknasilla, the elegant Great Southern Hotel is famed for its rock gardens and colorful sub-tropical blooms.

Continue east on the N70 for 17 miles to Kenmare.

The drive from Sneem along the banks of the Kenmare River has lovely views of the Caha and Slieve Miskish mountains on the opposite shore. Kenmare faces the broad Kenmare River estuary, with impressive mountains at its back.

Known as Ceann Mara (Head of the Sea) by the ancients, today it is a lively heritage town, particularly noted for its sea fishing, safe swimming, walks and climbs, homespun woolen industry and lace. Kenmare is one of Ireland's planned estate towns, dating from 1670. The Heritage Centre details its history, as well as covering such intriguing exhibits as the Nun of Kenmare, the Landlords of Kenmare, the Effects of the Famine, and Kenmare Lace Exhibition. A Heritage Trail map focusing on historical sites within walking distance from the center is furnished at no charge.

Turn north on the N71 to reach Moll's Gap.

The drive north to Moll's Gap is one of

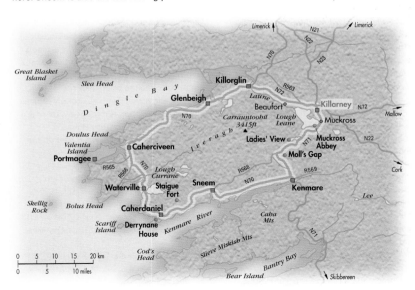

Molls Gap in Killarney

rugged mountains and stone-strewn valleys. The viewing point at this gap affords sweeping views of Macgillycuddy's Reeks and of Ireland's highest mountain, 3,414-foot Carrantuohill. The restaurant and craft shop make this a good refreshment stop.

Follow the N71 northeast for 3 miles to Ladies' View.

This mountainside viewing point overlooks the broad valley of the Killarney lakes. Queen Victoria and her ladies-in-waiting were so enthused about this view that it was promptly named in their honor.

Nine miles north on the return to Killarney are the well-preserved ruins of Muckross Abbey. The abbey dates from 1448 and was built on the site of an earlier religious establishment. About a 10-minute walk from the abbey, Elizabethan-style Muckross House is surrounded by landscaped gardens that slope down to the lake (see page 136).

The first two floors are furnished in the manner of the great houses of Ireland, while its upper floors hold fascinating exhibits of maps, prints and other documents, as well as a small wildlife and bird collection. In the basement there is a folk museum with a

country pub, print shop, dairy, carpentry shop and weaving shop. Craftspeople are at work in some, and you can purchase their products in the gift shop. Visit the adjoining Muckross Traditional Farms, a working museum which farms the land in the methods used in the 1930s (see page 136).

About 1 mile before Muckross House, a signpost on the N71 directs you to a scenic footpath up a mountain slope to the 60-foot Torc Waterfall in a beautiful wooded area. Continue to the top of the falls for magnificent views, if you've brought a picnic, this is the ideal spot. Alternatively, there is a good tea-shop at Muckross House.

Continue for 11 miles northeast on the N71 to Killarney.

Caherciveen Heritage Centre ✉ Bridge Street ☎ 066 947 2777 🕐 Mon.–Fri. 10–5, Sun. 12:30–5, Apr.–Oct.; phone to confirm winter hours 🅿 $$
Derrynane House ✉ Caherdaniel ☎ 066 947 5113 🕐 Mon.–Fri. 9–6, Sun. 11–7; ring to confirm winter hours 🅿 $$
Kenmare Heritage Centre ✉ The Square ☎ 064 41233 🕐 Mon.–Fri. 9–6, Sun. 10–1 and 2:15–5, Apr.–Sep. 🅿 Free

KINSALE

As picturesque a fishing and boating town as you're likely to encounter in the whole of Ireland, Kinsale (18 miles south of Cork city via N71) is a gateway to a meandering coastline drive through west Cork. From its beginnings in 1333, it has witnessed – and participated in – the ebb and flow of Irish history which is traced through exhibits and photos housed in Kinsale's Regional Museum in the Old Courthouse, built in 1600.

Today Kinsale is a popular yachting center, and home to several top-rated gourmet restaurants. Its narrow, winding streets make for great strolls through the town. The Earl of Desmond built Desmond Castle in the 1500s as a custom house, but over its long history it has served as a prison, wine storage depot and a workhouse during the famine years. These days it holds an interesting International Museum of Wine, illustrating Ireland's contribution to the international wine trade.

South of town at Castlepark, you can visit the remains of James Fort, which dates back to 1602. The Old Head of Kinsale is where a ruined 12th-century castle sits atop a high cliff overlooking the spot where in 1915 the *Lusitania* was sent to a watery grave by a German submarine, with the loss of 1,198 souls.

In Summer Cove on the eastern side of the estuary stands the still intact Charles Fort. Built in 1683 and in constant use until 1922, the fort is designed in the classic star-shaped style. It sits high on a clifftop, with spectacular views of Kinsale Harbour.

Timoleague Abbey, 10 miles southwest of Kinsale, is one of Ireland's best preserved Franciscan friaries, built in the mid-1200s. Nearby, the Castle Gardens have been maintained by one family for the past 150 years.

✚ B1

Tourist information ✉ Pier Road ☎ 021 477 2234 🕒 Mon.–Sat. 9–6, Sep.–Oct. and Apr.–Jun.; Mon.–Sat. 9–6:45, Sun. 10–5:45, Jul. and Aug.

Kinsale Regional Museum ✉ Market Square

Fishing boats resting in the still waters of Kinsale Harbour

Fine walking countryside around Lough Gur

☎ 021 477 2044 🕐 Daily 10:30–1 and 2–5, Apr.–Sep.;
Wed.–Fri. 10:30–1:30, rest of year 💷 $$
Desmond Castle ✉ Cork Street ☎ 021 477 4855
🕐 Daily 10–5:15, mid-Jun. to early-Oct.; 10–6, mid-
Apr. to mid-Jun. 🍴 The Vintage (☎ 021 477 2502,
✉ Main Street) 💷 $$
Charles Fort ✉ Summer Cove ☎ 021 477 2263
🕐 Daily 10–5:15, mid-Mar. to Oct.; Sat.–Sun. 10–5,
rest of year (last admission 45 min before closing)
🍴 Man Friday (see page 208) 💷 $$ 🛈 Wear
suitable shoes for the uneven terrain. Parking nearby

LIMERICK

Limerick, Ireland's third largest city (with
a population of 81,000), gets its name
from the Irish Luimneach (Bare Spot).
Centuries ago, that's just what was here –
a barren, hilly bit of land on an island, and
because the island sat at the lowest ford of
the Shannon, it is believed early Celts
built an earthen fort at its highest point.
Then came the Danes in AD 831 to build
a base from which to launch their
plundering. More than a century later,
Brian Ború sent them packing and
installed the O'Briens as rulers. St. Mary's
Cathedral, built in the oldest part of the
city, has a fine view from its bell tower
and holds some intriguing antiqities.

Next it was the Normans, with their
stout city walls and castles. Portions of

their walls remain to this day, as does
King John's Castle, whose impressive
fortification on the banks of the Shannon
has guarded Limerick since the early
1200s. The imaginative admissions
building sits atop excavated remains of
ancient city walls and homes of pre-
Norman residents. The massive gate
house, corner towers, curtain walls and
battlements reflect the authority of
royalty, while in the courtyard medieval
war machines usually seen only in
period movies beguile the imagination.
Don't rush through this one – it is a
definite "don't miss."

The marvelously restored 15th-century
Bunratty Castle was built for the
O'Briens, earls of Thomond, and its
restoration includes furnishings that look
as though they've been here since the days
of those first residents. Enter across a
drawbridge into the vaulted Great Hall,
the center of castle life where elaborate
feasts are served up nightly just as they
were in days of yore (see page 144). Some
of the reconstructions in the Folk Park
include a blacksmith shop, post office,
draper, tea room and a tiny pub.

During the 18th century, Limerick
took on its present-day form, with stylish
townhouses going up along broad avenues
extending far beyond the old boundaries
of Irish Town and English Town.

With 800 years of turbulent history
behind it, Limerick has in recent years
transformed itself from a town with a
slightly grubby image to one of
progressive modernity built around its
cherished monuments from the past.
There is a variety of sightseeing
attractions, with a plentiful supply of all
the facilities expected of a city of this size.

Modern places of interest include
the worthwhile Hunt Museum, one of the
finest art museums in the country outside
the National Gallery of Dublin (page 81).
It contains works by Picasso, Renoir and
Leonardo de Vinci. Along with medieval
statues in stone, bronze and wood, there
are Egyptian, Greek and Roman
artifacts, as well as Neolithic flints and
other Irish relics.

If flying is your passion, you'll know
that the first commercial direct flight

between the United States and Europe was flown by Pan Am's luxury flying boat *Yankee Clipper*, which landed at Foynes on the broad estuary of the Shannon. Now restored and preserved, the Foynes Flying Boat Museum translates nostalgia for that era into exhibits, an audiovisual show and the radio and weather room with original navigation equipment.

At Lough Gur, in addition to the lake dwelling that dates between AD 500 and 1000, there's a wedge tomb from 2500 BC, one of Ireland's largest stone circles and replicas of weapons, tools and pottery found in this area. The remains of animals no longer seen in Ireland (giant Irish deer and bear) have been unearthed in nearby caves. The center tells the story in detail.
➕ B2

Tourist information ✉ Arthurs Quay ☎ 061 317 522 🕐 Mon.–Sat. 9:30–5:30; also Sun., Jul.–Aug.

St. Mary's Cathedral ✉ Bridge Street ☎ 061 310 293 🕐 Daily 9–5 💷 Donation: $

King John's Castle ✉ Nicholas Street ☎ 061 360 788 🕐 Daily 9:30–5:30, Apr.–Oct.; Sun. only rest of year 💷 $$$

Bunratty Castle and Folk Park ✉ Shannon Airport Road (N18) ☎ 061 360 788 🕐 Castle: Daily 9–4:30; Park: 9–7, Jul.–Aug.; 9:30–5:30, rest of year 🍴 Tearoom in folk park 🚌 Limerick and Shannon Airport bus 💷 $$$

Lough Gur Stone Age Centre ✉ Lough Gur, 16 miles from Limerick ☎ 061 360 788 🕐 Daily 10–6 (last admission at 5:30), May–Sep. 💷 Access to lake: free; centre: $$ 🛈 Regular walking tours conducted to archeological features.

Hunt Museum ✉ The Custom House, Rutland Street ☎ 061 312 833 🕐 Daily 10–5 🍴 Restaurant 💷 $$

Foynes Flying Boat Musuem ✉ Foynes, 20 miles west of Limerick via N69 ☎ 069 65416 🕐 Daily 10–6, Apr.–Oct. 🍴 Café 💷 $$

The austere facade of Bunratty Castle, Limerick

LISMORE

Among the several scenic drives around the Cappoquin and Lismore area, undoubtedly the most spectacular is the one that takes you through a gap in the Knockmealdown Mountains, known as the Vee. From the outskirts of Lismore, it climbs through larch and rhododendron, and heather-covered mountainsides, to the V-shaped pass. The sweeping views from numerous stopping points overlook

Tipperary's Golden Vale, before descending to the little town of Clogheen in County Tipperary. High on one mountain slope stands a most curious grave, that of Samuel Grubb, one-time owner of Castle Grace, who so loved his lands that he decreed he should be buried upright overlooking them. There's a small pathway leading up to the stone cairn that is his final resting place.
➕ C2

LISTOWEL

There is a decidedly literary bent to this north Kerry town, 17 miles northeast of Tralee. It has nurtured several of Ireland's leading writers, including John B. Keane and Bryan McMahon. The tradition lives on during Writer's Week in late June or early July, when lectures and workshops are designed to encourage beginning writers. Theater thrives with performances by Irish and international troupes in St. John's Arts and Heritage Centre on the square. If you're visiting in September, don't miss the Listowel Races.
➕ A2

Tourist information ✉ St. John's Church ☎ 066 22590 🕐 Jun.–Sep. (phone to confirm times)

St. John's Arts and Heritage Centre ✉ The Square, Listowel ☎ 068 22566 🕐 Mon.–Sat. 10–1, 2–6

Munster

Enjoy an evening of feasting and merriment at Knappogue Castle

MEDIEVAL CASTLE BANQUETS AND TRADITIONAL *CÉILÍ*

The medieval banquets at Bunratty and Knappogue castles and the traditional *céilí* at Bunratty Folk Park are each a unique experience and appeal to all age groups. No matter which you choose, you'll not be disappointed – at least one should go on your "don't miss" list. You stand a good chance of being disappointed if you fail to make reservations through a travel agent or the banquet reservations manager, Shannon Castle Banquets before you leave home. If you arrive without a reservation, any tourist office in Ireland will try to make one for you (with as much advance notice as you can give them). There is free parking, and tourist offices in Ennis or Limerick can furnish information about bus transportation.

Any "lord and lady of the castle" spirit you might anticipate for the medieval banquet at Bunratty Castle quickly dissolves into one of great fun and hilarity. Even the stuffiest of type joins in as story follows story and song follows song. The internationally famed Bunratty Singers serve up enchanting melodies, and the golden notes of an Irish harp melt the stoniest heart.

Somewhat harder to reach than Bunratty (it's 19 miles from Limerick, 9 miles from Ennis, signposted from Quin, south on R469 and there's no public transportation), Knappogue Castle's banquet is slightly more sedate, but far from stuffy. The group is smaller and more intimate, and the colorful entertainment focuses on the women of Ireland, both mythical and real – queens, saints and sinners from a Celtic past.

In the great barn in the Bunratty Folk Park, the traditional Irish *céilí* are strictly not for upper-crust nobility! The traditional music of pipes, fiddle, *bodhran* and accordion is what the people of Ireland have made their own and handed down through the centuries. This is the most informal of the three feasts, where audience and performers join together in song and dance, the menu here features wholesome dishes such as Irish stew and fresh homegrown garden produce.

Shannon Castle Banquets ✉ Town Centre, Shannon ☎ 061 360 788 Twice nightly 5:30 and 8:45; Knappogue Castle's banquet: Apr.–Oct.; Bunratty Folk Park; year-round

THURLES

A large market town on the River Suir, Thurles (pronounced "Thur-less") has two castles and a splendid Italianate cathedral, based on the one at Pisa in Italy. The town's Semple Stadium is a major venue for all Gaelic games, and it was in the Hayes Hotel that the Gaelic Athletics Association was founded in 1884 to codify and encourage Irish sports. On the west bank of the River Suir 4 miles south of Thurles, Holy Cross Abbey was founded in 1168 and was ever after a revered place of pilgrimage. Among its treasures was a particle of the True Cross preserved in a golden shrine dating from 1110, now in the Ursuline Convent in Blackrock, Cork. Restored in 1971, the abbey still contains many interesting and religiously significant ruins, and Sunday pilgrimages continue to take place from May to September.

✠ C2

Tourist information ✉ Excel Building, Mitchell Street, Tipperary town ☎ 062 51457 🕐 Mon.–Sat. 9:30–5:30

TRALEE

Tralee grew around the 13th-century Desmond Castle, of which a tiny portion can be seen where Denny Street meets the broad Mall. The history and heritage of the area is revealed in three separate presentations at the multimedia exhibition called Kerry the Kingdom and housed in the Ashe Hall. "Kerry in Colour" spotlights the county's landscape and historic monuments; the Kerry County Museum follows the county's evolution over some 7,000 years, with exhibits of the Stone, Bronze, Iron, Celtic and early Christian ages, while "The Story of Kerry" charts the history of modern Ireland; and "Geraldine Tralee" is a time car ride that takes you through the streets of the town in the Middle Ages, when Kerry, Cork and Limerick were under the control of the powerful Desmond Fitzgeralds (Geraldines). Touring the narrow, winding streets of the town, you'll see the Gothic-style Holy Cross Church designed by Pugin, with splendid stained glass by Michael Healy. St. John's

Flower-clad pub entrance in Tralee

includes a statue of a notable Kerry saint – Brendan the Navigator.

Two miles out of town brings you along an old ship canal to a 65-foot-high windmill at Blennerville. Built in 1800, it worked continually until 1850, and was restored to full working order in the 1990s. The exhibition center tells the story of 19th-century emigration from Blennerville port. Train buffs will not want to miss the scenic, narrated 2-mile ride from Tralee to Blennerville on the beautifully restored narrow-gauge steam train, Europe's most westerly railroad. Trains leave Tralee on the hour, Blennerville on the half-hour.

For entertainment, don't miss the superb Siamsa Tíre (pronounced "Sheem-sa Tee-ra" – it means merrymaking), Ireland's National Folk Theatre troupe, who regularly perform in Tralee. This is Irish theater with a difference – a depiction of everyday rural life in the past through music, song, dance and mime. All this is done through the Irish language, but don't let that put you off – the meaning of every stage action is made perfectly clear. Another popular event is the summer Rose of Tralee Festival, when young women with Irish roots come from around the world and compete to become the "Rose" (see page 19).

The National Folk Theatre, Tralee

Twenty-one miles northwest of Tralee, Ballybunion is home to some of Kerry's most glorious beaches, overlooked by soaring cliffs, crowned by 14 Celtic promontory forts. For magnificent panoramic views, walk at least a portion of the cliff walk that climbs to the summit of Knockanore. Ballybunion is home to a seaside golf course that challenged President Clinton during his 1998 visit to Ireland. The Ballybunion Busking Festival is held in August.

✚ A2

Tourist information ✉ Ashe Memorial Hall, Denny Street ☎ 066 712 1288 ⏲ Mon.–Fri. 9–5, Nov.–May;

The Holy Cross Church, Tralee

Mon.–Fri. 9–6, Mar.–Jun.; Sep. and Oct.; Mon.–Fri. 9–7, Sun. 9–6, Jul. and Aug.

Kerry the Kingdom ✉ Ashe Memorial Hall, Denny Street ☎ 066 712 7777 ⏲ Daily 10–7, Aug.–Oct.; 10–6, mid-Mar. to Jul.; noon–5, Nov.–Dec. ▯ Café ▯ $$$ ℹ Tralee tourist office on site

Blennerville Windmill and Steam Train ✉ Windmill: on R559, 3 miles west of Tralee; steam train: Ballyard, Tralee ☎ 066 712 1064 ⏲ Windmill: daily 10–6, Apr.–Oct.; steam train: daily 11–5:30, Jun.–Aug.; noon–5:30, May and Sep. ▯ Coffee shop ▯ $$

Siamsa Tíre ✉ National Folk Theatre, Town Park ☎ 066 712 3055 ⏲ Daily 8 p.m., May to mid-Oct. ▯ $$$

TRAMORE

Tramore's 3-mile beach and 50-acre amusement park are ideal for families. Kids will love the beach and Splashworld, an enclosed swimming complex The Tramore Golf Club is nearby and welcomes visitors to its 18-hole course. That giant of a statue looking down from Great Newtown Head is known locally as "Metal Man," and although it was erected to protect mariners, legend has it that any unmarried female who hops three times on one foot around its base will hop down the aisle within the next 12 months.

✚ C2

Preparing for a pony sale, a serious business at a local country fair

KERRY'S FESTIVALS

For six days and nights in August, international beauties with Irish ancestry gather in Tralee to decide who best fits the time-honored description "...lovely and fair as the rose of the summer." The Rose of Tralee International Festival, however, is a far cry from other such competitions. This festival is one of light-hearted fun and frolic that entails parades, pipe bands, street entertainment and the crowning of the "Rose." It's six days and nights of sheer merriment and a grand time to be in County Kerry.

If you'd like to be part of the fun, there are several package deals that cover transportation and accommodations available from local tourist offices. Be sure to make arrangements well in advance, whether you plan to stay in Tralee or in Killarney, 20 miles to the south.

Lighthearted also best describes Killarney's Roaring Twenties Festival during St. Patrick's weekend in March. The streets teem with high-spirited high-society types, gangsters, bootleggers and other assorted Roaring Twenties characters for four days of revelry. Barbershop quartet competitions, an Al Capone party and the gala Gatsby Ball are just a few of the highlights.

In mid-August, the hillside market town of Killorglin lets its hair down in three days of what many Irish call sheer madness disguised under the name of the Puck Fair. This bacchanalian event has been held every year since 1613, originally to celebrate the beginning of the harvest. Things get off to a rowdy start when a tremendous male (or puck) goat is hauled up to a high platform in the square and crowned as "King of the Fair." What follows is a free-for-all carnival and country fair, with most pubs staying open around the clock. There are all sorts of street entertainment, and over on the green, you can witness some pretty serious horse and cattle trading.

Just how all this began is a matter of dispute: some say a goat bleated to alert a shepherd boy of approaching enemy forces and he then alerted the town. This is traditionally a gathering place for the country's traveling people, who come to drive hard bargains in the horse-swapping business, catch up with tinker gossip and indulge in non-stop revelry.

Rose of Tralee Festival Office ☎ 066 712 1322; fax 66 712 2654 ✉ Ashe Memorial Hall, Denny Street, Tralee

Munster

Crystal cutting at the Waterford Visitor Centre

WATERFORD

Waterford, Ireland's fourth-largest city with a population of 50,000, reflects virtually every phase of Irish history. Its fine harbor, which is the main seaport of the southeast, is as alive with freighters along the broad River Suir as it was in the days when Viking long-ships plied its waters.

Prehistoric dolmens, promontory forts and passage graves speak of the earliest settlers. Legends of valor and incredibly beautiful Iron Age metalwork mirror the two sides of the flamboyant, battle-loving and artistic Celtic clan of the Deise.

The most extensive remains of Viking walls in the country and massive Reginald's Tower (which has stood intact for a thousand years) remind us of those fierce sea-raiders who came in 853 for a safe sea-haven from which to launch their plundering forays. They stayed here and become settlers and traders for more than 300 years.

Dozens of towers are legacies of the Normans, who claimed the city in 1170. Reginald's Tower has stood sentinel at the end of the quay for 1,000 years. Originally, the River Suir lapped at its 12-foot-thick walls, and entry was only from inside the city walls. As the strongest fortification on the river, it has resisted attacks from a variety of forces, including those of Oliver Cromwell.

This fascinating museum's treasures include King John's mace and sword, many of the city's 30 royal charters and an interesting display on "Timbertoes," a wooden bridge designed by Boston architect Lemuel Cox in 1797. Rebels who participated in the 1798 uprising met their end hanging from its beams.

It is the modern Waterford Crystal Factory that is the city's most persistent claim to fame. Tours of production areas of the factory are one of Ireland's most popular attractions. Visitors are also invited to view a 17-minute audiovisual presentation, which details glassmaking from its ancient beginnings to the present.

In the 1980s, Waterford underwent extensive excavations that unearthed fascinating details of the lives of its ancient inhabitants. Special attention is given to the period AD 1000 to 1500. Housed in a 19th-century church, the Waterford Heritage Museum displays a marvelous model of the medieval city, as well as a drawing of Viking Waterford just before the Normans arrived. The exhibits that explain archeologists' excavation methods are eye-opening. Be prepared to linger longer than you might expect. Waterford Museum of Treasures – the massive riverside renovated stone granary that holds an overflowing cornucopia of Waterford's historic treasures – is also where you'll find the tourist information office. Viking jewelry, old glass and the ornately illustrated 14th-century Great Charter Roll are among this important collection of artifacts from Waterford's rich history.

In the heart of Waterford city on Barronstrand Street, the Holy Trinity Cathedral turns a plain, unadorned face to passersby. But a surprise awaits those who step inside to view extravagant decorations and numerous Waterford crystal chandeliers. The magnificent 1770's Christ Church Cathedral sits on the site of an 11th-century cathedral. Its Renaissance style was designed by John Roberts, a noted Waterford architect. Each Monday and Friday evening at 8 during July and August, there's a 45-minute audiovisual presentation of the city from its beginnings to the present.

As for the people of Waterford – an amiable blend of all those who came over the centuries as settlers, conquerors, and artisans – they are especially warm in their welcome to visitors. One-hour walking tours conducted by knowledgable and entertaining storytellers are scheduled

daily at 11:45 and 1.45 from the Granary and depart from the Granville Hotel on the quay at noon and 2. The Green Plaque Trail is a self-guided walking tour outlined in a helpful booklet and map available at the tourist office.

🔶 C2 (regional map on page 112)

Tourist information 🔶 B2 ✉ The Granary, Merchant's Quay ☎ 051 875 823; fax 051877 388 🕐 Mon.–Sat. 9–6, Sun. 11–5, Apr.–Oct.; Mon.–Sat. 9–5, rest of the year ⑪ Restaurant ✋ $$

Reginald's Tower 🔶 C1 ✉ The Mall, Waterford ☎ 051 304 220 🕐 Daily 10–5, Mar.–May and Oct.; 9:30–6:30, Jun.–Sep. ✋ $

Waterford Museum of Treasures 🔶 B2 ✉ The Granary, Merchant's Quay ☎ 051 304 500 🕐 Daily 10–5, Oct.–Apr.; 9:30–6, Sep. and May; 9:30–9, Jun.–Aug.

Christ Church Cathedral 🔶 B1 ✉ Cathedral Square ☎ 051 858 958 🕐 Mon.–Sat. 10–5, Sun. noon–5, Jun.–Sep. Restricted access to some areas during renovation ✋ Presentation: $$

Waterford Heritage Museum 🔶 C1 ✉ Greyfriars ☎ 051 304 500 🕐 Daily 10–6, Apr.–May; 9:30–9, Jun.–Aug.; 10–5, Sep.–Mar. ✋ $$

Waterford Crystal Visitor Centre 🔶 Off the map ✉ Kilbarry, Cork Road ☎ 051 332 500; fax 051 378 539 🕐 Daily 8:30–6, Mar.–Oct.; 9–5, rest of year; tours: daily 8:30–4, Mar.–Oct.; Mon.–Fri. 9–3:15, rest of year ✋ Tour $$

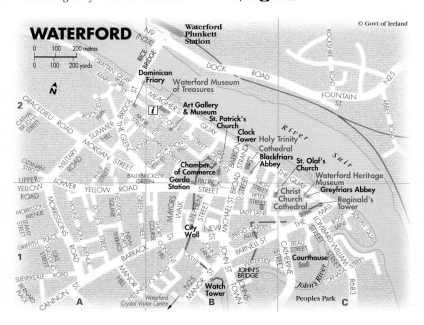

© Govt of Ireland

WATERFORD

ULSTER AND NORTHERN IRELAND

*" **U**LSTER'S landscape lends credence to the heroic myths and legends that have been spawned within its borders. "*

The astonishing hexagonal rock formations of the Giants' Causeway

ULSTER AND NORTHERN IRELAND

Since 1921, the ancient province of Ulster has consisted of the six counties of Northern Ireland – Antrim, Armagh, Down, Fermanagh, Londonderry and Tyrone – and the three Republic of Ireland border counties of Cavan, Donegal and Monaghan.

Border Counties

At the very top of Ireland, County Donegal is awash with scenic beauty, its jagged coastline bordered by wide strands backed by steep cliffs, inland mountains cut by deep valleys and a countryside filled with antiquities and legends. In the rhythmic patterns of Donegal speech can be heard the distinctive cadence of Ulster, and the Irish language thrives in *Gaeltacht* (Gaelic speaking) areas. From Donegal cottages come some of the world's most beautiful hand-woven woolens.

The great Irish poet Patrick Kavanagh was born in County Monaghan, and wrote of his home county, "O stoney grey soil of Monaghan, You burgled my bank of youth." Although early on, he managed to "escape" to make Dublin his home for 30 years, his poetry is sprinkled with references to and influences of the nearly flat, faintly rolling land that seems to nurture creative talent, from literature to exquisite hand-made lace.

In the end, he was brought back home to Inishkeen and laid to rest in his native county.

Cuilcagh Mountain, at the Northern Ireland border just south of Enniskillen, rises to 2,188 feet, the highest point in County Cavan's gently undulating landscape of water-splashed rolling hills. The Shannon, Ireland's longest river, rises on its southern slopes, and the Erne flows northward from Lough Gowna through the center of the county into the Upper Erne river, spreading its waters into myriad lakes along the way.

Fishing and water sports draw modern-day residents and visitors alike to the more than 365 lakes in the county. The Ulster Way provides excellent walking along 435 miles of interconnected and well-marked footpaths through all six counties.

Northern Ireland

Like the Republic to the south, Northern Ireland is a veritable cornucopia of travel treasures and experiences. Its green fields, cliff-studded and cove-indented coastline, forest-clad mountains and above all its hospitable inhabitants invite a visit to this unique part of Ireland.

Highlights not to be missed include the gentle shoreline of County Down with its romantic Mountains of Mourne that sweep down to the sea; its firm claim on a good part of St. Patrick's sojourn; quiet little villages on the Ards Peninsula that look across to Scotland (clearly visible in many places); a countryside dotted with Norman castles; Strangford Lough; County Fermanagh's Lough Erne and its 300 square miles of exquisite scenery; the fabulous Marble Arch

The Erne forms a stunning string of loughs and waterways from County Cavan to Donegal Bay

Ulster and Northern Ireland

Caves; Devenish Island; Armagh's two cathedrals – one Protestant, one Catholic, both named for St. Patrick; the Sperrin Mountains of County Tyrone; a unique folk park that depicts the rural lives of Irish immigrants on both sides of the Atlantic, and Londonderry's massive old city walls.

Northern Ireland spreads before the visitor a wealth of other scenic splendors throughout all six counties. Because the province is small (about the size of Connecticut), in the space of one week it is possible to comfortably visit most of the major attractions. Beyond all those, there are elements found only here that will add a special dimension to your Irish experience.

Myths

It was in this part of Ireland that the champion Cuchulainn singlehandedly guarded the border against the onslaught of Connaught's Queen Maeve when she set out to capture the Brown Bull of Cooley. This was home territory for Finn MacCool (see page 199) and his faithful Fianna warriors. And the beautiful Deirdre o' the Sorrows played out her life's tragedy within the borders of Ulster.

The People

The accents of the North fall on the ear with the soft burr of Scotland, mingled with the clipped speech of native English and the lilting Irish brogue of the Republic. It's an enchanting mix, and don't be at all surprised if you find yourself ending sentences with the distinctive lift that characterizes so much of what you hear.

Along with their speech, these descendants of Britain's plantation-era families have put into the mix strong elements of their cultures. Squash and cricket are sports you'll rarely find in the Republic, but they flourish above

the border; the strains of traditional Irish music are interspersed with music of a distinctly British or Scottish flavor. Belfast's magnificent Opera House is as likely to play an English drawing-room comedy as an Irish classic by O'Casey or Synge.

Although one-third of Northern Ireland's population is concentrated in Belfast, because of their largely rural heritage Ulster people tend to be outdoor people who make the most of the natural resources lavished on them by nature. With the British Isles' largest lake (Lough Neagh), 50 miles of tranquil cruising waters on Lough Erne and rivers teeming with fish, water sports rank high in leisure activities, from fishing, both fresh water and coastal sea angling, to boating and water skiing. Golf, hiking and cycling follow closely behind.

Politics

There is no question that long-standing tensions exist around, among other things, such Unionist activities as the Orange parades of July 12 (to celebrate their beloved King Billy's victory at the 1690 Battle of the Boyne) and the Catholic St. Patrick's Day parade on March 17 and, on August 15, the Ancient Order of Hibernian parade to celebrate the Feast of the Assumption. Now the strife that has infected Northern Ireland since 1969 is much muted since political parties from both sides have begun to talk and work together for a peaceful solution.

One thing is certain: both traditions welcome visitors warmly and are equally proud of the natural beauty and historical monuments of their homeland. Perhaps because of their turbulent recent history, Northern Ireland natives are also especially anxious that visitors return home with positive memories.

Belfast

In ancient times, Belfast was a castle built at a ford of the River Lagan. Its name in Irish is Beal Feirste, Mouth of the Sandy Ford. A small village developed around the castle, and in the 17th century Protestant settlers from Scotland and parts of England moved in, and native villagers were moved out by order of English rulers, thus establishing the character of the city that grew at a steady pace until the end of the 1700s, thanks in large part to a thriving linen industry.

In 1791 Wolfe Tone founded the United Irish Society in Belfast to bring together Protestants and Catholics who chafed under the repressive Penal Laws. In 1798 their efforts led to an uprising, one which was quickly squelched by English forces. The shipyard that was to contribute so much to the city's growth was opened in 1791. By the time the Industrial Revolution was in full bloom during the 19th century, both shipbuilding (the *Titanic* was built here) and the linen trade welcomed newer, more modern operating methods. Both prospered, and Belfast's population grew by leaps and bounds.

The city today is a bustling, energetic center of industry. The unique

Ulster and Northern Ireland

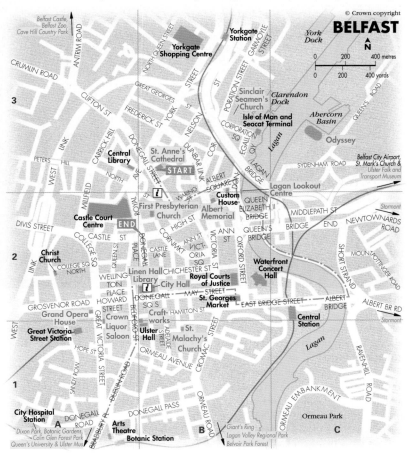

© Crown copyright

Built in Portland stone, the Victorian Belfast City Hall dominates Donegall Square

character of the place has been brought about through the combination of economic and polital struggle, hard work and a special brand if Irish humor. Yet for the visitor it is easy to get around and holds many points of interest, most prominent landmark of which must be credited to good Queen Victoria, whose statue adorns Donegall Square and whose architectural style is in evidence around the city. Belfast's ambience today, however, is far from Victorian. Both the city center and the riverfront are taking on a new face, incorporating widespread pedestrian areas dotted with benches and street entertainers. The big millennium building project "Odyssey" has had a huge impact (see page 164).

The city center has also developed as a first-rate shopping mecca, with many of Britain's leading stores represented along with shops featuring native crafts.

Belfast city center is fairly compact and most of the important sights are within easy walking distance. To explore the city on foot, take it neighborhood by neighborhood – the city center, university area, and so on – and use local buses to get you from one to another. The Shankill Road area (Protestant, loyalist) is northwest of the center; the Falls Road area (Catholic, nationalist) is to the west; Malone and Ballynafeigh areas are to the south; and the Sydenham, Bloomfield, Belmont and Ballymacarrett areas are to the east.

The City Hall marks Donegall Square as the hub of Belfast city center.

From the square, Donegall Place leads north to the important shopping area along Royal Avenue, while to the south, Bedford Street leads into Dublin Road and the Queens University area.

With the easing of political tensions in recent years, a vibrant cultural scene has emerged in this relatively young city. It caters to all tastes, from classical music and theater to the latest in popular music led by native son Van Morrison, who began his career with a Belfast rhythm-and-blues group.

Venues are as varied as performances. The Waterfront Hall and Conference Centre on the Lagan river presents a variety of entertainment, as does the Grand Opera House on Great Victoria Street (see page 164). Ulster Orchestra

and Northern Ireland Symphony Orchestra concerts are regularly scheduled in Ulster Hall on Bedford Street, while you'll find superstar concerts are likely to be in Kings Hall Exhibition and Conference Centre.

Less structured performances of traditional, folk, jazz, blues and rock music are found in such pubs as the Duke of York (off Lower Donegall Street), the Front Page (Donegall Street) and Kelly's Cellars (Bank Street just off Royal Avenue).

Irish plays and international theatrical productions are staged in the Lyric Theatre on Ridgeway Street, and musicals and other popular shows are produced in the Belfast Civic Arts Theatre on Botanic Avenue.

Tracing Your Roots

If tracking down your Northern Ireland ancestors is your top priority, collect as much information about your forebears as possible before leaving home. It is also a good idea to contact Northern Ireland genealogical organizations well in advance of your arrival in the province. They will reply to every letter, but you are requested to enclose three international reply coupons with your query to help with postage.

The Public Record Office is the main source for genealogical research in Ulster. While they do not conduct individual genealogical research, members of the public are welcome to search the records themselves.

The General Register Office has records of births and deaths from 1864 and marriage registrations since 1922. For a small fee, the Registrar General will arrange searches of any births, marriages or deaths in Northern Ireland prior to 1922.

You can, of course, employ a professional to do your research. For a list of members and the services they offer, write to:
Association of Ulster Genealogists and Record Agents,
AUGRA, Glen Cottage, Glenmachan Road,
Belfast BT4 2NP.

Public Records Office
✉ 66 Balmoral Avenue, Belfast BT9 6NY ☎ 028 9025 5905; fax 028 9025 5999
◷ Mon.–Fri. 9:15–4:45, Thu. until 8:45

The General Register Office
✉ Oxford House, 49 Chichester Street, Belfast BT1 4HL ☎ 028 9025 2000
◷ Mon.–Fri. 9:30–4

Richly carved woodwork, colored tiles and mirrors adorn the interior of a typical Irish pub

ESSENTIAL INFORMATION

TOURIST INFORMATION
Northern Ireland Tourist Information Office ✉ 59 North Street, Belfast ☎ 028 9023 1221 ⊙ Mon.–Fri. 9–5:15, Sat. 9–2, Easter–Sep. (closed Sat., rest of year)

✉ Castle Place ☎ 028 9045 8484 ⊙ Living History: daily, 1 p.m. in summer; Thu., Tue., and Sun., rest of year (2.5 hours); City Tour: Mon.–Sat., 1 p.m. in summer; Wed. and Sat., rest of year (3.5 hours)

URBAN TRANSPORTATION
In Belfast, Citibus operates a network to all parts of the city, with departures from Donegall Square East, West and North, Upper Queen Street, Wellington Place, Chichester Street and Castle Street. Information on which buses go where is posted at Donegall Square West, and routes are listed on the Belfast city map available from the tourist office.
For details of bus services (both Citybus and Ulsterbus), contct Translink Call Centre ☎ 028 9066 6630 ⊙ Daily 7a.m.–11p.m. Translink can also provide information on Northern Ireland Railways.

During the summer months there are guided coach tours of Belfast and its environs, they are an excellent way to gain an overview of the city. The pick of the crop are the Belfast Living History Tour and the Belfast City Tour.

There are taxi stands at main rail stations, ports and airports. Black cabs are metered and service stands are at Central Station, both bus stations and City Hall. When using a taxi without a meter, be sure to agree on a price before you enter the taxi.

AIRPORT INFORMATION
Belfast International Airport is 19 miles northwest of the city center in Crumlin. The Belfast City Airport is 4 miles to the northeast. Most flights from the U.S. and Canada set down at Belfast International Airport, and there's frequent Airbus services to and from the city. Passengers arriving at Belfast City Airport will have to take a taxi into the city. ☎ Belfast International Airport: 028 9442 2888; Belfast City Airport: 028 9093 9093 🚌 Airbus fare £5 one-way, £8 round trip; taxi fare from Belfast City Airport starts at £6

CLIMATE – Average highs and lows

JAN.	FEB.	MAR.	APR.	MAY	JUN.	JUL.	AUG.	SEP.	OCT.	NOV.	DEC.
8°C	9°C	11°C	13°C	16°C	18°C	19°C	19°C	17°C	14°C	11°C	8°C
46°F	48°F	52°F	55°F	61°F	64°F	66°F	66°F	63°F	57°F	52°F	46°F
3°C	3°C	4°C	6°C	8°C	10°C	13°C	13°C	11°C	8°C	6°C	4°C
37°F	37°F	39°F	43°F	46°F	50°F	55°F	55°F	52°F	46°F	43°F	39°F

The 1865 Albert Memorial Clock Tower, named after Queen Victoria's husband

BELFAST SIGHTS

Key to symbols

✛ map coordinates refer to the Belfast map on page 155; sights below are highlighted in yellow on the map

✉ address or location ☎ telephone number

🕐 opening times

🍴 restaurant on site or nearby

🚌 nearest bus or tram route

✋ admission charge: $$$ = more than £4, $$ = £2 to £4, $ = under £2

ℹ information

ALBERT MEMORIAL

The Albert Memorial Clock Tower designed by W. J. Barre, looks towards the river on High Street and pays tribute to Queen Victoria's consort. It is affectionately known as Belfast's "leaning tower" because it is slightly less than straight (more than a yard off true vertical). You'll have to admire the lean from the outside as the tower is not open to the public.

✛ B2

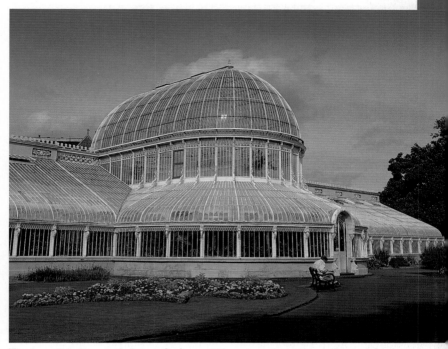

The elegant Palm House in the Botanic Gardens – a 19th-century technical marvel of iron and glass

BELFAST CASTLE

From its perch on Cave Hill, 400 feet above sea level, Belfast Castle was built in the late 1800s as a family residence and was a gift to the city in 1934 from the Earl of Shaftesbury. Used primarily for private functions, its Scottish baronial architecture features a six-story square tower, but the Victorian arcade cellar holds shops, a bar and a bistro eatery open to the public daily. The Heritage Centre has information on Cave Hill as well as the castle itself. There are also pleasant walkways in the castle's 200-acre estate.
➕ A3 ✉ Antrim Road (2.5 miles from the city center, signposted from Antrim Road) ☎ 028 9077 6925 🕐 Daily 9–10 👆 Free

BELFAST ZOO

The Belfast Zoo, with its dramatic mountain site and marvelous views of the city, is a delight. Its gorilla and chimp houses have won animal welfare awards, and some species roam free. Don't miss

the penguin and sea lion enclosures with underwater viewing. Of note, too, are the spectacled bears – this is the only zoo in the United Kingdom that keeps them.
➕ A3 ✉ Antrim Road (4 miles north of city on slopes of Cave Hill) ☎ 028 9077 6277 🕐 Daily 10–5, Apr.–Sep.; 10–2:30, rest of year 🍴 Restaurants 👆 $$$

BELVOIR PARK FOREST

Comprehensive information on Ireland's feathered population is readily available at The Royal Society for the Protection of Birds Visitor Centre in the pleasant woodland of Belvoir Park Forest. This is a must for dedicated bird watchers.
➕ B1 ☎ 028 9049 1264 🕐 Dawn–dusk 👆 Free

BOTANIC GARDENS

Established in 1827, these outstanding gardens are noted for the Victorian-style 1839 Palm House glass house and its rare plants, including banana, aloe, rubber, bamboo and bird of paradise flower. In

Victorian facade of the Crown Liquor Saloon, decorated with splendid mosaic tiles

the 1889 Tropical Ravine, or Fernery, a profusion of tropical plants in a sunken glen can be viewed from the observation balcony. The outdoor gardens, first planted in 1927, feature herbaceous borders and fragrant, colorful rose beds.

⊞ A1 ✉ Stranmillis Road (signposted from M1/M2, Balmoral exit) ☎ 028 9032 4902 ⏱ Daily 10–5 🚌 69, 70, 71, 83, 84, 85 💷 Free

CAVE HILL COUNTRY PARK

Neolithic men carved the five caves that give this popular public park on the slopes of a 1,200-foot basalt cliff its name, and the caves have provided shelter for generations that followed. Persevere to the very top and you will be rewarded with spectacular panoramic views of Belfast and the Lagan river valley. Not views, but rebellion was on the minds of Wolfe Tone, Henry Joy McCracken and other United Irishmen when they met here for two days in 1795 to plot the 1798 uprising. There are more gentle walks in the park (be sure to remember which color arrow you need to follow for your specific route) and for children there's an adventure playground.

⊞ A3 ✉ 3 miles north of city, off Antrim Road. Numerous access points; parking at Befast Castle or Belfast Zoo ☎ 028 9077 6925 or 9037 1013 ⏱ Daily dawn–dusk. Visitor center 9–6 💷 Free

CITY HALL

This massive two-story Portland stone building crowned with a copper dome and set around a central courtyard in Donegall Square was 10 years in construction (begun in 1888). Inside is all elegance with Greek and Italian marble; the dome rises above the central staircase at the heart of the exuberant interior of rich mosaic, stained glass, marble and wood paneling. The city's industrial history is traced in a large mural. If you don't recognize it otherwise, you'll know it by the bust of Queen Victoria out front. She was a guest of the city in 1846 and is much revered. A Great War Memorial sits on the west side, with a memorial sculpture to the *Titanic*, the Belfast-built liner that went to the bottom in 1912.

⊞ B2 ✉ Donegall Square South ☎ 028 9027 0456 ⏱ Guided tours; Mon.–Fri. 10:30, 11:30 and 2:30, Sat. 2:30; Jun.–Sep.; Mon.–Sat. 2:30, rest of year 💷 Free

COLIN GLEN FOREST PARK

It is well worth a stop at the visitor center in this 200-acre park at the foot of Black Mountain to view the audiovisual presentation and other displays before setting out on the several nature trails.

⊞ A1 ✉ Stewartstown Road (5 miles west of the

Ornamentation on the wall of the Grand Opera House

city) ☎ 028 9061 4115 ⏰ Park: daily dawn–dusk; center: Mon.–Fri. 9–5, Sat. –Sun. 10–2 🖐 Free

CRAFTWORKS

Craftspeople from around Ireland display their work in this showplace and shop located behind Belfast City Hall. Hand-woven clothing, linen and hand-painted silk products are available, as are limited edition prints, jewelry, ceramics and baskets. Don't leave without picking up the helpful booklet *Crafts in Northern Ireland* that lists where to find local crafts in the six counties of Northern Ireland.
✚ B2 ✉ Bedford House, Bedford Street ☎ 028 9024 4465 ⏰ Mon.–Sat. 9:30–5:30 (Thu. until 7) 🖐 Free

CROWN LIQUOR SALOON

Bend an elbow at least once or go by for lunch at the Crown Liquor Saloon, which dates from 1849. It's a marvelous old Victorian pub, the Corinthian pillars flanking the entrance give way to the ultimate in casual elegance with an interior of carved woodwork, marble counters and painted ceramic tiles. Some chrome-and-mirror addicts got their hands on it a few years back and nearly modernized the character out of it, but the National Trust conservation organisation came to the rescue and it is now back to its original state. The saloon is still lit by gas lamps and to call for service you'll need to use the antique system of bell pulls.
✚ A1 ✉ Great Victoria Street ☎ 028 9027 9901 ⏰ Daily 11:30 a.m.–midnight 🍴 Restaurant

DIXON PARK

Named for Sir Thomas and Lady Dixon, the beautiful rose gardens in this park have won international acclaim and are widely acknowledged to be among the world's finest. From July to September, the City of Belfast International Rose Trials are held here. In addition to more than 20,000 rose bushes, there's an interesting Japanese garden and wooded areas and shrubberies on several levels and a play area for the youngsters.
✚ A1 ✉ Upper Malone Road ☎ 028 9061 1506 ⏰ Daily dawn–dusk 🍴 Restaurant 🖐 Free

FIRST PRESBYTERIAN CHURCH

Situated in the pedestrianized main shopping center, this 1783 church is notable for its elliptical interior with enclosed pews, each entered by a door and designed by John Wesley. Free lunchtime concerts are occasionally offered.
✚ B2 ✉ Rosemary Street

GIANT'S RING

This impressive Bronze Age antiquity is within easy reach of Belfast. The huge circular structure is more than 600 feet in diameter, and the enigmatic Druid's Alter dolmen inhabits its center. Its original purpose is a matter of speculation. Prehistoric rings were commonly thought to be the home of fairies, and consequently treated with respect, but locals back in the 18th century found it made a terrific race course. The earthen bank surrounding the ring, 20 feet wide and 12 feet high, is a natural grandstand.
✚ B1 ✉ Near Edenderry village, a mile south of Shaw's Bridge, off B23 🖐 Free

GRAND OPERA HOUSE

Even if it means enduring a mediocre production, try to catch a performance in this marvel of rich, rococo eccentricity. There are 24 gilt elephant heads separating boxes sporting canopies, Buddhas scattered about the draperies, and lots of gold and maroon. Closed from 1972 to 1981, its beautiful restoration was worth the wait.

➕ A2 ✉ Great Victoria Street ☎ 028 9024 1919 🕐 Daily 7–11 🎫 Free

LAGAN VALLEY REGIONAL PARK AND MINNOWBURN BEECHES

A walk over the 9 miles of paths along the banks of the River Lagan from Belfast to Lisburn takes you past old locks and lock houses from the late 1700s, when the horses towing coal barges used these pathways. If you are lucky enough to be here in the fall, the blazing colors of the Minnowburn Beeches woodlands are a spectacle not to be missed. You can enjoy pleasant walks from the Beeches to Edenderry village and the Giant's Ring.

➕ B1 ✉ Towpath begins near Belfast Boat Club in Stranmillis and runs upstream from Moore's Bridge, Hillsborough Road in Lisburn. Minnowburn Beeches are 3.5 miles south of Belfast at Shaw's Bridge on Milton Road ☎ 028 9049 1922

LAGAN LOOKOUT CENTRE

To understand the River Lagan's influence on Belfast's history, spend some time here examining the videos and hands-on computer exhibits, then step outside for platform views of river activities.

➕ B3 ✉ Donegall Quay ☎ 028 9031 5444 🕐 Mon.–Fri. 11–5, Sat. noon–5, Sun. 2–5, Apr.–Sep.; Tue.–Fri. 11–3:30, Sat. 1–4:30, rest of year 🎫 $

LINEN HALL LIBRARY

Established in 1788 to "improve the mind and excite a spirit of general enquiry," this is the oldest library in the city. It began life as a charitable project and is still supported by public subscription. Among its notable collections are books on heraldry, books by Robert Burns, important documents of local history and an impressive array of press coverage during the long period of the "Troubles" that began in 1969. Thomas Russell, librarian here in 1803, was executed for his revolutionary activities.

➕ A2 ✉ 17 Donegall Square North ☎ 028 9032 1707 🕐 Mon.–Fri. 9:30–5:30, Sat. 9:30–4. Tours must be arranged in advance 🍴 Café 🎫 Free

ODYSSEY

Belfast's big millennium project is a complex covering 23 acres of the riverfront. It includes a science center with over 100 interactive exhibits, an IMAX theater, a 12-screen multiplex cinema and huge arena, and the Pavilion has restaurants, bars and shops.

➕ C3 ✉ 2 Queen's Quay ☎ 028 9045 0545 🕐 Science center: Mon.–Fri. 10–6, Sat.–Sun. noon–6. Phone for times of other attractions 🎫 $$–$$$

QUEEN'S UNIVERSITY AND VISITOR CENTRE

South of Belfast's city center, Queen's University is the hub for a cluster of art galleries, restaurants, accommodations and shops. The campus is a charming mixture of little mid-Victorian row houses, complete with front gardens (largely occupied by arts and law faculties), and the very formal Tudor-revival-style main building designed by Charles Lanyon in 1849. There's a strong emphasis on science studies, and the full-time student body numbers about 14,000, with another 10,000 part-time students. Queen's Visitor Centre features exhibitions and memorabilia associated with the university.

➕ A1 ✉ University Road ☎ 208 9033 5252 🕐 Visitor centre: Mon.–Fri. 10–4, (also Sat. 10–4, May–Sep.) 🎫 Free

SINCLAIR SEAMEN'S CHURCH

Charles Lanyon, who designed so many Belfast buildings, was the architect for this unique 1857 church, whose interior is very much like a maritime museum. Sailors home from the sea must feel right

Stormont stands proudly overlooking its sweeping drive on the outskirts of Belfast

at home as they listen to sermons delivered from a pulpit built like a ship's prow. The nautical theme is carried over to the organ, which has port and starboard lighting.

✚ B3 ✉ Corporation Square ☎ 028 9071 5997
🕐 Daily 2–5 and Sunday services

St. Anne's Cathedral

Belfast Cathedral (St. Anne's) was built between 1899 and 1904 and has a particularly fine mosaic showing St. Patrick landing at Saul in AD 432, which you will find over the entrance to the Chapel of the Holy Spirit.

✚ B3 ✉ Donegall Street ☎ 028 9032 8332
🕐 Phone to confirm

St. Malachy's Church

Its striking turrets overlooking the Upper Markets area, St. Malachy's Roman Catholic Church opened in 1844 and boasts a fine fan-vaulted ceiling.

✚ B1 ✉ Alfred Street ☎ 028 9032 1713
🕐 Daily 8–6

Stormont

A mile-long avenue leads up to the massive, gleaming white building that has

been, since it opened in 1932, the seat of Northern Ireland self-governing parliaments that come and go, as negotiations for self-rule wax and wane with the political climate. This is where the Good Friday Agreement of 1997 was hammered out, and it was also the seat of the resultant executive committee of the Northern Ireland Assembly. The statue standing squarely in the middle of the avenue is of Sir Edward Carson, who was largely responsible for maintaining Northern Ireland's position as a part of the United Kingdom when he led the opposition of Irish home rule in 1912. The building itself is not open to the public, but the beautifully maintained grounds are open to all.

✚ C2

Ulster Folk and Transport Museum

The unique Ulster Folk and Transport Museum is set on 176 acres of the beautiful parkland estate of Cultra Manor. The open-air museum is composed of a fascinating collection of buildings and rural and urban shops, all furnished in 1900s style. Many were moved stone by stone from original locations and rebuilt here. The result is a microcosm of Ulster

Ulster Folk Museum re-creates 19th-century Ireland

life from the 18th to the 19th century. Traditional Irish cottages, watermills, farms, a 1792 church, a flax-scutching mill, schools, printer's workshops, even a small town in addition to many other buildings make this enchanting place well worth a visit of half a day or more.

The Transport Museum includes the largest locomotive (*Old Maeve*) built in Ireland, trams, buses, cars, horse-drawn carts and all sorts of other means of transportation. Perenially popular is the *Titanic* exhibition on the "unsinkable" liner that was built in Belfast's shipyards and foundered after hitting an iceberg on her maiden voyage. Take in the Flight Experience, an interactive exhibition. In addition to the permanent exhibitions and buildings, the museum has lots of special events during the year.

✚ C3

✉ Bangor Road, Cultra Manor, Holywood, Co. Down (7 miles east of Belfast on A2, the road to Bangor) ☎ 028 9042 8428 or 9042 1444 ⊕ Mon.–Fri. 10–5, Sat. 10–6, Sun. 11–6, Mar.–Jun.; Mon.–Sat. 10–6, Sun. 11–6, Jul.–Sep.; Mon.–Fri. 10–4, Sat. 10–4, Sun. 11–5, rest of year (last admission one hour before closing) 🍴 Tearoom 🎫 Combined ticket: $$$

ULSTER MUSEUM

In the lovely surroundings of the Botanic Gardens, the Ulster Museum gives remarkable insight into the life and history of the province. One of the most interesting of the museum's collections of Irish art, history, natural sciences and archeology is the Early Ireland Gallery, which concentrates on the flora and fauna of 10,000 BC to 1500 BC. Also fascinating is the collection of armada treasures recovered from the 1588 shipwrecked *Girona* in 1968, lost off the Giant's Causeway. Items include a ruby-encrusted salamander and an inscribed gold ring. Allow several hours to fully take in the museum's exhibits.

✚ A1

✉ Stranmillis Road, next to Botanic Gardens ☎ 028 9038 3000 ⊕ Mon.–Fri. 10–5, Sat. 1–5, Sun. 2–5 🍴 Café 🚌 69, 70, 71 🎫 Free

Harland and Wolff shipyard maintains the strong ship-building tradition

WALK: BETWEEN OLD AND NEW

Refer to route marked on city map on page 155.

This walk combines some of Belfast's major attractions and a portion of the exciting and ongoing rejuvenation of the city's waterfront. As you walk, notice the contrast between Belfast's distinctive Georgian, Victorian and Edwardian buildings and the newer structures along the river. Begin your tour at the tourist information center, 59 North Street. Allow about one-and-a-half hours.

Just behind the information center on Lower Donegall Street, imposing Hiberno-Romanesque St. Anne's is sometimes called Belfast Cathedral. Take a look at the striking mosaic inside depicting the arrival of St. Patrick on his return to Northern Ireland (see page 182).

> *From the cathedral, turn left and walk down Donegall Street to Waring Street, then left to reach Albert Square.*

Poor old Prince Albert lists slightly to one side, due to the fine silty soil on which he stands, an unstable underpinning left by a glacier at the end of the last Ice Age (some of Belfast's substantial Victorian buildings have fallen victim to this same instability). Giant cranes of nearby Harland and Wolff, the United Kingdom's largest shipyard, loom against the Belfast skyline behind Prince Albert.

> *From the Albert Memorial, turn right to reach Donegall Quay.*

The Lagan Weir, beautifully spotlighted at night, is located close to the spot where Belfast began and maintains the river level

Ulster and Northern Ireland

close to the high-tide mark. The small conical building at the west end of the weir houses the Lagan Lookout, an information center that focuses not only on the river's importance to the city and the workings of the weir, but also has displays of riverfront commercial developments (see page 164). Camera buffs will surely want to snap the 30-foot ceramic Belfast salmon by local sculptor John Kindness.

Leaving the Lagan Lookout, cross the bridge and follow the signposted Riverside Walk.

Notice the huge block of art nouveau flats, quite a departure from Belfast's traditional architectural style. At the beginning of a curve in the river, look across to the opposite bank for a view of the Waterfront Hall, the most strikingly modern new resident of Belfast's riverfront. There's a bit of irony that its location is Lanyon Place, named for Sir Charles Lanyon, the architect largely responsible for the city center's overwhelmingly Victorian buildings. A wonder of glass and metal, the badly needed concert and conference center seats 2,500 and is sometimes the venue for Belfast-born rock star Van Morrison.

Next-door neighbors to the Waterfront Hall, the massive Hilton hotel and huge British Telecom Call Centre offices are tall, red-brick structures that could be called Belfast's skyscrapers. Both represent great commercial confidence in the city's future.

Cross the river at Albert Bridge and walk along East Bridge Street to the intersection with Oxford Street.

One peek inside St. George's Market and it's a sure bet you'll linger to explore this covered marketplace that has been a Belfast tradition for generations. It was recently renovated and revitalized. There's everything from fresh produce and fish to discount and used clothing to second-hand videos and odds-and-ends.

Exit the market and turn left on May Street and walk to Donegall Square.

Built of white Portland stone in 1906, the Edwardian City Hall facade is 300 feet long, with a copper dome rising 173 feet. Equally impressive interior features are the marble grand staircase and main entrance. The city council meets here, and in its custody is the Charter of Belfast granted by King James I in 1613 (see page 162).

Cross to Donegall Square North.

If you're interested in Irish politics or any phase of Northern Ireland culture, you'll want to allow time to browse through the collections at Linen Hall Library, one of the oldest subscription libraries in the United Kingdom (see page 164).

End your tour here, or walk north to Donegall Place for shopping, or head south on Bedford Street and Dublin Road to reach the Queen's University area.

Waterfront Hall is set in the city's commercial area, close to the river

The 19th-century Mount Stuart House surrounded by splendid gardens

DRIVE: STRANGFORD LOUGH

Duration: 1 day

This is an 87-mile drive around Belfast city encompassing its strong industrial ship-building tradition. The city is rich in Victorian and Edwardian architecture, from the magnificent City Hall to the atmospheric 1849 Crown Liquor Saloon.

> *Start at the tourist office on North Street in Belfast. Take the A2, following signposts for Bangor, and after 7 miles turn left for the Ulster Folk and Transport Museum.*

The Ulster Folk and Transport Museum, in the grounds of Cultra Manor, tells the story of the province's past through buildings that have been saved and meticulously reconstructed at this site. You can wander through a thatched cottage, a rectory and a terraced house, and watch demonstrations of traditional crafts. A church, schoolhouse, water-powered mills and other buildings give a vivid picture of the past. The transport section spans the history of transport, from creels used by a donkey carrying turf, through the grand ocean-going liners built in Belfast, to ultra-modern aircraft from the Belfast firm Short Brothers and Harland. This is undoubtedly one of the best museums in Ireland (see page 165).

> *Turn left and follow the A2 for 4 miles. Turn right following the signpost for Newtownards, 3 miles farther.*

This thriving town lies among some of the richest arable land in Ulster. St. Finnian founded Movilla Abbey in AD 540, and the Dominican priory was established by the Normans in the 13th century. The hollow, octagonal, 17th-century market cross also served as the town watch and jail. The impressive town hall was built around 1770 by the Londonderry family who also built Scrabo Tower overlooking the town. The surrounding country park has pretty woodland walks, sandstone quarries and panoramic views.

> *Take the A20, following signs for Portaferry to Greyabbey.*

The village derives its name from the 12th-century Cistercian abbey. North of the village is Mount Stewart, a magnificent garden where, enjoying the mild climate of the peninsula, many exotic plants flourish in formal terraces and parterres or in natural settings. Lady Londonderry, the renowned hostess and leader of London society, created this unique garden after World War I, and it is considered one of the finest in these islands. Each garden is given a name such as Tir n'an Og (the Land of Eternal Youth), the Mairi

Ulster and Northern Ireland

Garden, Peace Garden, the Dodo Terrace and the Italian Garden. The lake is particularly beautiful. The house, the early home of Lord Castlereagh, contains the 22 chairs used at the Congress of Vienna and a masterpiece by the painter Stubbs ranks among its treasures. Designed as a banquet house, the Temple of the Winds is an exquisite piece of 18th-century landscape architecture. The shoreline is an excellent place for viewing birds, including thousands of Brent geese that winter on the lough.

Follow the A20 for 4 miles to Kircubbin. Take a left turn on to the B173 for 3 miles, then turn left for Portavogie.

Up to 40 boats fill the attractive harbor of Portavogie when the fleet is in. Shellfish are plentiful and hotels also serve a good variety of fresh fish. Seals regularly follow the boats into the harbor to scavenge for food before the load is auctioned on the harborside.

Take the A2 south for 2 miles. At Cloughey turn left and follow signposts to Kearney. After 1 mile, turn left for Kearney and follow signposts at two left turns for Kearney, about 3 miles.

Kearney is a tiny village of whitewashed houses in the care of the National Trust conservation organisation. Once a fishing village, it now offers fine walks along its rocky shoreline.

At Temple Cowey and St. Cowey's Wells on a remote and peaceful shore are a penance stone and holy well at a site founded in the seventh century and later used for worship in penal times. Mass is still celebrated here from time to time.

Turn left and left again to follow the road around the tip of the peninsula by Barr Hall and Quintin Bay to Portaferry.

One of Ulster's most beautiful villages, Portaferry's attractive waterfront of colorful row of cottages, pubs and shops is framed by green meadows and wooded slopes. No fewer than five defensive tower houses guard the narrow neck of the lough. The Marine Biology Station, part of Queen's University in Belfast, is opposite the ferry jetty. Nearby is the Northern Ireland Aquarium, Exploris, beside a pleasant park, which explains the unique nature of the marine life of Strangford Lough. More than 2,000 species of marine animals thrive in the waters of Strangford, including large colonies of corals and sponges in the fast-flowing tides of the Narrows, with sea anemones and brittle stars in the quieter waters. The lough is home to large fish, including tope and skate. A regular, five-minute car-ferry service to Strangford gives stunning views of the lough.

Take the car ferry to Strangford. Boats leave at half-hour intervals.

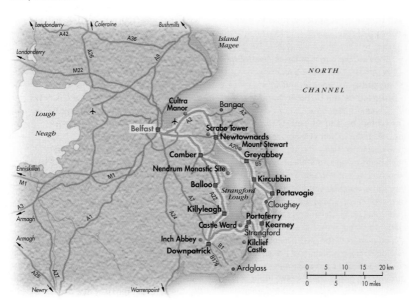

Scrabo Hill, toppd by a 135-foot tower in memory of the 3rd Marquess of Londonderry

Strangford is a small village with two bays, pretty houses and a castle. Close by is Castle Ward, set in a fine parkland with excellent views over the lough. This fascinating 18th-century mansion is an architectural hodgepodge – part pseudo-Gothic and part Classical – the result of disputed tastes between Lord and Lady Bangor. Restored estate buildings show the busy organization that once supported a country house including formal gardens, a Victorian laundry and theater in the stableyard, and a sawmill.

One mile south on the A2 to Ardglass, a stop-over to Cloughy Rocks is a great place for viewing seals when the tide is right. Farther south is Kilclief Castle and Killard Point at the narrowest point of the neck to the lough. This lovely grassland area with low cliffs and a small beach is rich in wild flowers.

Take the A25 to Downpatrick.
Down Cathedral stands on the hill above the town, while English Street, Irish Street and Scotch Street jostle together below (see page 183). Quoile Pondage is an area of meandering freshwater wetland between wooded shores, with fine walks. Southwest is the popular Downpatrick race course.

Follow the A22 to Killyleagh.
A fairy-tale castle with towers and battlements overlooks this quiet loughside village. The Hamilton family has lived here for 300 years, and although the original castle was built by the Normans, its present appearance owes more to the 19th century. Sir Hans Sloane, the physician and naturalist whose collection formed the nucleus of the British Museum, was born in Killyleagh in 1660 and educated in the castle.

It is said that the famous Emigrant's Lament: "I'm sitting on the stile, Mary," written by Lady Dufferin, a guest at the castle during the Famine, was inspired by the stile at Killowen Old Churchyard.

Follow the A22 for 5 miles to Balloo crossroads. Turn right at the sign for Killinchy, and continue for 4 miles, turning right three times for Comber. After 2.5 miles, turn right, following the sign for Nendrum Monastic Site.
A place of great tranquility, Nendrum monastic site was established on one of the many islands sprinkled along Strangford's calm middle waters; it is now reached by a causeway. The site is one of the most complete examples of an early monastery, and the ruins, in three concentric rings, include the stump of a round tower, monks' cells and a church with a stone sundial.

Return across the causeway, and after 3 miles turn right for 3 miles to join the A22 to Comber, then back to Belfast.

Mount Stewart Gardens ✉ Portaferry Road (A20 from Newtownards towards Greyabbey) ☎ 028 4278 8387 🕐 Gardens: daily 10–8, May–Sep.; 10–4, rest of year 🎫 $$

Exploris Aquarium ✉ The Ropewalk, Castle Street, Portaferry ☎ 028 4272 8062 🕐 Mon.–Fri. 10–6, Sat. 11–6, Sun. 1–6, Apr.–Aug.; until 5, rest of year 🍴 Café 🎫 $$$

Castle Ward ✉ 1.5 miles west of Strangford Village on A25 ☎ 028 4488 1204 🕐 House: daily noon–6, Jun.–Aug.; Wed.–Mon. 1–6, May; Sat.–Sun. noon–6, Apr., Sep.–Oct. 🍴 Tearoom 🎫 $$

The handsome observatory at Armagh is the oldest meteorological station in the British Isles

REGIONAL SIGHTS

Key to symbols

➕ map coordinates refer to the region map on page 152; sights below are highlighted in yellow on the map

✉ address or location ☎ telephone number

🕐 opening times 🍴 restaurant on site or nearby

💷 admission charge: $$$ = more than £4, $$ = £2 to £4, $ = under £2 ℹ️ information

ARDS PENINSULA

Some 23 miles of unspoiled countryside, the Ards Peninsula lies between Strangford Lough and the Irish Sea and runs from Bangor to Ballyquintin Point. Only about 5 miles wide, this long finger of land is dotted with picture-postcard villages, windmills and ancient ring forts. A bird sanctuary and wildlife reserve emphasize the peninsula's natural beauty. Of the two roads running down the peninsula, the lough road (A20) is more scenic than the coast road (A2). Drive out to the little 19th-century village of Kearney for a taste of history. The car ferry that crosses from Portaferry to Strangford gives you a look straight out to sea, but look quickly because the crossing takes only four minutes.

➕ C2 ✉ 10 miles east of Belfast

ARMAGH

Your exploration of County Armagh's sightseeing treasures will be more meaningful if you make St. Patrick's Trian and Land of Lilliput your first stop. Dramatic presentations of the Armagh Story and Least of the Faithful provide an insightful background for other attractions, and the Land of Lilliput's gigantic reclining Gulliver surrounded by Lilliputians will delight the entire family.

Myths and legends of Queen Macha and the Red Branch Knights surround Armagh, but historical fact outshines them all. At first glance, Navan Fort, a grassy 250-yard enclosure around a large mound, gives few clues to the fabulous kingdom that inhabited this site. You have to use your imagination to unfold the stories of Queen Macha's palace: Deirdre of the Sorrows, who first met her lover Naisi here; Cuchulain, who polished his martial arts skills here; and the Red Branch knights. A 120-foot wide by 40-foot high Celtic temple once crowned its top. Navan was the capital of the kings of Ulster from 600 BC to AD 332, and the burial in 1014 of the high king of Ireland, Brian Ború, is commemorated in the Church of Ireland Cathedral of St. Patrick. Standing on the site of a church founded in AD 445 by St. Patrick himself, this cathedral has been altered and added to over the centuries, whereas the Roman Catholic St. Patrick's Cathedral, built between 1838 and 1873, is a light Gothic-style building with a lavish interior.

The town's excellent county museum houses outstanding collections reflecting Northern Ireland life from prehistoric times to the present in an Ionic schoolhouse that dates from 1833. In addition to an extensive library, there are maps, photographs, paintings by Armagh-born James Sleator and George Russell.

Armagh is without doubt Northern Ireland's most interesting cathedral town (St. Patrick called it "my sweet hill"), with imposing Catholic and Protestant edifices facing each other from their respective hilltops. Red hats of every cardinal archbishop of Armagh and medallions for each of Ireland's saints can be seen in the Catholic cathedral.

The city also has many beautiful buildings and some delightful old streets – Abbey Lane, lined with quaint shops, the Cathedral Close and Castle Street, which follows the contours of an ancient ring fortress. The tree-lined Mall, once a racecourse, is now one of Ireland's finest parks and is surrounded by Armagh's best Georgian buildings including the imposing Court House, the splendid Public Library and the Royal Irish Fusiliers Museum, where a large model of the Battle of Barossa in 1811 is only one of the exhibits that tell the story of the Royal Irish Fusiliers regiment from 1793 to 1968.

In the Palace Stables Heritage Centre, costumed guides successfully re-create and bring to life the activities in the archbishop's palace in 1786. At the entrance to the house is Ireland's longest friary, now in ruins – the 13th-century 153-foot-long Franciscan friary that was founded by Archbishop O'Scanail.

A 10-minute walk from town, off the Friary Road, will bring you to the grounds of Armagh Observatory, which although not open to the public does take groups around on request. It is a modern astronomical research institute with a rich heritage and you can see the Robinson

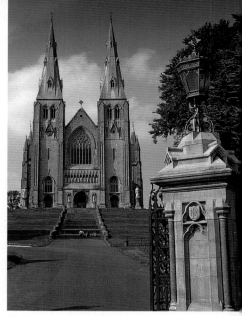

The elegant entrance to St. Patrick's Roman Catholic Cathedral

dome and the Lindsay sundial. On the grounds is the Armagh Planetarium, at present undergoing a major renovation.

Southeast of Armagh is Gosford Forest Park, where rare breeds of cattle and deer rome in open paddocks and there are marked nature trails and an arboretum.

🔁 B2

Tourist information ✉ 40 English Street ☎ 028 3752 1800 🕐 Daily 9:30–5

St. Patrick's Trian and Land of Lilliput ✉ 40 English Street ☎ 028 3752 1801 🕐 Mon.–Sat. 10–5, Sun. 2–5 🍴 Restaurant 🖐 $$

Armagh County Museum ✉ The Mall East ☎ 028 3752 3070 🕐 Mon.–Fri. 10–5, Sat.–Sun. 10–1 and 2–5 🖐 Free

Palace Stables Heritage Centre ✉ Friary Road ☎ 028 3752 9629 🕐 Mon.–Sat. 10–5:30, Sun. 1–6, May–Aug.; Mon.–Sat. 10–5, Sun. 2–5, rest of year 🍴 Restaurant 🖐 $$

Armagh Friary ✉ At entrance to Palace Stables Heritage Centre 🖐 Free

Armagh Observatory ✉ College Hill ☎ 028 3752 2928 🕐 Grounds open all year. Observatory: group tours on request 🖐 Free

Royal Irish Fusiliers Museum ✉ Sovereign's House, The Mall East ☎ 028 3752 2911 🕐 Mon.–Fri. 10–12:30 and 1:30–4 🖐 $

Gosford Forest Park ✉ Markethill, off A28 ☎ 028 3755 1277 🕐 Daily 10–dusk 🍴 Restaurant 🖐 $

Ulster and Northern Ireland

BALLYCASTLE AND THE GLENS OF ANTRIM

Under the Fair Head promontory, the beautiful seaside town of Ballycastle has a wide strand to the east and the lovely Glens of Antrim stretching away inland. At the heart of the town is The Diamond (Market Square), packed with the stalls, entertainments and horse dealing of the famous Ould Lammas Fair at the end of August each year. For about a hundred years St. Patrick's Day has been celebrated with a horse show, and in June there is a festival of Irish music, dancing and games. Just outside the town are the ruins of Bonamargy Friary, founded by Rory MacQuillan around 1500 and burial place of the MacDonnell chiefs, including the notorious Sorley Boy. Amazingly, the eastern range of cloister, gatehouse and church are virtually intact, lacking only the roof. Beyond Fair Head is the scenic Murlough Bay, in the care of the National Trust conservation organization.

Ballycastle's museum illustrates the folk and social history of the Glens of Antrim. At the harbor is a memorial to Gugliemo Marconi, who carried out the first practical test on radio signals between White Lodge, on the clifftop at Ballycastle, and Rathlin Island in 1898. You can travel by boat to Rathlin and savor the life of the 30-odd farming families who live here. The island is a mecca for divers and birdwatchers.

Water of Life

Spelling apart, Irish whiskey is distinctively different from its Scottish sister. In Scotland, the malted barley is dried over an open peat fire, imparting its characteristic smoky flavor. Irish whiskey is distilled three times and dried in smoke-free kilns producing a clear, clean taste; most spirits are distilled twice. The art of distillation was introduced to Ireland by Christian missionaries around AD 600. The elixir was originally named *Uisce Beatha* (pronounced "Ish'ke Ba-ha", meaning water of life).

From the shore you can follow the B15 coastal route west to Ballintoy, then turning right, following the signpost to Carrick-a-Rede.

The mainland clifftops are connected to the small rocky island of Carrick-a-Rede by a swinging rope bridge that is strung across a deep 60-foot-wide chasm. The water here is too treacherous to cross in any other way. You'll not be charged to cross over the wooden planks as you grip the rope handrails, but be warned, this is definitely not for the fainthearted. The bridge is put up each year by salmon fishermen who use Carrick-a-Rede, "the Rock in the Road," as a good place to net the fish in their path to the Bush and Bann rivers. The rope bridge is approached from Larry Bane, a limestone head that was once quarried. Some of the quarry workings remain at Larry Bane, the quarry access to the magnificent seascape that provides guaranteed birdwatching. You can sit in your car and spot kittiwakes, cormorants, guillemots, fulmars and razorbills, though you might need binoculars to see the puffins on Sheep Island farther out to sea.

The nine green Glens of Antrim run through mountainous terrain from Cushendun to Larne before reaching the sea. All nine have individual names and virtually all have stories to tell: Glentaisie (Taisie's glen, named for a daughter of the king of Rathlin), Glenshesk (sedgy glen), Glendun (brown glen), Glencorp (glen of the dead), Glenaan (blue glen), Glenballyeamon (Eamonn's townland glen), Glenariff (ploughman's glen), Glencloy (glen of hedges) and Glenarm (glen of the army). "The Capital of the Glens," Cushendall sits on a pleasant, sandy bay below Glenballyemon, Glenaan and Glencorp and in the curve of the Dall River. The rugged peak of Lurigethan broods over the village, while the softer Tieveragh Hill is supposed to be the capital of the fairies. Cushendall owes much to an East Indian nabob, Francis Turnley, who built the Curfew Tower in the center as a "place for the confinement of idlers and rioters."

Larne is the terminus for the shortest sea-crossing between Ireland and Britain.

Intrepid visitors cross the Carrick-a-Rede rope bridge, 80 feet above the sea

It also marks the start of the scenic Antrim Coast Road, constructed in the 1830's to link the remote Glens of Antrim to the rest of Ulster. To the north is Carnfunnock Park, which has a maze in the shape of Northern Ireland.

Ballycastle ✚ C3

Tourist information ✉ 7 Mary Street ☎ 028 2076 2024; fax 028 2076 2515 🕐 Mon.–Fri. 9:30–7, Sat. 10–6, Sun 2–6, Jul.–Aug.; Mon.–Fri. 9:30–5, rest of year

Ballycastle Museum ✉ 59 Castle Street ☎ 028 2076 2942 🕐 Mon.–Sat. noon–6, Jul.–Aug. (or by arrangement) 🖐 Free

Bonamargy ✉ A2, half a mile east of Ballycastle 🖐 Free

Larne tourist information ✉ Narrow Gauge Road, Larne ☎ 028 2862 0088

Carrick-a-Rede Rope Bridge ✉ Larrybane, County Antrim (5 miles northwest of Ballycastle off A2) 🖐 Parking $$

Ulster and Northern Ireland

AMERICAN CONNECTION

America's military links to northern Ireland date back as early as 1778, when John Paul Jones scored America's first naval victory when he sailed the USS *Ranger* up Belfast Lough and captured the HMS *Drake* within sight of the 12th-century Carrickfergus Castle (see page 177). During those turbulent times, America's Declaration of Independence was printed by John Dunlap from Strabane, County Londonderry (who went on to found the *Philadelphia Gazette*, America's first daily newspaper). At least five of those who signed the Declaration of Independence were from Northern Ireland.

Among American presidents, Andrew Jackson's parents came from Carrickfergus; Andrew Johnson's grandfather was from Larne; Chester A. Arthur's father was born near Ballymena; Grover Cleveland's grandfather was a County Antrim merchant; William McKinley's great-great-grandfather emigrated from Conagher, near Ballymoney; and Theodore Roosevelt's maternal ancestors were from Larne. Quite an impressive score.

Plenty of other American heroes had Northern Ireland roots, including Davy Crockett, Sam Houston, Mark Twain and Neil Armstrong. The founder of the American Presbyterian Church, Francis Makemie, sailed from Northern Ireland for America in 1682, and John Hughes, first Roman Catholic archbishop of New York, emigrated in 1817.

In June 1942 American troops arrived in Northern Ireland to begin intensive training in preparation for World War II battles.

All those connections take on even more meaning at the Ulster-American Folk Park at Camphill just north of Omagh, County Tyrone (see page 194). The re-created cottages and working conditions of 250,000 18th-century emigrants give a real insight into their reasons for crossing the Atlantic, and the replicas of their log cabin settlements in America kindle a new appreciation of their contribution to U.S. history. Also, ask at tourist information centers for the Heritage Trail brochure that lists restored ancestral homes of U.S. presidents.

American hero with Irish roots: Neil Armstrong, the first man on the moon

The lough beside Carrickfergus Castle provides a harbor for small boats

CARRICKFERGUS

The main landmark of this small seaside town is its massive Norman castle. Dating from the late 12th and early 13th centuries, the almost perfectly preserved fortress was actually garrisoned until 1928. In 1778, Commander John Paul Jones of the fledgling American Navy stood offshore just below Carrickfergus Castle in the *Ranger* and captured the much larger British *Drake*. In 1611, a defensive stone wall was built around Carrickfergus (the only place in the North where English was spoken at the time), and more than half of the wall is still intact.

A good beginning for your exploration of Carrickfergus is to take Knight Ride, after which there won't be much about Carrickfergus' history you won't know. Beginning in AD 581, the town's maritime, military and historical stories unfold before your eyes during the monorail ride. There is also an excellent exhibition of gas equipment and other machinery as well as an audiovisual presentation at Flame – The Gasworks Museum of Ireland. Built in 1855 to light street lamps, these are the only Victorian coal-fired gasworks in Ireland and were in service until 1964.

The ancestral home of American President Andrew Jackson was just beyond the north end of Carrickfergus' seafront promenade at Boneybefore, a site now marked by a plaque. Just a few yards away, the Andrew Jackson Centre, in a replica of a simple thatched cottage of the 1700s, gives insight into the life of his forebears before they left for America in 1765, as well as his career and that of other U.S. presidents with Ulster connections. In the grounds of the Jackson Centre, the U.S. Rangers Centre has an exhibition on the First Battalion U.S. Rangers, (the U.S. Army's most decorated unit) and their connections with Carrickfergus in 1942.

✠ C2

Tourist information ✉ Heritage Plaza, Antrim Street ☎ 028 9336 6455 🕐 Mon.–Sat. 10–6, Sun. 12–6, Apr.–Sep.; Mon.–Fri. 10–5, rest of year

Carrickfergus Castle ✉ Marine Highway ☎ 028 9335 1273 🕐 Mon.–Sat. 10–6, Sun. 2–6, Apr.–Sep.; 10–4 and 2–4, rest of year 🍴 Café ✋ $$

Flame – The Gasworks Museum of Ireland ✉ Irish Quarter West ☎ 028 9336 9575 🕐 Daily 10–6, Jun.–Aug.; 2–6, Apr.–Jun.; Sat.–Sun. 2–6, Mar., Oct. ✋ $

Knight Ride ✉ The Heritage Centre, Antrim Street ☎ 028 9336 6455 🕐 Mon.–Sat. 10–6, Sun. noon–6, Apr.–Sep.; 10–5 and noon–5, rest of year ✋ $

Andrew Jackson Centre and U.S. Rangers Centre ✉ Boneybefore ☎ 028 9336 6455 🕐 Mon.–Fri. 10–1 and 2–6, Sat.–Sun. 2–6, Jun.–Sep.; 10–1 and 2–4, Apr.–May and Oct. ✋ $

Breathtaking Atlantic views from Mussenden Temple, Downhill

THE CAUSEWAY COASTLINE

The most distinguishing feature of the north Antrim coast is undoubtedly the Causeway Coast and a string of such small towns as Ballycastle, Ballymena, Ballymoney, Larne and Portrush. Ballymena, the county town of Antrim, boasts as one of its sons Timothy Eaton, who founded Eaton's Stores in Canada.

The fantastic Giant's Causeway is much more impressive when you walk its basalt columns (there are 37,000!) than any photograph can possibly convey. How they came to be packed so tightly together that they form a sort of bridge from the shoreline out into the sea, submerge, and then surface on the Hebrides island of Staffa is a matter of conjecture. Scientists will tell you unequivocally that they're the result of a massive volcanic eruption 60 million years ago, when molten lava cooled and formed into geometric shapes. But Irish legend will tell you that it was the giant, Finn MacCool (see page 199), who built the causeway between Ulster and Scotland and it was his Scottish counterpart, Finn Gall, who destroyed all but the bit you see today.

Be that as it may, you will not want to miss this mass of symmetrical basalt columns jutting out into the sea from the foot of a steep cliff. The visitor center houses a 25-minute audiovisual show telling the story of the formation of the Causeway, together with fascinating pictoral exhibits, a tourist information office and book shop and tearooms. A minibus service from the visitor center to the foot of the cliff is a decided bonus if you don't want to walk.

Generations of imaginative guides have embroidered stories and created names for the remarkable formations – the Giant's Organ, the Giant's Harp, the Wishing Chair and Lord Antrim's Parlour. One story absolutely based on fact is of the *Girona*, a fleeing Spanish Armada galleon, wrecked in a storm one night in October 1588. A diving team retrieved a treasure hoard from the wreck in 1967, and it's now on display in the Ulster Museum in Belfast (see page 166). The wreck still lies under cliffs in Port na Spaniagh, one of a magnificent array of bays and headlands on the causeway.

Portrush, west of Giant's Causeway, is a typical seaside resort that flourished with the rise of the railways. It has three good bays, with broad stretches of sand, ranges of dunes, rock pools, white cliffs and a busy harbor. Nearby, there could hardly be a more dramatic sight than the craggy headland crowned by the great

lump of ruined 13th-century Dunluce
Castle sitting on – almost overhanging –
the very edge of the cliff. Back in 1639 a
storm actually dumped the kitchens, the
cooks and all the pots into the sea below.
Silhouetted against the skyline, it was in
its day the largest castle in the north.

Here also is the Dunluce Centre,
which was refurbished in 2002. It features
the Finn McCool Playground, a themed
and interactive game environment, and
the Treasure Fortress, Motion Simulator
and Turbo Tours that supply unexpected
thrills. Panoramic views from the tower
are spectacular and there's a shopping
arcade all of which makes for a good
family day out. Portrush's indoor water
center, Waterworld, is the perfect place to
take a break from the rigors of travel and
enjoy the fun pools. There are giant water
flumes, water cannon, swings, a rope
bridge and even a pirate ship.

The neat village of Bushmills close by
is the home of the world's oldest legal
distillery. Licensed since 1608, it's still
turning out the "wine of the country" after
all these centuries. There's a marvelous
exhibition of its history, and a whiskey
tasting nicely rounds off the one-hour
guided tour through the distilling process.
The water from St. Columb's Rill, or
stream, is said to give the whiskey its
special quality. The Bush River is rich in
trout and salmon, and its fast-flowing
waters not only supported the mills that
gave the town its name, but they also
generated electricity for the world's first
hydroelectric tramway, which carried
passengers to the Giant's Causeway
between 1893 and 1949.

Panoramic views of the coast are
nothing short of breathtaking at
Downhill, which is perched on the very
edge of a cliff overlooking the Atlantic.
Mussendon Temple, a beautiful 18th-
century rotunda modeled on Tivoli's
Temple of Vesta is only part of this ruined
estate that once belonged to the 4th Earl
of Bristol, Frederick Hervey. He was an
eccentric collector and traveler who gave
his name to the Bristol hotels throughout
Europe. A scenic glen walk leads from the
Bishop's Gate to the temple.

➕ C3

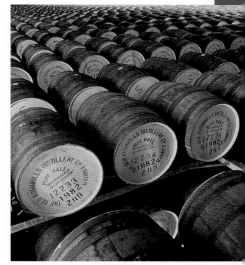

**Whiskey barrels waiting for delivery in the ware-
house at Old Bushmills Distillery**

Giant's Causeway ✉ 44 Causeway Road, County
Antrim (2 miles north of Bushmills on B146) ☎ 028
2073 1855 🕐 Daily 10–7, Jul.–Aug.; 10–6, Jun. and
Sep.; 10–5, Mar.–May and Oct.; 10–4.30, rest of year
🍴 Tearoom open Mar.–Nov. 💷 Causeway: free;
audiovisual: $

Dunluce Castle ✉ On A2, 3 miles east of Portrush
☎ 028 2073 1938 🕐 Tue.–Sat. 10–4, Sun. 2–4,
Oct.–Mar.; Mon.–Sat. 10–6, Sun. 2–4, Apr., Jun.
and Sep.; Mon.–Sat. 10–6, Sun 2–6, Jul. and Aug.
💷 $

Dunluce Centre ✉ 10 Sandhill Drive, Portrush
☎ 028 7082 4444 🕐 Daily 10–8, Jul.–Aug.; Mon.–Fri.
10–5, Sat.–Sun. noon–7, Jun.; Sat.–Sun. noon–5,
Sep.–Mar. 🍴 Café 💷 $$$

Waterworld ✉ Portrush, end of Portrush harbor
☎ 028 708 2001 🕐 Mon.–Sat. 10–6:45, Sun.
noon–6:45, Easter–Aug.; weekends only, Sep.
🍴 Café 💷 $$$

Old Bushmills Distillery ✉ 2 Distillery Road,
Bushmills ☎ 028 2073 1521 🕐 Mon.–Sat. 9:30–5:30,
Sun. noon–5:30 (last tour at 4), Apr.–Oct.; reduced
tours Nov.–Feb. (phone for details) 🍴 Coffee shop
💷 $$

Mussendon Temple ✉ Mussenden Road,
Castlerock, County Londonderry ☎ 028 7084 8728
🕐 Daily 11–6, Jul.–Aug.; Sat.–Sun. 11–6, Apr. and
Sep.; grounds are always open

Tourist information ✉ 76 Church Street, Ballymena
☎ 028 2563 8494 🕐 Mon.–Fri. 9–5, Sat. 10–4,
Apr.–Sep.; winter times vary (phone for details)

DONEGAL

At the head of Donegal Bay, on the estuary of the River Eske, Donegal is a pleasant town with the splendid central Diamond Square. Historically, it was the seat of the O'Donnells and Donegal Abbey, now in ruins, which was a Franciscan friary founded by Red Hugh O'Donnell and his mother, Nuala O'Connor. Red Hugh also built the west tower of Donegal Castle (1505) on the banks of the Eske beside the Diamond (town square) when he rebuilt an earlier castle on the site. He made this the chief O'Donnell stronghold. The rest was added by Sir Basil Brooke in 1607 and features a mammoth Jacobean fireplace, and windows and gables in the handsome house he built around the old tower. The extensive remains have been beautifully restored.

Donegal is an attractive and strategic place for exploring the northwest, and is known worldwide for its shopping. Its main store, Magee's is one of the best-known places to buy the regional specialty, tweed, a quality fabric still produced in the town. Other craftsmanship such as jewelry, handweaving, ceramics, batik and crystal can be found at the Donegal Craft Village. Other factory shops in the area include the Donegal Parian China factory in Ballyshannon, which since 1985 has specialized in the delicate brand of china known as Parian ware (because it resembles the clear white Greek marble from the island of Paros). You can take guided tours through the workshop where such diverse items as thimbles and complete tea and coffee services are fashioned, decorated, fired and polished – look for the distinctive graceful shapes and soft green shamrock, rose, hawthorn and other Irish floral designs.

East of Ballyshannon, you'll find the distinctive china of Belleek Pottery. Their intricate "basket weaving" has to be seen to be believed. There's a small museum (some pieces on display are more than 100 years old), and the visitor center conducts guided tours to let you see craftspeople creating, glazing and decorating the world-famous porcelain. The shop features tableware, vases, clocks,

ornaments and a host of other products – this is the place to buy a future heirloom to carry home!

The drive to Glencolumbkille travels west of Donegal through lonely mountain country with occasional glimpses of the sea. It is a journey that goes back as far as 5,000 years through a culture that has changed little since the days of Bonnie Prince Charlie. Try to get to the picturesque little harbor town of Killybegs (west of Donegal on the R263) in the late afternoon, and go down to the pier to watch the fishing fleet come in – it's a memorable experience, seagulls swarm and screech overhead and half the town gathers to greet the fishermen.

Modest in size, Glencolumbkille Folk Village is one of Ireland's most authentic, with cottage dwellings built and

Lying below Beefan Mountain, Glencolumbkille Folk Village displays the story of Irish peasant life

furnished to depict the daily lives of people who lived here from 1700 to the 1900s. There are guided tours that explain the workings of each cottage. The home of a 1720 cotter is earthen-floored, and its open hearth has no chimney; by the 1820s the cotter's home has a flagstone floor, chimney and oil-lamp lighting; the 1920 cottage is much like many you'll see in today's Irish countryside. The Old National Schoolhouse from a century ago and a country pub, or *sheebeen* (where the drink on sale was illegal poteen, more often than not), complete the village.

🕂 A2

Tourist information ✉ Quay Street ☎ 073 21148 🕘 Mon.–Sat. 9–6, Jun.–Aug.; Mon.–Fri. 9–5 Mar.–May and Sep.–Oct.; winter times vary

(phone for details)

Donegal Castle ✉ Donegal (beside the River Eske) ☎ 073 22405; fax 073 22436 🕘 Daily 10–6, mid-Mar.–Nov. 👋 $$

Belleek Pottery ✉ Belleek, Co. Fermanagh (just across the Donegal border) ☎ 028 6865 8501 🕘 Mon.–Sat. 9–6, Sun. 2–6, Mar.–Jun. and Oct. (Sun. 11–8, Jul.–Aug.); Sat.–Sun. 9–5:30, rest of year 🍴 Restaurant 👋 $

Donegal Parian China ✉ Ballyshannon, Co. Donegal (south of town on N15) ☎ 072 51826; fax 072 52429 🕘 Mon.–Fri. 9–6 , Jun.–Sep.; Mon.–Fri. 9–5:30, Oct.–May. 🍴 Tearoom 👋 Free 🛈 Mail order service, exchange bureau and Cash Back and V.A.T. refunds

Glencolumbkille Folk Village ✉ Glencolumbkille Co. Donegal (on outskirts of village) ☎ 073 30017; fax 073 30334 🕘 Mon.–Sat. 10–6, Sun. noon–6, Easter–Sep. 🍴 Tearoom 👋 $$

St. Patrick's birthplace is uncertain, but it was probably Scotland or Wales. Son of a Roman centurion, he was taken into slavery while still a young boy. After six years of tending sheep on Slemish mountain in County Antrim, he escaped and studied for several years with Martin of Tours in Gaul before fulfilling his deep wish to bring the message of Christianity to Celtic Ireland.

Legend says that his arrival in County Down was quite by accident – his destination was the Antrim coast farther north, but Strangford Lough's strong tidal currents drew his boat through the narrows and he was deposited where the River Slaney flows into the Lough (the Slaney is now a stream near Ringbane townland, north of Saul).

Undaunted, he quickly converted Dichu, a local chieftan, who gave Patrick a barn in which to hold services. For the next 30 years, he traveled the length and breadth of Ireland preaching the gospel to Celtic chieftains and peasants while generating hundreds of legends – there are many "St. Patrick slept here" stories in Ireland. At the end of his life, he returned to his abbey at Saul, northeast of Downpatrick, the place his Irish ministry began, that he returned and died in AD 461.

A round tower adjoining the chancel of a Celtic-revival church of Saul marks the place where St. Patrick preached his first sermon to the Irish. He was reputedly buried in Down cathedral graveyard (see page 184), where pilgrims bring daffodils

Ireland's patron saint

IN ST. PATRICK'S FOOTSTEPS

each St. Patrick's Day (March 17).

County Down, especially in the Downpatrick area, is strewn with reminders of St. Patrick. Perhaps the best introduction to his history is the excellent St. Patrick Centre close to Down County Museum, next door to Down cathedral, where his life story is recounted in his own words. In the cathedral graveyard, pause by the grave that is said to be his, and you'll find an overwhelming sense of reverence that will dispel any importance you may have placed on whether or not the saint's remains actually lie there.

He is also linked with nearby Struell Wells, which is said to have healing properties. Fed by an underground spring, it continues to draw those afflicted with eye ailments and other infirmities to collect their waters in hope of a cure. Near the site there are ruins of an 18th-century church and bath houses for bathing in the holy waters.

As you travel around County Down, it may come as a surprise to learn just how many places have associations of one sort or another with St. Patrick, some marked with historical plaques, others recorded only in the verbal history of a locality. Visit Saul, a place that meant so much to him during his lifetime, and you may discover that the very earth itself seems to be imbued with his spirit even today.

Saul ✉ About halfway between Downpatrick and Strangford on A25
Streull Wells ✉ 1.5 miles east of Downpatrick off the B1

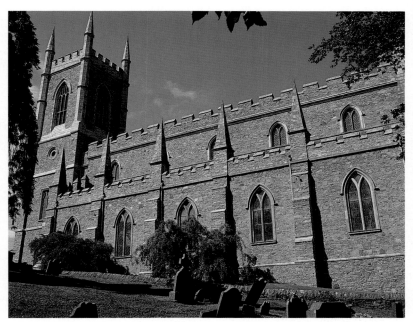

Downpatrick's Church of Ireland cathedral contains traces of earlier churches from the sixth century

DOWNPATRICK

Radiating from the center of Downpatrick are three streets – English Street, Irish Street and Scotch Street – which recall the Elizabethan system of dividing settlements racially. Fine Georgian and Victorian buildings line these streets, notably the High Victorian Gothic Assembly Rooms, with a large clock tower and an arcaded ground floor, the Regency-style Judge's House, the Court House of 1834, and Southwell Charity Schools and Almshouses, about 100 years older. Northwest of the town are the ruins of the Cistercian Inch Abbey, founded in the late 1180s by John de Courcy on a strategic island in the Quoile Marshes within sight of the Hill of Down. Now reached by a causeway, the monastic ruins include an interesting pointed triple window.

Downpatrick, as its name suggests, has links with Ireland's patron saint (see opposite). The present Down cathedral is a reconstruction of its 13th- and 16th-century predecessors, and a large stone in the churchyard purports to mark St.

Patrick's grave (it's the one under a gigantic weeping willow tree). The gravestone is actually a granite monolith placed on the holy spot in 1901 to protect it from pilgrims who persisted in taking away scoops of earth from the grave. It is said that the bones of Sts. Columbanus and Bridgit were transferred here in the 12th century.

St. Patrick's first stone church is thought to have been erected on the historic Mound of Down site that held a Bronze Age fortification. The St. Patrick Centre, a new exhibition center close to the Down County Museum premises, explores the legacy of the good saint and tells his story in his own words.

Other attractions of the town include the Railway Museum with working engines and steam locomotives, and where on July and August Sunday afternoons the steam locomotive Guinness runs trips over a restored half-mile section of the Belfast-Newcastle main line railway to the grave of a Viking king, Magnus Barefoot.

Downpatrick is popular for its access to Strangford Lough (see drive page 169), a beautiful inlet of the sea separating the

Ards Peninsula (see page 172) and the rest of County Down. Dotted with numerous islands formed by submerged drumlins, it was named Strang Fiord (Violent Inlet) by the Vikings because of the tidal surges up and down the Narrows between the lake and the open sea. The lough extends for about 12 miles to the north and measures up to 5 miles wide. It's a serene landscape with gleaming white farmhouses, and several nature reserves, including the delightful Delamont Country Park, which has Ireland's longest miniature railway. Strangford Castle, a 16th-century tower house, is one of a cluster of strongholds built at strategic points on the lake.

✚ C2

Tourist information ✉ 74 Market Street ☎ 028 4461 2233 ⏰ Mon.–Fri. 9–6, Sat. 10–6, Jul. and Aug.; Mon.–Fri. 9–5, Sat. 10–5, Jun. and Sep.

Downpatrick Cathedral ✉ The Mall, English Street ☎ 028 4461 4922 ⏰ Mon.–Sat. 9:30–5, Sun. 2–5 💷 Donations requested

Down County Museum ✉ The Mall (next to the cathedral) ☎ 028 4461 5218 ⏰ Mon.–Sat. 10–5, Sat.–Sun. 1–5 🍴 Café 💷 Free

St. Patrick Centre ✉ The Mall ☎ 028 4461 9000 ⏰ Mon.–Sat. 9:30–7, Sun. 10–6, Jun.–Aug.; Mon.–Sat. 9–5:30, Sun. 1–5:30, Apr.–May, Sep.; Mon.–Sat. 10–5, rest of year 💷 $$

Downpatrick Railway Museum ✉ Railway Station, Market Street ☎ 028 4461 5779 ⏰ Call for ride schedules and fares

Inch Abbey ✉ 1 mile northwest of Downpatrick, off A7 ⏰ Free access all year 💷 $

Strangford Castle ✉ Strangford, 6 miles northwest of Downpatrick on A25 ⏰ Tue.–Sat. 10–6, Sun. 2–6, Jul.–Aug.

Delamont Country Park ✉ Downpatrick (On A22, 3 miles north of Downpatrick) ☎ 028 4482 8333 ⏰ Daily 9–dusk 🍴 Tearoom and restaurant 💷 Car $$

DUNGANNON

The county town of Tyrone, Dungannon is a large, attractive place, built on several hills. It occupies the site of the ancient seat of the O'Neill chieftains, and there are remains of O'Neill Castle, an 18th-century house on the site of 16th-century fortifications. Dungannon prospered on the linen industry, and this and other

town history can be explored in the Donaghmore Heritage Centre.

There's a 200-year tradition behind the fine crystal produced at Killybrackey's Tyrone Crystal factory, one of the oldest in Ireland. Visitors can follow the process from the time the glass is blown until the finished product is engraved.

The town has many fine buildings, including the former Northern Bank building in Market Square, Dungannon Royal School, founded by Charles I in 1628 and the elaborately designed police station in Market Square, which has been known as the "Khyber Pass" since its plans were mistaken for a fortress in India by a clerk in Dublin.

West of Dungannon is the ancestral home of Ulysses S. Grant, victorious Civil War general and 18th U.S. president (1869–77). The maternal great-grandfather of Grant left this two-room farm cottage in 1738 and settled in Pennsylvania. The mud-floor cottage has been restored, and its period furnishings include a settle bed and dresser.

East of Dungannon is Peatlands Park. Peat has been vital in the Irish home for centuries and this park in the southwest corner of the Lough Neagh basin is the place to learn the 10,000-year history of the peat bogs. Wooded drumlins (rounded hills) break through the surface, and small lakes have been formed in boglands that have been cut over. The rides into the bog on the narrow-gauge railroad, uses a locomotive that once transported the peat.

✚ C2

Tourist information ✉ Kilmaddy Centre, Ballygawley Road ☎ 028 8776 7259 ⏰ Mon.–Fri. 9–7, Sat. 10–6, Sun. 10–5, Jul.–Sep.; Mon.–Fri. 9–5, Nov.–Feb.; Mon.–Fri. 9–5, Sat. 10–5, Mar.–Jun.

Tyrone Crystal ✉ Coalisland Road, Killybrackey, (2 miles east of Dungannon) ☎ 028 8772 5335 ⏰ Mon.–Sat. 9–6, Sun. 1–5. Phone for tours 🍴 Restaurant 💷 $$

U.S. Grant Ancestral Homestead and Visitor Centre ✉ Dergina, Ballygawley (off A4, 13 miles west of Dungannon) ☎ 028 8555 7133 ⏰ Mon.–Sat. noon–5, Sun. 2–6, Apr.–Sep. 🍴 Tearoom 💷 $

Peatlands Park ✉ 7 miles east of Dungannon, exit 13 from M1 ☎ 028 3885 1102 ⏰ Park: daily 9–9 Easter–Sep.; 9–dusk, rest of year; cente: daily 2–6, Jun.–Aug.; Sat.–Sun. 1–6, Apr.–May, Sep. 💷 $

ENNISKILLEN AND LOUGH ERNE

This appealing little town owes much of its attractiveness to its setting on an island where the two sections of Lough Erne constrict to their narrowest point. Overlooking the lough is Enniskillen Castle, a magnificent 15th-century stone fortress sporting a unique two-turret water gate, down in the vault, lifesize figures depict castle life. Surrounded by great stone barracks, the keep now houses the Museum of the Royal Inniskillin Fusiliers, which features battle trophies of the Dragoons and Fusiliers from the Napoleonic Wars, arms and a host of colorful uniforms.

The county museum features exhibits on the history, wildlife and landscape of this area. The delicate handmade lace for which Ulster is renowned is beautifully displayed in the Sheelin Lace Museum, with items dating from 1850 to 1900.

The River Erne and its Upper and Lower Loughs are linked to the Shannon river as part of a 500-mile leisure waterway. Video presentations at the Explore Erne Exhibition explain how the lough was formed, its part in the most extensive inland waterway in western Europe, and the effects its history and customs have had on the people who live and work on its shores. The river and the loughs are dotted with 154 intriguing and historical islands, many with ancient monastic ruins (see drive page 186). In summer, two-hour waterbus cruises ply the Lower Lough, departing Enniskillen Round O pier and calling at Devenish Island. Cruising trips of several days are popular, and the tourist office can arrange boat rentals.

You can take the 7-mile drive through Lough Navar Forest for a marvelous panoramic view of Lower Lough Erne. Or follow marked trails to viewpoints, the best (and steepest walk) leads to a view across the lough to Donegal and Sligo. Keep an eye out, whether you're walking or driving, for the red deer and wild goats that roam the forest freely.

➕ B2 and A2

Tourist information ✉ Wellington Road ☎ 028 6632

3110 🕐 Mon.–Fri. 9–7, Sat. 10–6, Sun. 11–5, Jul. and Aug.; Mon.–Fri. 9–5:30, Sat. 10–6, Sun. 11–5, Mar.–Jun. and Sep.; Mon.–Fri. 9–5:30, Oct.–Feb.

Enniskillen Castle ✉ Castle Barracks ☎ 028 6632 5000 🕐 Sat.–Mon. 2–5, Tue.–Fri. 10–5, Jul. and Aug.; Mon. and Sat. 2–5, Tue.–Fri. 10–5, May., Jun. and Sep. 🅿 $$

Sheelin Lace Museum ✉ Bellanaleck (5 miles south of Enniskillen on A509) ☎ 028 6634 8052 🕐 Daily 10–6 🅿 $$

Explore Erne Exhibition ✉ Erne Gateway Centre, Corry, Belleek ☎ 028 6865 8866 🕐 Daily 11–5, May–Sep.; (last admission 4:30) 🅿 $

Lough Erne Cruises: ☎ 028 6632 2882 🕐 Call for sailing schedules and fares

Lough Navar Forest ✉ 5 miles northwest of Derrygonnelly, signposted off A46 ☎ 028 6634 3032 🕐 Daily 10–dusk 🅿 Car $$

Enniskillen Castle reflected in Lough Erne

Ulster and Northern Ireland

DRIVE: FERMANAGH LAKELAND

Duration: 1 day

This 84-mile drive explores the major monastic sites in Ulster, the awesome Marble Arch Cave and a magical boat ride through 300 million years of history.

> *Start this drive at the tourist center in Enniskillen. Take the A32 toward Omagh for 2 miles until you reach the signpost for the ferries to Devenish. Take a ferry from Trory to get to Devenish Island.*

The sixth-century Augustinian abbey founded by St. Molaise is a noteworthy monastic ruin. There is also a 12th-century round tower that has survived the centuries in perfect condition and is regarded as one of the finest in Ireland. Beautifully proportioned with finely cut stones and precise lines is the intricately carved 15th-century high cross in the graveyard. The small museum focuses on the monastic history of the island. The great treasure of Devenish, the book shrine of Molaise, a masterpiece of early Christian art, is kept at the National Museum in Dublin.

> *Take the B82 for 7 miles for Castle Archdale and Kesh.*

In the old estate of the Archdale family is an arboretum, butterfly park and farm with rare breeds. The ruins of the old castle, burned in the Williamite wars of 1689, can be seen in the forest. Castle Archdale is one of the busiest places around Lough Erne. The focus is the marina, where concrete jetties and slipways, built for flying boats taking off for the Battle of the Atlantic in 1941, have been turned to more peaceful use. Here you can hire a boat with a *gillie* (a man to help you with the fishing).

It is possible to reach White Island from here to see the enigmatic carved stones that for centuries have puzzled experts and fascinated visitors. Set in the little 12th-century church, they seem to represent biblical figures, with the exception of *Sheil-na-gig*, a female fertility figure, a strange meeting of Celtic pagan art and Christianity.

> *Turn left onto the B82. After 2 miles, turn left for Kesh via the scenic route for 4 miles. At Kesh turn left for Belleek, onto the A35, then after 1 mile turn on to the A47 and drive for 8 miles to Boa Island (pronounced "Bo").*

Two bridges connect Boa Island to the mainland. Just before the bridge at the west end is a track on the left to Caldragh graveyard, where there are two pagan idols in stone. One is called a Janus figure because it is double-faced and could be 2000 years old; the other, a small, hunched figure, was moved here from Lusty Beg Island. Long before Christianity began to populate the islands of Lough Erne, the Celts recognized their mystical qualities. Boa Island, with its echoes of pre-Christian Ireland, is said to be named after Badhbh, the Irish goddess of war.

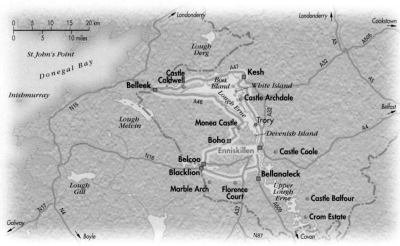

The carved stone figure of Janus in Caldragh churchyard

Continue on the A47 for 5 miles to Castle Caldwell.

The Fiddler's Stone at the entrance to Castle Caldwell is in memory of the fiddler Dennis McCabe, who fell out of Sir James Caldwell's family barge in August 1770 and was drowned. The obituary ends: "On firm land only exercise your skill that you may play and safely drink your fill." The castle, now in ruins, had the reputation of enjoying one of the most beautiful situations of all Irish houses. The fine views are still the same, across water rich in wildlife, with bird hides that allow an opportunity to catch sight of many ducks, geese and grebes.

Continue on the A47 to Belleek (see page 180). Take the A46 for Enniskillen. After 13 miles turn right on the Slavin scenic route for 2 miles. Rejoin the A46 and after 6 miles, turn right and follow signs to Monea.

The ruins of this superb plantation castle (pronounced "Mon-ay"), built in 1618, sit at the end of a long avenue of beech trees. Its builder, Malcolm Hamilton, became Archbishop of Cashel. Surrounded by bog and overlooking a lake, the castle has an impressive entrance, twin circular towers with square turrets and interesting Scottish-type corbels. Occupants came and went until 1750, when a fire made it uninhabitable and it was abandoned. There are still remnants of the old wall that surrounded the castle, and an ancient crannóg, or artificial island dwelling, can be picked out in the marsh in front of Monea.

The ruined tower of a 13th-century priory on Devenish Island

Turn left leaving Monea, then left for Enniskillen. Turn right, following signs to Boho for 5 miles, then right again for Belcoo.

Belcoo sits neatly between the two Lough Macneans, surrounded by mountains and adjacent to its neighboring village, Blacklion. The two loughs are large and very beautiful.

To the south of Lower Lough Macnean is the limestone cliff of Hanging Rock, and by the road is the Salt Man, a great lump of limestone, which, it is said, fell off the cliff and killed a man pulling a load of salt. Just north of Belcoo is the Holywell, traditionally visited by pilgrims in search of the curative powers of St. Patrick's Well.

From Belcoo, cross the border into the Republic and Blacklion for a very short distance, then cross back into Northern Ireland, taking the road along the south shore of Lower Lough Macnean. Turn right along Marlbank Scenic Loop and drive for 3 miles to Marble Arch.

The highlight of Fermanagh is one of the most awesome sights in all of Europe. The mysterious beauty of Marble Arch Cave is

Turn left, then right and drive for 4 miles to Florence Court.

Home of the Enniskillen family, Florence Court is one of Northern Ireland's most impressive great houses. A three-story 18th-century mansion, with pavilions connected to the house by open, arched walkways, the interior is especially notable for its fine rococo plasterwork. The mountainous woodland setting is as dramatic as the house, and is now Florencecourt Forest Park, with a landscaped "pleasure" garden as well as the original Irish yew from which cuttings were first taken to propagate the species and oaks that were planted some 200 years ago.

From Florence Court, turn right. After a mile turn left on the A32, then after 2 miles turn right for Bellanaleck.

A base for cruising, Bellanaleck gives a glimpse of the winding, mazy ways of Upper Lough Erne, as its waters thread through 57 islands between Enniskillen and Galloon Bridge to the southeast. Here are hidden remote treasures such as ruins of Castle Balfour and the 1,350-acre estate at Crom, a conservation area rich in history and rare in wildlife.

Return to Enniskillen via the A509.

Devenish Island ✉ 1.5 miles north of Enniskillen, embark at Trory Point, down a lane to the lough shore from the junction of A32 and B82 ⏰ Daily 10, 1, 3 and 5 💷 $$, includes ferry crossing and admission to round tower and museum

Castle Archdale Country Park ✉ 3 miles south of Kesh on B82 ☎ 028 6862 1588 ⏰ Park always open; center: daily 11–6, Easter–Jun.; Tue.–Sun. 11–7, Jul.–Aug. 💷 Free

Marble Arch Caves and Marble Arch Forest
✉ Caves: Marbank Scenic Loop Road, Florencecourt (off A4/A32, 12 miles southwest of Eniskillen); forest: near Marble Arch Caves, entrance off main Florence Court – Blacklion road ☎ 028 6634 8855 ⏰ Daily 10–4:30, mid-Mar.–Sep. (weather permitting) 🍴 Café 💷 $$$

Florence Court and Florence Court Forest Park
✉ 8 miles southwest of Enniskillen via A4 and A32 ☎ 028 6634 8249 or 6634 8497 ⏰ House: daily noon–6, Apr.–May, Sep.; park: daily 10–8, May–Sep.; 10–4, rest of year 🍴 Tearoom 💷 $$

Crom Estate ✉ 3 miles west of Newtownbutler off A34 ☎ 028 6773 8118 or 6773 8174 ⏰ Mon.–Sat. 10–6, Sun. noon–6, Apr.–Sep. (closes Jul. 8–Aug.) 🍴 Tearoom 💷 $$ (car or boat $$)

enhanced by a ride on a quiet, flat-bottom boat through still, dark waters. Over 300 million years of history are here: the boat travels through a spectacular underground world of rivers, waterfalls, lakes, lofty chambers and winding passages with wonderful stalagmites and stalactites. It's chilly down there, so take a sweater, plus good walking shoes for the uneven surfaces. Nearby Marble Arch Forest, laced with nature trails, includes a walk along the Claddagh Glen and a dramatically beautiful waterfall. Common wild flowers as well as some Irish rarities are seen here in glorious abundance.

Climb to the summit of Mount Errigal, Donegal's highest peak – tough, but rewarding

LETTERKENNY

Overlooking the River Swilly, which is said to be named after a 400-eyed monster, Suileach, killed by St. Columcille, is the cathedral town and commercial center of north Donegal. Letterkenny claims to have the longest main street in the country, which is overlooked by the Cathedral of St. Eunan. This turn-of-the-20th-century cathedral has a lofty spire, one of the tallest in the country, and stands on Sentry Hill, where secret Masses were held during penal times. Letterkenny is also the home of the Donegal County Museum which, housed in a section of what was the local workhouse back in sadder times, displays artifacts from the prehistoric to the early medieval periods in addition to the Folklife of the county and the story of Donegal Railways.

If you are using Letterkenny as a base for the countryside of north County Donegal, don't miss the splendors of Atlantic Highlands, a landscape of jagged, cliff-filled coastline, rocky mountain pastures and breathtaking mountain passes. Mount Errigal, Donegal's highest at 2,466 feet, is an almost straight climb up to the summit that overlooks spectacular views.

Nearby in Dunlewy, there is something for all the family at Ionad Cois Locha, a charming cottage center beside Dunlewy Lake. There are demonstrations of carding, spinning and weaving of wool, tours, storytelling and boat trips on the lake.

At some point in your Donegal rambles, take in the deeply wooded reaches of Glenveagh National Park. Set between the Derryveagh and Glendowan mountain ranges, the park covers 25,000 acres of wilderness, set like a jewel on the edge of Lough Veagh. At the main entrance near Churchill Village, the Regency-style Glebe Gallery houses the collection of the late noteworthy painter Derek Hill, and include works by Picasso, Bonnard and Kokoshka, together with works by Irish and Italian artists.

➕ B3

Tourist information ✉ Derry Road, Letterkenny ☎ 074 21160 🕐 Mon.–Sat. 9–5, Sun., 10–2 Jul.–Aug.; Mon.–Sat. 9–5, Jun., Sep.; closed Sat.–Sun., rest of year

Donegal County Museum ✉ High Road (turn right at Courthouse in town center) ☎ 074 24613; fax 074 26165 🕐 Mon.–Fri. 10–4:30, Sat. 1–4:30 🎟 Free

Errigal Mountain ✉ Dunlewy, County Donegal

Glebe Gallery and Glenveagh National Park and Castle ✉ Churchill, about 18 miles northwest of Letterkenny on the Churchill road (R251) ☎ Park: 074 37090; gallery: 074 37071 🕐 Park and castle: daily 10–6:30, mid-Mar.–Nov.; gallery: Sat.–Thu. 11–6:30, mid-May–Sep. 🍴 Restaurant and tearoom in castle 🎟 Park: $$; castle $$; gallery $$

Ionad Cois Locha (Lakeside Centre) ✉ Dunlewy. From Letterkenny take N56 and turn left at Termon on to R251 ☎ 075 31699; fax 075 31698 🕐 Mon.–Sat. 10:30–6, Sun. 11–7, Easter–Oct.; weekends only mid-Mar.–Easter 🍴 Tearoom, restaurant 🎟 Cottage tour: $$; boat ride: $$; combination ticket: $$$

LONDONDERRY

Londonderry is widely known by its original name of Derry, especially by its mostly Catholic population. Derry's notorious Bogside district has seen much unrest, for it is here that Catholic and Protestant factionalism is most sharply polarized. Catholics, stranded right on the Republic's border, have suffered much discrimination under Protestant control. However, for all its political ill-feelings, Derry is a fascinating city, retaining intact the 17th-century walls that played such a significant role in its history.

The walls are about a mile in circumference and a walk around them is recommended. They are the only unbroken city walls in the British Isles, and this was the last city in Europe to build protective wall fortifications. The walls measure 20 to 25 feet high and 14 to 30 feet thick, with seven gates. The old, walled section of modern-day Londonderry is west of the River Foyle, as are the main business and shopping districts, with ancient winding lanes and rows of charming Georgian and Victorian buildings. In the northeastern walls, Shipquay Gate is only two blocks from

the river, and the historic old Guildhall with its turrets and tower clock is midway between river quays and this gate. Most of what you'll want to see will be within a short walk of these two points. Walk them on your own, or join a guided tour that begins at the tourist information center.

Derry's St. Columb's Cathedral was built in the mid-1600s. It's a splendid neo-Gothic structure, but much of what you'll see today has been added since. One of its most important features is the memorial window showing the relief of the siege in 1689.

At Fifth Province, the very Irish talent of fleshing out images of the mind into full-blown stories is put to good use in a fascinating multimedia presentation. The multistage, high-tech tour explores Celtic history, takes a look at what might have been had ancient Ireland contained a fifth province. Exhibitions also center on the history of Derry and the impact of Irish emigrants on the United States.

A small cottage in Ballyarnet (2 miles from the center of Londonderry) is dedicated to the memory of Amelia Earhart, the first woman to fly solo across the Atlantic. She landed in an adjacent field in May 1932, and there's a

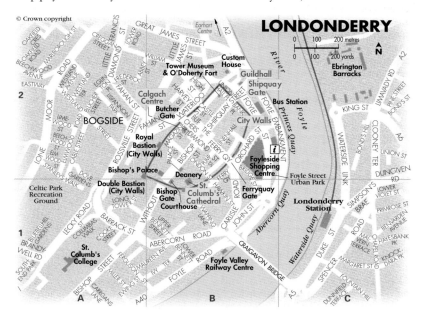

Londonderry's Peace *statue symbolizes hope for a land where politics and religion divide*

commemorative sculpture at the landing site. The cottage holds exhibitions centered around the famous American aviatrix. There is also a wildlife sanctuary on the grounds.

✚ B3 (regional map on page 152)

Tourist information ✚ B2 ✉ 44 Foyle Street ☎ 028 7126 7284 🕐 Mon.–Fri. 10–7, Sat. 10–6, Sun. 10–5, Jun.–Sep.; Mon.–Fri. 9–5, Sat. 10–5, rest of year

City Walls ✚ B2 ✉ Tours: 44 Foyle Street ☎ 028 7126 7284 🕐 Tours: daily 11:15 and 3:15, Jun.–Sep.; at 2:30, rest of year 🎟 $$

St. Columb's Cathedral ✚ B1 ✉ London Street (near Bishop's Gate) ☎ 028 7126 7313 🕐 Mon.–Sat. 9–5, Apr.–Sep.; 9–1 and 2–4, rest of year 🎟 $

Fifth Province ✚ B2 ✉ Calgach Centre, Butcher Street ☎ 028 7137 3177 🕐 Showing times 11:30, 2:30 (Sat. by arrangement) 🎟 $$

Earhart Centre ✚ Off the map ✉ Ballyarnet, 1.5 miles beyond Foyle Bridge, off B194 ☎ 028 7135 4040 🕐 Center: Mon.–Thu. 9–4:30, Fri 9–1 (call to confirm); wildlife sanctuary: Mon.–Fri. 9–dusk, Sat.–Sun. 9–4:30 🎟 Free; sanctuary: donation

MOUNTAINS OF MOURNE

The Mourne Heritage Trust at Newcastle provides lots of information and guided walks. One of the nature trails follows the "Brandy Pad," a notorious smugglers' route that links Hilltown, notable for its many pubs, with the coast south of Newcastle. There is more woodland in the Tollymore and Castlewellan Forest parks. Castlewellan is an outstanding feature with a 3-mile trail around the lake that features scultpures created from the park's natural materials. There are tropical birds and the world's longest and largest hedge. To the south the beautiful stone-walled countryside is evocatively named Silent Valley.

Slieve Donard, at 2,800 feet, is the highest mountain, and clothing its slopes is the Donard Forest Park. It's a gorgeous 8-mile drive up to and around the thickly wooded Slieve Gullion Forest Park. Walkers who follow the mountaintop trail will be rewarded by views of the Ring of Gullion and both the Mourne and Cooley mountains. Two dams form the Silent Valley and Ben Crom reservoirs, which supply 30 million gallons of water daily to County Down and Belfast. This is worth a visit just for the scenery, which includes lovely parkland before the dams. During July and August, a shuttle bus runs from the information center to the top of nearby Ben Crom.

Eastern coastal resorts of Dundrum, Annalong and Kilkeel provide alternative bases to Newcastle. Dundrum Castle, built by John de Courcy about 1177, is one of Northern Ireland's finest Norman castles. From its hilltop perch, the castle overlooks Dundrum Bay, with splendid views of the sea and the Mourne mountains. Bird-watchers should visit Murlough Nature Reserve where sea birds and a wide variety of botanical specimens flourish in an outstanding habitat of woodland and heath surrounded by the estuary and the sea. You can opt for organized guided walks or follow a self-guided marked trail.

The wild, steep granite hills of the Mountains of Mourne present an unforgettable aspect when seen across Carlingford Lough from the Republic. One of several fortifications guarding the entrance to the lough is Greencastle and it has not had an easy time over the centuries. It was besieged by Edward the Bruce in 1316, sacked twice in the 14th century, later garrisoned for Elizabeth I, fell to Cromwell in 1652 and then fell into disuse. In today's more peaceful climate, the castle offers terrific views of the lough and the mountains.

There are number of literary associations in this area too. Before moving to Yorkshire, Patrick Brontë, father of the novelist sisters, taught at Drumballyroney school and preached in the local church; both structures have been preserved. Brontë was born in 1777 at Emdale, and the 8-mile Homeland Drive starts from this point.

If you are visiting the Mountains of Mourne, cross over into Inniskeen, in the next-door county of Monaghan, to the birthplace of Patrick Kavanagh, one of Ireland's greatest poets, who was often inspired by its rich heritage of legends and myths, as well as the physical demands the stony land made on rural life in the county. In the old parish church that was frequented by Kavanagh, now a resource center, the colorful past of this part of Ireland and the poet's own background are recounted in exhibitions and there is an extensive research library.

➕ C2

Annalong's deep-water harbor sits beneath the Mountains of Mourne

Mourne Heritage Trust ✉ 87 Central Promenade, Newcastle, Co Down ☎ 028 4372 4059 🕐 Mon.–Fri. 9–5 💷 Free

Castlewellan Forest Park ✉ Main Street, Castlewellan ☎ 028 4377 8664 🕐 Daily 10–dusk 💷 $$

Slieve Gullion Forest Park ✉ 5 miles southwest of Newry on B30 ☎ 028 3755 1277 🕐 Daily 10–dusk, Easter–Sep. 🍴 Café 💷 Car: $$

Silent Valley Mountain Park ✉ Head Road, Annalong, Co. Down ☎ 028 9074 1166 🕐 Daily 10–6:30, Easter–Sep.; 10–4, rest of year. 🍴 Restaurant 💷 $

Dundrum Castle ✉ 5 miles north of Newcastle, Co. Down ☎ 028 4372 2222 🕐 Tue.–Sat. 10–6, Sun. 2–6, Apr.–Sep.; Sat. 10–4, Sun. 2–4, rest of year 💷 $$

Murlough Nature Reserve ✉ 2 miles south of Dundrum on A24, Co. Down ☎ 028 4375 1467 🕐 Reserve always open; center: daily 10–5 (weather permitting), May to mid-Sep. 💷 Free

Greencastle ✉ Kilkeel, Co. Down (4 miles southwest of town, off A2) ☎ 028 4372 2222 🕐 Tue.–Sat. 10–6, Sun. 2–6, Jul.–Aug. 💷 $

Bronte Homeland Interpretative Centre ✉ Drumballyroney, Rathfriland, Co. Down (9 miles southeast of Banbridge, off B10) ☎ 028 4063 1152 or 028 4062 3322 🕐 Tue.–Fri. 11–5, Sat.–Sun. 2–6, mid-Mar.–Sep. 💷 $$

Patrick Kavanagh Rural and Resource Centre ✉ Innishkeen, Co. Monaghan ☎ 042 937 8560 🕐 Mon.–Fri. 11–5, Sun. 2–7 💷 $$

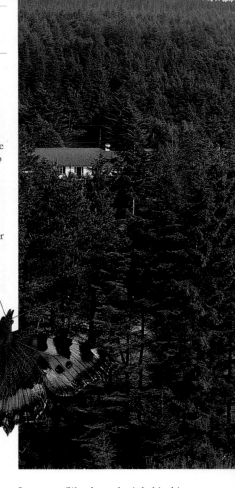

OMAGH

Omagh has long been an important
center for the extensive agricultural
area which surrounds it. High Street is
the undisputed heart of the town, with
the best shops and architecture, but the
Strule River is a major artery, with some
fine old bridges and excellent views of the
city. The best townscapes include a group
of four churches, the most prominent
being the Church of the Sacred Heart
with its twin asymmetric towers. To the
north of the town are two museums,
which are among the top attractions in
Northern Ireland. The well-known Ulster
American Folk Park is a unique
outdoor museum
that has as its
main theme
the history of
18th- and
19th-century
emigration from
Ulster to North
America. Rural
Ulster thatched
cottages contrast
with log cabins in the
New World, and there's
a full-scale replica of an emigrant
ship at a dock surrounded by buildings
from the Ulster ports of Londonderry,
Belfast and Newry. Reconstructions
include the ancestral home of the Mellon
family of Pittsburgh, whose forefathers
were from Ulster. They endowed the folk
park, as well as the home of John Joseph
Hughes, the first Catholic archbishop of
New York, who was instrumental in
building St. Patrick's Cathedral in New
York City. The Ulster History Park puts
you right into the widely varying stages of
Ulster history from the Stone Age (8,000
BC) to the 17th-century Plantation Period.
You can enter the full-scale models of
buildings, crannogs, and a plantation
manor house, and see megalithic tombs.

When you have had your fill of
history, take a 5-mile drive through the
woodlands of Gortin Glen Forest Park,
with its off-the-road scenic viewing
points. En route, keep an eye out for
wildfowl and an unusual herd of

Japaneese Sika deer who inhabit this
forest park. The visitor center supplies
informative booklets. Alternatively, given
Ireland's unpredictable weather, Aladdin's
Kingdom, a children's adventure
playground, can be a welcome alternative
if you have children. There are pendulum
swings, a spiral glide, crawl tunnels, a
mountain climb, rope bridges and even
a haunted house.

Omagh's other attractions lie east
toward Cookstown. You'll hear all about
"scutching," "hackling," "weaving" and
"beetling" at the linen-making
demonstrations at Wellbrook Beetling
Mill. Beetling, the final part of the
process, is when the cloth is beaten
unmercifully with wooden hammers, or
beetles, to produce a sheen. "Linen-speak"

Ulster History Park has fascinating models of hide huts, ancient farms and stockades
Inset: Small tortoiseshell butterfly

has been used in this water-powered hammer mill since the 18th century, when it must have been literally deafening for the employees.

Nearby is Drum Manor Forest Park, a haven for nature lovers, featuring a shrub garden, an arboretum, a lake, heronry, a walled butterfly garden and a self-guided nature trail.

✚ B2

Tourist information ✉ 1 Market Street ☎ 028 8224 7831 ◉ Mon.–Sat. 9–5

Ulster American Folk Park ✉ Castletown, on A5, 3 miles north of Omagh ☎ 028 8224 3292 ◉ Mon.–Sat. 11–6:30, Sun. 11–7, Easter–Sep.; Mon.–Fri. 10:30–5, rest of year 🍴 Café 🚻 $$

Ulster History Park ✉ Cullion, Co. Tyrone (on B48, 7 miles north of Omagh) ☎ 028 8164 8188 ◉ Daily 10–6:30, Jul.–Aug.; 10–5:30, Apr.–Jun. and Sep.; Mon.–Fri. 10–5, rest of year; last admission 1 hour before closing 🍴 Restaurant 🚻 $$

Gortin Glen Forest Park ✉ 7 miles north of Omagh on B48 ☎ 028 8167 0666 ◉ Daily 10–dusk 🍴 Café 🚻 Parking: $$

Aladdin's Kingdom ✉ Mountjoy Road, north out of Omagh ☎ 028 8225 1550 ◉ Sun.–Thu. 2–6:30, Fri. 3–7:30, Sat. 10:30–6:30 🚻 $

Wellbrook Beetling Mill ✉ 23 miles east of Omagh off A505 ☎ 028 8674 8210 or 8675 1735 ◉ Daily noon–6, Jul.–Aug.; Sat.–Sun. noon–6, mid-Mar.–Jun. Sep. 🚻 $$

Drum Manor Forest Park ✉ 23 miles east of Omagh on A505 towards Omagh ☎ 028 8676 2774 or 8775 9311 ◉ Daily 8–dusk 🚻 Parking $$

Ulster and Northern Ireland

The Sperrin Mountains

Nobel Prize-winning poet Seamus Heaney grew up on the edge of the Sperrin Mountains, and their softly rounded beauty figures in much of his work. The range, bounded by the towns of Omagh, Magherafelt, Cookstown and Strabane, runs about 40 miles east to west, and the highest point rises only 2,240 feet at Sawel. Although the hillsides tend to be a bit bare, you can drive through the fertile, wooded valleys for as much as 200 miles.

Nature is the focal point at Sperrin Heritage Centre, and natural history and gold-mining exhibits may well whet your appetite for a little panning for gold yourself. Pans are available for you to dabble in the iron pyrite stream, but what you're likely to get is "fool's gold," not the real stuff. South of the mountain range is the mysterious complex of ritualistic stone circles at Beaghmore. The three pairs of circles, a single circle, and stone rows known as "alignments" were discovered in AD 130, but are believed to date back to the Bronze Age or possibly earlier.

Discovered beneath a peat layer, the origins of the Beaghmore Stone Circles are still unknown

West of the mountains, near Strabane, is the Wilson Ancestral Home. Judge James Wilson, grandfather of Woodrow Wilson, 28th president of the United States and an early winner of the Nobel Prize, left for America in 1807 from this small thatched whitewashed cottage. Members of the Wilson family still live next door in a modern farmhouse. The cottage holds some of the original furniture, including a portrait of James Wilson and large curtained beds.

A good source of reliable information on the Sperrin Mountains is Altmore Open Farm, where in addition to guided tours of the farm, there are facilities for fly fishing, crazy golf and pony rides. The thatched cottage on this sheep farm is a museum reflecting rural life in this area. ✚ B3

Sperrin Heritage Centre ⊠ 274 Glenelly Road, Cranagh, Gortin, Co. Tyrone (on B47, 9 miles east of Plumbridge) ☎ 028 8164 8142 ⏱ Mon.–Fri. 11–5:30, Sat. 11:30–6, Sun. 2–6, Apr.–Oct. 🍴 Café 💷 $$

Beaghmore Stone Circles ⊠ Between Cookstown and Gortin, Co. Tyrone (signposted off A505)

Wilson Ancestral Home ⊠ Dergalt, 2 miles southeast of Strabane, off Plumbridge road ☎ 028 7138 2204 ⏱ Tue.–Sun. 2–5, Jul. and Aug. 💷 $

Altmore Open Farm ⊠ 32 Altmore Road, Pomeroy (3 miles south of Pomeroy, signposted) ☎ 028 8775 8977 ⏱ Daily 9–dusk 🍴 Café 💷 $

Ulster and Northern Ireland

The bewitching coastline from Doah Isle, where the elements have cut myriad shapes in the rock

THE INISHOWEN PENINSULA

Buffeted by the Atlantic Ocean, the long stretches of sandy beaches make up the Inishowen peninsula, Ireland's northernmost point. Backed by sheer cliffs, inland are some of the country's most impressive mountains. The peninsula's heritage reaches back beyond recorded history, leaving relics of those distant days scattered across its face.

On the 800-foot-high Greenan Mountain sits the Grianan of Aileach, an ancient stone circular fort *(cashel)* affording spectacular panoramic views of this part of Ulster. As far as archeologists can determine, the dry stone structure was built about 1700 BC and during the Iron Age served as a temple of the sun. High kings of Ireland regarded it as a sacred spot. At the foot of the access road, Burt church's circular design follows that of the fort itself. The church houses the visitor center, which has information on the eventful past of this mysterious fort.

A few miles to the north, at the little resort town of Fahan, the old graveyard holds a flat, two-faced cross from the seventh century and two rather curious carved stones.

Buncrana is the principal town of Inishowen, the ruins of 16th-century Buncrana Castle, where Wolfe Tone was imprisoned after his capture in 1798, overlook the Crana River. Close by are the ruins of O'Doherty's Castle. North of Buncrana is Dunree Head and Fort Dunree, a restored coastal defense battery that commands superb views of Lough Swilly, and was in use from the Napoleonic era to the departure of the British militia in 1938.

Magheramore Hill near Clonmany is the home of the huge capstone of a Bronze Age dolmen and reputed to have been thrown by Ireland's legendary giant hero, hence its local name of "Finn McCool's Finger Stone." North of Clonmany in the delightful seaside resort of Ballyliffin. Irish music nights are often held in local hotels and pubs.

The prosperous town of Carndonagh has been an important ecclesiastical center since the fifth century. The striking 1945 Church of the Sacred Heart holds exceptionally fine statuary by the famous sculptor Albert Power, and the nearby Church of Ireland occupies a site on which St. Patrick founded one of his churches. If you're picnicking, there's a picnic area in lovely woods on the outskirts of town on the Ballyliffin side.

A drive to Malin Head takes you as far north as you can go on Ireland's mainland. While this northerly point lacks the spectacular clifftop heights you've seen en route, it provides marvelous panoramic views of the peninsula and the sea. Southwards takes you through the picturesque village of Culdaff with lovely sandy beaches to Moville.

Grianan of Aileach ✉ Signposted from Burt, 3 miles south of Bridgend, 10 miles south of Buncrana on N13 Letterkenny/Londonderry road (main access to Inishowen peninsula) ☎ 077 68080; fax 077 68012 🕐 Daily 10–7, summer; 10–4:30, winter 🍽 Restaurant 💷 $$

If there's anything the Irish love it's a good story. It seems only natural, then, that gaps in their long history are quickly filled with stories that evolve into legends. At the top of the list is the legend of Fionn MacCumhaill, "The Fair One," whose name has several spellings, the easiest of which is simply Finn MacCool. Was he a real man who lived in the third century, or a figment of the lively Irish immagination

Ireland's legendary hero

FINN MACCOOL

of the highest moral character and courage. Even today you may run across a huge stone in a field believed by locals to have been flung there by Finn or one of the Fianna, and there are those who will tell you that the Isle of Man is actually a sod of Irish soil hurled by Finn MacCool, leaving a great hole that became the largest of Glendalough's sparkling lakes.

His stories are legend, but by far the most widely told (and half believed) is the one of the Giant's Causeway. Forget the scientific theory behind its creation (see page 178), as far as the Irish are concerned, the causeway would still be above water all the way across had it not been for a ferocious tiff between the Ulster giant, Finn MacCool, and his Scottish counterpart, Finn Gall. Finn MacCool actually built the causeway, but when he went home to rest, the wily Scotsman tripped across, club in hand, to catch his foe unawares. When Finn Gall burst into Mrs. MacCool's kitchen and demanded to know if the sleeping giant was her husband, she – in a master stroke of quick thinking – assured him that it was only her wee baby. Imagining the father of such a gigantic babe put such a fright into the Scotsman that he hightailed it back across the water, destroying the causeway behind him to keep Finn MacCool in Ireland where he belonged. Fact or fiction, either way you'll agree, it is one whale of a story!

To learn more about Ireland's intriguing, legendary figures, look for Lady Gregory's fascinating book *Gods and Fighting Men*, published by Colin Smythe and available in bookshops specializing in Irish publications.

whose exploits were first written about in the seventh and eighth centuries? That weighty question matters not one whit to the Irish – he is their hero, real or fanciful fiction, and that is that.

Decended from the gods through his mother, he was of gigantic statue, noble of nature, and fearless in battle. He also possessed infinite wisdom and accumulated the knowledge of the ages. The story goes that while cooking the Salmon of Knowledge, Finn burned his thumb and stuck it in his mouth to ease the pain, whereupon the salmon's wisdom became his own. From then on, he had only to put his thumb in his mouth to find the answer to any perplexing matter.

Finn was also a romantic who rescued his beloved wife Saba from an enchantment that had turned her into a fawn. They had seven supremely happy years together before she fell victim to a wicked spell while she was carrying Finn's son Oisin, and the story of the boy's birth and return to his father through a magical sequence of events forms an important element of Finn's legend.

One of his most significant acheivements was the gathering of his Fianna band of faithful and skilled warriors (this is where the modern-day Fianna Fail political party gets its name)

HOTELS AND RESTAURANTS

The hotels and restaurants in this book were selected by local specialists and include establishments in several price ranges. Since price is often the best indication of the level of facilities and quality of service, a three-tiered price guide appears at the beginning of the listings. Because variable rates will affect the amount of foreign currency that can be exchanged for dollars (and therefore affect the cost of the room or meal), price ranges are given in the local currency.

Although price ranges and operating times were accurate at press time, this information is always subject to change without notice. If you're interested in a particular establishment, it is always advisable to call ahead to book.

Facilities suitable for travelers with disabilities vary greatly, and you are strongly advised to contact an establishment directly to determine whether it can meet your needs. Older buildings may not be adequately designed or equipped for visitors with limited or impaired mobility.

Accommodations

Accommodations have been selected with two considerations in mind: a particular sense of character or sense of local flavor, or a central location that is convenient for sightseeing. Remember that centrally located hotels fill up quickly, especially during busy summer vacation periods; make reservations well in advance. In-room bathrooms (sometimes referred to as "en-suite bathrooms") may not be available in budget hotels. Room rates normally include a full breakfast meal of bacon, sausage, eggs, fried potatoes and toast that should leave you feeling well-fed most of the day. Some hotels offer a price for overnight accomodations that includes an evening meal (known as "half-board" in Ireland).

Eating Out

Listed restaurants range from upscale places suitable for an elegant evening out to small cafés where you can stop and take a leisurely break from a busy day of sightseeing. Most Irish meals are meat based, although some enticing vegetarian alternatives are now finding a place on the menus in town and city restaurants A delicious tradition not to be missed is the popular plate of oysters accompanied by a pint of Guinness. You can sample epicurian seafood delights in Kinsale, often considered to be Ireland's gourmet capital.

Powerscourt Town House in Dublin is a delightful shopping mall with a selection of eateries

Connacht

KEY TO SYMBOLS

- ⊞ hotel
- ⫪ restaurant
- ✉ address
- ☎ telephone number
- ◔ days/times closed
- AX American Express
- DC Diners Club
- MC MasterCard
- VI VISA

Hotel

Price guide: double room with breakfast for two people:

- **$$$** over €180
- **$$** €110–€180
- **$** up to €110

Restaurant

Price guide: dinner per person, excluding drinks

- **$$$** over €50
- **$$** €25–€50
- **$** under €25

THREE SQUARE A DAY

Traditionally the Irish have always had their heartiest meal at midday. That's primarily because, as an agricultural nation, those working in the fields felt the need for sustenance to see them through a long afternoon. Lunch ("dinner" to the Irish) was the main meal, and the early evening "tea" was often as light as soup and brown bread or sandwiches. That still holds true today, and a full restaurant or pub lunch will provide as much to eat as most dinners. However, Irish eating habits have changed, and if you are simply not ready for a full meal at midday after that sumptuous breakfast, just look for the nearest pub offering "pub grub," order a cup of hearty soup and a sandwich or salad plate and save your main meal for the evening.

Connacht

BALLINASLOE, CO. GALWAY

⊞ Hayden's Gateway $$

Built around 1803, this fine hotel offers excellent service. Meals are served throughout the day, either in the Gorbally Restaurant or the award-winning coffee shop.
✉ On the N6, Dublin–Galway Road
☎ 0905 42347; fax 0905 42347
◔ Closed Dec. 24–26 AX, DC, MC, VI

BALLYCONNEELY, CLIFDEN, CO. GALWAY

⫪ Erriseask House $–$$

Award-winning classical-style restaurant overlooking the sea. Local produce is used creatively in dishes such as fillet of smoked beef, Connemara lamb and local seafood.
✉ 7 miles south of Clifden on Clifden–Ballyconneely coast road
☎ 095 23553 ◔ Dinner only. Not suitable for children under 10 AX, DC, MC, VI

BALLYNAHINCH, CO. GALWAY

⊞ Ballynahinch Castle $$$

Ballynahinch stands at the foot of Ben Lettery on the banks of the famous salmon river, the Ballynahinch. The extensive grounds offer woodlands and scenic walks. The individually designed bedrooms are spacious and comfortable, and game and fresh local produce are a treat in the charming restaurant. Facilities include tennis, fishing, croquet, and river and lakeside walks.
✉ From N59, take Roundstone exit – hotel is 3 miles from turnoff
☎ 095 31006; fax 095 31085
◔ Closed Feb. and Dec. 20–26 AX, DC, MC, VI

CASTLEBAR, CO. MAYO

⊞ Welcome Inn $–$$

This town-center hotel offers a range of modern facilities behind its Tudor frontage. The bedrooms are spacious and well equipped and you can enjoy traditional music played in the nightclub on summer evenings.
✉ N5 to Castlebar. Hotel is just past the Church of the Holy Rosary
☎ 094 22288; fax 094 21766
◔ Closed Dec. 24–27 AX, MC, VI

CLIFDEN, CO. GALWAY

⊞ Alcock and Brown $$

The bar and restaurant are particularly inviting and pleasant in this comfortable town-center hotel. The extensive menu offers many fish specialties and service is friendly.
✉ N59 Galway–Clifden road via Oughterard ☎ 095 21206; fax 095 21842 ◔ Closed Dec. 22–26 AX, DC, MC, VI

⫪ O'Grady's Seafood Restaurant $–$$

This is Clifden's oldest restaurant, and it has won all kinds of awards, including the Bórd Fáilte Tourist Excellence Award. Chef Elliot Fox produces modern Irish cuisine with seafood and vegetarian specialties.
✉ Lower Market Street ☎ 095 21450 ◔ Closed Sun. and Nov.–Apr. AX, DC, MC, VI

⊞ Quay House $$

The Quay House is Clifden's oldest building, constructed around 1820. It comprises 14 individually furnished rooms, some with balconies and working fireplaces. It also has a wonderful collection of Georgian furniture and family portraits. Just seven minutes walk into town. Fishing, golf and pony-rides are all nearby.
✉ Beach Road ☎ 095 21369; fax 095 21608 ◔ Closed early Nov. to mid-Mar. MC, VI

COLLOONEY, CO. SLIGO

⊞ Markree Castle $$$

This magnificent castle dates back to 1640. Restoration work has transformed this grand building into a hotel with the imposing Knockmuldowney Restaurant. Facilities include horseback riding.
✉ Off N4 at Collooney crossroads just north of the N17 exit, 7 miles south of Sligo. Hotel gates on right side after half a mile ☎ 071 67800; fax 071 67840 ◔ Closed Dec. 24–27 AX, DC, MC, VI

GALWAY, CO. GALWAY

⫪ Galleon $

Small, cozy restaurant with widely varied menu emphasizing seafood, grills, Irish and vegetarian dishes.
✉ Salthill ☎ 091 522 963 AX, MC, VI

Connacht, Leinster

🏨 Glenlo Abbey $$$
Standing in a landscaped 134-acre estate, this restored 18th-century abbey overlooks a beautiful loch. The bedrooms are in a modern wing along with a library, restaurants, cocktail and cellar bars. Leisure facilities are situated in the grounds and include golf, fishing, boating and clay-pigeon shooting.
✉ Bushypark – 2.5 miles from Galway city center on N59 ☎ 091 526 666; fax 091 527 800 AX, DC, MC, VI

🍴 Kirwan's Lane $$
Very popular with locals. The chef-proprietor features international dishes adapted to local ingredients. Reservations required.
✉ Kirwan's Lane ☎ 091 568 266 🕐 Closed Sun. AX, MC, VI

🍴 McSwiggans $
An upstairs restaurant features seafood, sirloin steak, pork and grilled food. Bar food is served in ground-floor pub.
✉ 3 Eyre Street ☎ 091 568 917 🕐 Closed Good Friday AX, DC, MC, VI

🍴 The Malt House $$$
Local favorite. Traditional fare plus vegetarian menu. Hot seafood dishes such as pan-fried crab claws and garlic mussels are outstanding.
✉ Old Malt Shopping Mall, High Street (in quiet deadend) ☎ 091 567 866 🕐 Closed Sun. AX, DC, MC, VI

🏨 Victoria $$$
Bedrooms are well equipped; facilities include 24-hour room service, a good bar and pleasant restaurant. Friendly atmosphere.
✉ Beside railroad station, Victoria Place, off Eyre Square ☎ 091 567 433; fax 091 565 880 AX, MC, VI

KILCOLGAN, CO. GALWAY

🍴 Moran's Oyster Cottage $
Internationally famed seafood restaurant in a 200-year-old thatched cottage. Oysters are a specialty, with smoked salmon and mussel soup featured.
✉ The Weir, about 10 miles south of Galway town, signposted from N18 (Galway–Limerick road) ☎ 091 796 113 🕐 Closed Good Friday and Dec. 25 AX, MC, VI

ROSCOMMON, CO. ROSCOMMON

🏨 Abbey $$
Set in its own grounds just outside Roscommon, this fine manor house dates back more than 100 years. The bedrooms are well decorated, with a choice of period-style rooms in the original part of the house, while those in the newer wing are more contemporary. Service is attentive and the hotel has a friendly atmosphere. Popular brasserie-style restaurant. Traditonal home-cooked meals feature local ingredients such as beef, lamb and pork.
✉ Just outside Roscommon on N63 Galway Road, opposite railroad station ☎ 0903 26240; fax 0903 26021 🕐 Closed Dec. 25–26 AX, DC, MC, VI

ROUNDSTONE, CO. GALWAY

🏨 Eldons $$
This distinctive building stands on the main street of a picturesque fishing village. Guests receive a warm welcome and good service. The seafood restaurant, Beola, serves a good choice of dishes.
✉ Off N59 through Toombedla to Roundstone village ☎ 095 35933; fax 095 35722 🕐 Closed Nov. 3–Mar. 14 AX, DC, MC, VI

SLIGO, CO. SLIGO

🍴 Bistro Bianconi $
Pleasant informal restaurant with heavy emphasis on Italian and international dishes that include quite spicy meals.
✉ 44 O'Connell Street (on main street) ☎ 071 41744 🕐 Dinner only. Closed Sun., Good Friday and Dec. 2–26 AX, DC, MC, VI

🏨 Silver Swan $$
A family-owned hotel beside the Garavogue River in the heart of Sligo. The bedrooms are well furnished, and some include spa baths. The Horseshoe Bar is a popular spot for snacks and drinks and there is a parking lot to the rear.
✉ Hyde Bridge, in city center beside the post office, at the intersection between N4, N15 and N16 ☎ 071 43231; fax 071 42232 🕐 Closed Dec. 25–28 AX, DC, MC, VI

🏨 Sligo Park $$$
Set on seven acres of parkland on the southern edge of Sligo, this hotel is an ideal base for exploring Yeats country. Offering excellent "executive" rooms, there are good beaches, an indoor heated pool, tennis, snooker, sauna, solarium and hot tub.
✉ Pearse Road, on N4 ☎ 071 60291; fax 071 69556 AX, DC, MC, VI

WESTPORT, CO. MAYO

🏨 Knockranny House $$$
Overlooking Westport with Clew Bay in the distance, this family-run hotel makes full use of the lovely views, offering a luxurious lounge, bar and the restaurant, La Fougère, offers excellent seafood.
✉ N5 Westport–Castlebar Road, close to Westport ☎ 098 28600; fax 098 28611 🕐 Closed Dec. 23–27 AX, MC, VI

🍴 Quay Cottage $
Charming quayside restaurant known for its seafood chowder, choice fish dishes, mountain lamb and steaks. Excellent vegetarian choices.
✉ The Harbour (beside gate to Westport House) ☎ 098 26412 🕐 Dinner only. Closed Sun. and Mon. in winter, Jan., Dec. 24–26 AX, MC, VI

Leinster

ARTHURSTOWN, CO. WEXFORD

🏨 Dunbrody Country House and Restaurant $$–$$$
Surrounded by parkland, you can expect tranquility and generous hospitality in this elegant Georgian manor house. The bedrooms are individually styled and there is an award-winning restaurant, beaches nearby, golf, horseback riding, croquet and clay-pigeon shooting.
✉ From N11 follow signs for Duncannon and Ballyhack (R733). Hotel is 20 miles on from the turnoff. Turn left at gate lodge on approaching Arthurstown ☎ 051 389 600; fax 051 389 601 🕐 Closed Dec. 25–27 AX, DC, MC, VI

BETTYSTOWN, CO. MEATH

🏨 Neptune Beach Hotel and Leisure Club $$$
Overlooking the sea with access to a

Leinster

KEY TO SYMBOLS

- 🏨 hotel
- 🍴 restaurant
- ✉ address
- ☎ telephone number
- ⏰ days/times closed
- 🚉 nearby train or bus route(s).
- AX   American Express
- DC   Diners Club
- MC   MasterCard
- VI   VISA

Hotel
Price guide: double room with breakfast for two people:
$$$ over €180
$$ €110–€180
$ up to €110

Restaurant
Price guide: dinner per person, excluding drinks
$$$ over €50
$$ €25–€50
$ under €25

CHANGING TASTES

There is little doubt that tourism has had a notable impact on the cuisine in Ireland. Until recently there was hardly any tradition of eating out, except on rare occasions at a local hotel. Patterns of diet were conservative, based on "meat and two veg" (somewhat overcooked), potatoes (of course) and large quantities of dairy fat. Now demands for predictable, inexpensive fast food are met, as everywhere, with burgers and pizzas – a better bet being fish and chips (fries). The restaurant scene reflects the country's broadening cosmopolitan population, and French, Italian, Chinese, Russian and Indian restaurants have blossomed throughout the country. Sophisticated tastes have also introduced whole foods and vegetarian restaurants – once unheard of. In fact it seems hard to imagine the grim days of the 19th century when so many of the population were starving and food preparation amounted to little more than boiling a potato!

sandy beach. Many bedrooms enjoy sea views and facilities include an indoor heated pool, sauna, solarium and gym.
✉ Bettystown. Off N1 Dublin–Belfast Road ☎ 041 982 7107; fax 041 982 7412 AX, MC, VI

DUBLIN, CO. DUBLIN

🏨 The Clarence $$$
The hotel is located in the heart of Dublin city center within walking distance of many restaurants and theaters, galleries, museums, shopping areas and Temple Bar. This is an individual and very tasteful hotel offering richly furnished bedrooms. For sheer luxury, the two-bedroom penthouse suite is outstanding, and the public area has a long gallery. The bar is smart and the restaurant serves fine cuisine.
✉ 6–8 Wellington Quay ☎ 01 407 0800; fax 01 407 0820 ⏰ Closed Dec. 24–26 AX, DC, MC, VI

🍴 Le Coq Hardi $$
Top-ranking restaurant for classic French dishes and innovations to traditional Irish cuisine. Service and decor are elegant and sophisticated. Superb coq au vin and baked white fishes with a whiskey cream sauce. Outstanding wine list.
✉ 35 Pembroke Road, Ballsbridge ☎ 01 668 9070 ⏰ Closed Sun., 2 weeks in Aug. and Christmas AX, DC, MC, VI

🍴 L'Ecrivain $$–$$$
Fine restaurant with emphasis on superb classic French cuisine. Excellent desserts. Good wine list. Reservations recommended.
✉ 109A Lower Baggot Street (near Merrion Square) ☎ 01 661 1919 🚉 10 or 5-minute walk from St. Stevens Green AX, DC, MC, VI

🏨 Harding $
At the heart of the fascinating Temple Bar area of Dublin, this friendly, purpose-built hotel offers a Peruvian-style bar and Fitzers Restaurant, which have become popular meeting places.
✉ Copper Alley, Fishamble Street, Temple Bar ☎ 01 679 6500; fax 01 679 6504 ⏰ Closed Dec. 23–27 AX, MC, VI

🍴 Locks Restaurant $$
Country house-style, canalside

restaurant featuring classical and country French and New Irish cuisine. Fish soup and roast loin of lamb with dauphinoise potatoes, caramelized onions, mushrooms and rosemary sauce are specialties.
✉ 01 454 3391 ⏰ Closed from Easter Sun for one week and Dec. 24–Jan. 6 AX, DC, MC, VI

🏨 Longfield's $$$
This intimate townhouse hotel lies close to the city center and serves good food.
✉ Fitzwilliam Street. Take Shelbourne Hotel exit from St. Stephens Green, continue down Baggot Street for half a mile, turn left at Fitzwilliam Street exit. The hotel is on the left ☎ 01 6761367; fax 01 6761542 ⏰ Closed Dec. 24–27 AX, DC, MC, VI

🍴 The Lord Edward $$
This informally elegant, upstairs restaurant is one of Dublin's oldest, with a traditional menu featuring a host of seafood dishes (their specialty) balanced by an excellent Irish stew, and corned beef and cabbage.
✉ 22 Christchurch Place (in the Liberties, near Christ Church Cathedral) ☎ 01 454 2420 ⏰ Closed Sun. and Dec. 24–Jan. 2 AX, DC, MC, VI

🏨 Marine $$$
On the north shore of Dublin Bay with attractive gardens and seashore walks, this hotel features spacious public rooms and well-equipped bedrooms. It is near to the Sutton rapid railroad into the city center and the famous Portmarnock Golf Course; there is an indoor heated pool and sauna.
✉ Sutton Cross. Take road from M1 toward Dublin city center, turn off at 2nd exit for Coolocil, continue until T-junction and turn left, after 1 mile the hotel is on right ☎ 01 839 0000, fax 01 839 0442 ⏰ Closed Dec. 25–27 AX, DC, MC, VI

🏨 The Merrion $$$
The four Georgian townhouses, with a modern garden wing, include an indoor heated pool, gym and steam room.
✉ Upper Merrion Street, on the east side, beyond government buildings on the right side

Leinster

☎ 01 603 0600; fax 01 603 0700
AX, DC, MC, VI

🏨 Temple Bar $$$

This stylish hotel in the heart of old Dublin is ideally situated for experiencing the cultural life of the city. Comfortable bedrooms are competitively priced, and good food is served throughout the day.
✉ Fleet Street, Temple Bar. From Trinity College, head for O'Connell Bridge and take the 1st left onto Fleet Street. Hotel is on the left ☎ 01 677 3333; fax 01 677 3088 ⊘ Closed Dec. 24–27 AX, DC, MC, VI

DUNDALK, CO. LOUTH

🏨 Ballymascanlon House $$–$$$

A Victorian mansion whose 130-acre grounds include an 18-hole golf course. Use the elegant restaurant and spacious lounge. There is a new wing of luxurious bedrooms, an indoor heated pool, tennis, sauna, gym and hot tub.
✉ North of Dundalk take T62 to Carlingford ☎ 042 937 1124; fax 042 937 1598 ⊘ Closed Dec. 24–27 AX, DC, MC, VI

DUN LAOGHAIRE, CO. DUBLIN

🏨 Royal Marine $$$

Set on 4 acres overlooking Dun Laoghaire harbor with easy access to Dublin city center, the Victorian Royal Marine is a local landmark and features a restaurant, bars, the popular Bay Lounge, attractive gardens and a gym.
✉ Marine Road (follow signs for "Car Ferry") ☎ 01 280 1911; fax 01 280 1089 🚆 DART, south of Dublin AX, DC, MC, VI

ENNISCORTHY, CO. WEXFORD

🏨 Riverside Park $$

In a picturesque position beside the River Slaney, the hotel is easily distinguished by its terracotta and blue color scheme. Public areas, including the dramatic lobby, take full advantage of the riverside views. The spacious, attractively decorated bedrooms have every convenience.
✉ The Promenade. One third mile from Newbridge, center of Enniscorthy, N11 Dublin–Rosslare

Road ☎ 054 3780; fax 054 37900 ⊘ Closed Dec. 24–26 AX, DC, MC, VI

GOREY, CO. WEXFORD

🏨 Marlfield House $$$

This distinctive Regency house was once the residence of the Earl of Courtown. Bedrooms are in keeping with the luxurious and well-proportioned day rooms, which include a library, drawing room, dining room and conservatory. Druids Glen and several golf courses are nearby.
✉ 1 mile outside Gorey on the Courtown Harbour Road ☎ 055 21124; fax 055 21572 ⊘ Closed Dec. 15–Jan. 25 AX, DC, MC, VI

HOWTH, CO. DUBLIN

🍴 Abbot Restaurant $$

Adjacent to a 16th-century pub. The decor features fires, gas lights and original stone walls. Excellent variety of seafood creations and traditional Irish meals. Try the seafood chowder and brown bread. Irish music every night.
✉ Abbey Street (9 miles from Dublin city center) ☎ 01 839 0307 ⊘ Closed Good Friday and Dec. 25 🚆 DART, north of Dublin AX, DC, MC, VI

KILKENNY, CO. KILKENNY

🏨 Club House $$–$$$

This 200-year-old hotel has a private parking lot and the suites have all been refurbished. Supervised by the owner, this is a comfortable and friendly hotel, with open fire, Georgian dining room and gym.
✉ Patrick Street, city center, near Kilkenny Castle. ☎ 056 21994; fax 056 71920 ⊘ Closed Dec. 24–27 AX, DC, MC, VI

🏨 Kilkenny $$$

Set on 5 acres of wooded land on the outskirts of Kilkenny, this hotel has refurbished bedrooms and an attractive restaurant with views of the landscaped gardens. There is also a comfortable bar and conservatory lounge. Health club and pool.
✉ College Road. Follow ring road to Callan and Clonmel traffic circle, hotel is on the right ☎ 056 62000; fax 056 65984 AX, DC, MC, VI

KILLINEY, CO. DUBLIN

🏨 Fitzpatrick Castle $$$

This converted castle with modern extensions is set in its own attractive gardens, with views over Dublin Bay. There is an indoor heated pool, sauna, gym, beauty salon, a helipad, and a courtesy bus to and from the Dublin airport. The hotel is only 20 minutes from Dublin city center.
✉ Killiney Hill Road ☎ 01 205 5400 fax 01 230 5466 ⊘ Closed Dec. 24–26 AX, DC, MC, VI

LUCAN, CO. DUBLIN

🏨 Lucan Spa $$

Set in its own grounds, the Lucan Spa is a fine Georgian House where guests have complimentary use of Lucan Golf Course, next to the hotel.
✉ On N4, about 7 miles from city center, 20 minutes from Dublin airport ☎ 01 628 0494; fax 01 628 0841 ⊘ Closed Dec. 25 AX, DC, MC, VI

MULLINGAR, CO. WESTMEATH

🍴 Crookedwood House $$

This whitewashed cellar of a 200-year-old former rectory draws loyal local following. Owner-chef features local beef, lamb, venison and seafood in exquisite dishes. Reservations recommended.
✉ One hour's drive from Dublin, third exit on Mullingar bypass, signposted Castlepollard, to Crookedwood village, turn right at Wood pub, Crookedwood House about 1 mile on right ☎ 044 72165; fax 044 72166 ⊘ Closed three days over Christmas. AX, DC, MC, VI

NEWBRIDGE, CO. KILDARE

🏨 Keadeen $$$

A family-owned hotel set on 9 acres of landscaped gardens and well placed for Dublin airport and the Mondello racing circuit. The hotel is equipped with an indoor heated pool, sauna, solarium, gym, hot-tub and massage. Comfortable public areas include a spacious drawing room, and two bars. Only one mile from the Curragh racecourse.
✉ M7 exit 10 Newbridge, Curragh, towards Newbridge. Hotel is on left, half a mile from traffic circle ☎ 045 431 666; fax 045 434 402 ⊘ Closed Dec. 24–27 AX, DC, MC, VI

KEY TO SYMBOLS

- ⊞ hotel
- ❙❙ restaurant
- ✉ address
- ☎ telephone number
- ⊕ days/times closed
- AX American Express
- DC Diners Club
- MC MasterCard
- VI VISA

Hotel

Price guide: double room with breakfast for two people:
- **$$$** over €180
- **$$** €110–€180
- **$** up to €110

Restaurant

Price guide: dinner per person, excluding drinks
- **$$$** over €50
- **$$** €25–€50
- **$** under €25

IRISH CUISINE

You may be surprised to learn that the hallowed "corned beef and cabbage" is wholly a figment of the Irish American image of Ireland. The Irish tradition is boiled bacon and cabbage, along with Irish stew, made with lamb and absolutely delicious. The equally hallowed potato is still high on the list of Irish culinary preferences, but these days the old spud comes to the table roasted, baked, boiled, mashed or as french fries (call them "chips," potato chips are "crisps"). And far from being the main dish as it was for generations, your potato is accompanied by local beef, lamb, chicken (often a curry), prawns or fish. Salads often include cold meats such as turkey, chicken or ham, and vegetables complete the heaping plates of "mains." Don't-miss foods include locally made cheddar, blue or herb soft cheese. Fish (trout and salmon) can be found throughout the country: Dublin Bay prawns and plaice, a lovely saltwater fish, are specialties and you don't have to be rich to enjoy oysters.

ROSSLARE, CO. WEXFORD

⊞ Kelly's Resort $

This popular seafront hotel sports a leisure center, health treatments, tennis courts, a children's nursery and spacious gardens. Choose between La Marine Bistro and the main award-winning restaurant. Public rooms are adorned with contemporary Irish art.
✉ Town center on seafront ☎ 053 32114; fax 053 32222 ⊕ Closed Dec. to late Feb. AX, MC, VI

SLANE, CO. MEATH

⊞ Conyngham Arms $$

In the picturesque village near the famous prehistoric tombs of New Grange, this hotel is ideal for exploring the historic local area of Tara and the Boyne Valley. Fishing, horseback riding and tennis are available locally.
✉ From N2 turn onto N51, hotel is just on the left ☎ 041 988 4444; fax 041 982 4205 AX, DC, MC, VI

WEXFORD, CO. WEXFORD

❙❙ La Riva $$

Bright, informal upstairs eatery. Blackboard menu features seafood, pasta and rack of lamb.
✉ Crescent Quay ☎ 053 24330 ⊕ Closed lunch, Sep.–mid-May MC, VI

⊞ White's $$–$$$

This former coaching inn has comfortable modern facilities, while it retains much of its historic charm. Entertainment is provided in the converted saddlery and forge.
✉ George Street. On entering Wexford town from the N11 or N25 follow directional signs for Whites ☎ 053 22311; fax 053 45000 AX, DC, MC, VI

WOODENBRIDGE, CO.

⊞ Woodenbridge $

Comfortable hotel in the Vale of Avoca, about an hour's drive from the ferry ports of Dun Laoghaire and Rosslaire and close to the N11. Renovations have given this hotel a new lease on life. Hospitality and good food are the focus of their concerns. Golf and fishing are on the doorstep.

✉ Vale of Avoca. Between Avoca and Arklow ☎ 0402 35146; fax 0402 35573 ⊕ Closed Dec. 25 MC, AX, VI

Munster

BALLYLICKY, CO. CORK

⊞ Sea View $$–$$$

Sample Irish hospitality at this delightful country house overlooking Bantry Bay. Set in well-tended gardens, it has cozy lounges with turf fires and pleasant bedrooms. The hotel is a good touring base for west Cork and Kerry. Award-winning food. Seafood from local waters is excellent; lamb, beef and veal are also featured.
✉ 3 miles from Bantry, 7 miles from Glengarriff on N71 ☎ 027 50073 or 027 50462; fax 027 51555 ⊕ Closed mid-Nov.–mid-Mar. AX, DC, MC, VI

BALLYVAUGHAN, CO. CLARE

⊞ Gregans Castle $$$

At the foot of Corkscrew Hill overlooking Galway Bay, this hotel is in an area rich in archeological, geological and botanical interest. Emphasis is on good food using fresh local produce.
✉ 3.5 miles south of Ballyvaughan on N67 ☎ 065 7077 005; fax 065 7077 111 ⊕ Closed Dec.–mid-Feb. 31 AX, MC, VI

BANTRY, CO. CORK

❙❙ O'Connor's Seafood Restaurant $–$$

Cozy restaurant in the town center. Live-lobster tank and good meat selections. Mussels cordon bleu is very good.
✉ The Square ☎ 027 50221 MC, VI

BLARNEY, CO. CORK

❙❙ Blairs Inn $

Winner of the World Pub Lunch Award, this popular riverside country pub has Irish music on Sundays after 9:30 p.m. Seafood from local waters, local lamb and other meats and game in season.
✉ Cloghroe, Blarney (3.5 miles from Blarney on R578) ☎ 021 381 470 AX, DC, MC, VI

Munster

BUNRATTY, CO. CLARE

🏨 Fitzpatrick Bunratty $$$
Set in picturesque Bunratty with its famous medieval castle, and surrounded by lawns and flowers, this modern ranch-style building is richly timbered inside and has an indoor heated pool, sauna, gym and hot-tub.
✉ Take Bunratty bypass, exit off Limerrick–Shannon divided highway ☎ 061 361177; fax 061 471252 AX, DC, MC, VI

CAHERDANIEL, CO. KERRRY

🏨 Derr $$
Strategically placed halfway around the famous Ring of Kerry, this modern hotel overlooking the sea is relaxed and friendly, and ideal for touring. There is an outdoor heated pool, tennis, fishing, snooker, sauna, solarium, gym and pool table.
✉ 2 minutes walk off the main road ☎ 066 947 5136; fax 066 947 5160 🕐 Closed early Oct. to mid-Apr. AX, DC, MC, VI

CLONAKILTY, CO. CORK

🏨 The Lodge and Spa at Inchydoney Island $$$
Chosen as hotel of the year for Ireland, this luxurious hotel is located on the stunning coastline, with steps down to a sandy beach. Bedrooms are warm, contemporary in style, and many have sea views. There is a cocktail bar, patio, library and restaurant.
✉ N71 West Cork Road to Clonakilty. Take second exit at the traffic circle and follow signs to Lodge and Spa ☎ 023 33143; fax 023 35229 AX, DC, MC, VI

CLONMEL, CO. TIPPERARY

🏨 Minella $$$
This mansion on 9 acres of grounds on the banks of the River Suir has comfortable bedrooms with good views; some bathrooms are furnished with hot tubs.
✉ Colleville Road ☎ 052 22388; fax 052 24381 🕐 Closed Dec. 24–26 AX, DC, MC, VI

CORK, CO. CORK

🏨 Ambassador $$
This distinguished sandstone and granite 19th-century building is a fine hotel with city views. Some bedrooms have balconies, and there is a cocktail lounge, bar and restaurant.
✉ Militry Hill, St. Lukes, just off Wellington Road ☎ 021 455 1996; fax 021 455 1997 🕐 Closed Dec. 24–25 AX, DC, MC, VI

🏨 Arbutus Lodge $$–$$$
This friendly suburban period townhouse overlooks the city and has many bedrooms with period furnishings. The elegant dining room has a good reputation for food and wine. Four suites of rooms with kitchens are ideal for guests who want privacy and the convenience of hotel amenities.
✉ Middle Glanmire Road, Montenotte ☎ 021 450 1237; fax 021 450 2893 🕐 Closed Dec. 24–28 AX, DC, MC, VI

🍴 Isaacs $–$$
Informal restaurant in an 18th-century warehouse. Mediterranean and other international influences, traditional Irish cuisine, daily blackboard specials, and vegetarian specialties are offered.
✉ 48 MacCurtain Street ☎ 021 450 3805 🕐 Closed Christmas week AX, DC, MC, VI

🍴 Restaurant Rossini $–$$
Excellent Italian cuisine. Extensive menu includes some Continental non-Italian dishes. Veal dishes are exceptional.
✉ Princes Street ☎ 021 427 5818 MC, VI

COURTMACSHERRY, CO. CORK

🏨 Courtmacsherry $–$$
This family-run Georgian house is set in attractive grounds near the beach. Quality meals served in the kitchen and a riding school is available to all ages, there are also fishing and tennis facilities.
✉ M71 to Bandon, then R602 to Timoleague – head for Courtmacsherry. Hotel is by the beach at the far end of the town ☎ 023 46198; fax 023 46137 🕐 Closed Oct.–Mar. MC, VI

DOOLIN, CO. CLARE

🏨 Aran View House $$
Situated on 100 acres of rolling farmland and commanding panoramic views of the Aran Islands. A welcoming hotel with a convivial atmosphere, attractive accommodations and comfortably furnished. Enjoy traditional music in the bar three times a week.
✉ Coast Road ☎ 065 707 4061 or 065 707 4420; fax 065 707 4540 🕐 Closed Nov.–Apr. 1 AX, DC, MC, VI

DUNGARVAN, CO. WATERFORD

🏨 Lawlors $
An ideal touring center, this family-run streetside hotel caters to both leisure and business guests. There is live evening entertainment.
✉ Off N25 ☎ 058 41122; fax 058 41000 🕐 Closed Dec. 25 AX, DC, MC, VI

ENNIS, CO. CLARE

🏨 Temple Gate $
This smart new hotel incorporates a 19th-century Gothic-style building with attractive bedrooms. The public areas include a lounge library, Preachers Pub and Le Bistro Restaurant. It shares the grounds with the Clare Museum and is set back from the center of the historic, yet progressive, town of Ennis.
✉ The Square. From Ennis follow signs for Temple Gate ☎ 065 682 3300; fax 065 682 3322 🕐 Closed Dec. 25 AX, DC, MC, VI

GOUGANE BARRA, CO. CORK

🏨 Gougane Barra $$
Right on the lake shore, this hotel is popular for its improved restaurant, bedrooms and bathrooms, all of which have lovely views. Guests can be met from their train, boat or plane by prior arrangement.
✉ Off N22 ☎ 026 47069; fax 026 47226 🕐 Closed mid-Oct. to mid-Apr. AX, DC, MC, VI

KENMARE, CO. KERRY

🏨 Park Hotel Kenmare $$$
This luxurious country house on the famous Ring of Kerry stands above terraced gardens that overlook the estuary of the Kenmare River, with a glorious mountain backdrop. A warm, professional service draws guests back regularly. The restaurant offers very good food and fine

Munster

KEY TO SYMBOLS

🏨	hotel
🍴	restaurant
✉	address
☎	telephone number
🕙	days/times closed
AX	American Express
DC	Diners Club
MC	MasterCard
VI	VISA

Hotel
Price guide: double room with breakfast for two people:
$$$ over €180
$$ €110–€180
$ up to €110

Restaurant
Price guide: dinner per person, excluding drinks
$$$ over €50
$$ €25–€50
$ under €25

THE BEST-VALUE MEAL

One thing is certain: You won't leave Ireland hungry. A "traditional Irish breakfast" (or the "Ulster fry" north of the border) is, simply put, overwhelming. Even if you're a coffee-and-toast person at home, you're not likely to resist the repast spread before your eyes every morning that includes a brimming plateful of bacon, eggs, broiled tomatoes with soda and potato breads and butter. Accommodation rates are nearly always quoted with a full breakfast included, so you might as well stoke up for the day!

---

wines. Leisure facilities include golf, tennis, gym and croquet.
✉ On R569, beside golf course
☎ 064 41200; fax 064 41402
🕙 Closed Jan. 3–Apr. 13 and Oct. 29–Dec. 23   AX, DC, MC, VI

🏨 Riversdale House $$
Nestling on the shores of Kemare Bay, this hotel has wonderful views. Its closeness to the town makes it an ideal base for family excursions. In the bedrooms, floor-length window alcoves take advantage of the clarity of light for which Kenmare is famous.
✉ Kenmare town center. Half a mile west on the Glengarriff Road
☎ 064 41299; fax 064 41075
🕙 Closed Nov.–Mar.   AX, MC

KILLARNEY, CO. KERRY

🏨 Aghadoe Heights $$$
In a superb setting overlooking the Killarney Lakes, this hotel is a luxurious and hospitable haven concealed behind an austere facade. The award-winning restaurant continues to receive well-deserved recognition, and standards of service have also brought accolades. There is an indoor heated pool, tennis, fishing, sauna, solarium, gym, and spa.
✉ 10 miles south of Kerry airport and 3 miles north of Killarney. Signposted off the N22 Tralee Road
☎ 064 31766; fax 064 31345
🕙 Closed Nov.–Mar.   AX, DC, MC, VI

🍴 Gaby's $$–$$$
Offering tempting seasonal menus in classic French style: Specialties include cassolette of shrimps and monkfish in a lightly gingered sauce, Gaby's famous smoked salmon pâté, lobster "Gaby" (made with a secret recipe), and classics like sole meunière. Availability of seafood depends on daily landings, but there's always a choice.
✉ 27 High Street   ☎ 064 32519
🕙 Closed Sun. and mid-Feb. to mid-Mar.   AX, DC, MC, VI

🏨 Killarney Park $$$
On the edge of town, this charming hotel has rich colors, open fires and welcoming staff. Also there's an indoor heated pool, sauna, gym, hot tub, outdoor hot tub and pool.
✉ Kenmare Place. N22 from Cork–

Killarney   ☎ 064 35555; fax 064 35266   🕙 Closed Nov. 28–Dec. 15 and Dec. 24–26   AX, DC, MC, VI

🏨 Lake $–$$
Approached by a wooded drive, this former mansion stands in lovely countryside with a lake, mountain views and woodland walks. Some bedrooms have balconies and four-poster beds.
✉ Muckross Road. Kenmare Road out of Killarney   ☎ 064 31035; fax 064 31902   🕙 Closed Dec. 16–Feb. 8   AX, DC, MC, VI

KINSALE, CO. CORK

🏨 Actons $$
Set in gardens overlooking the water front and marina, this hotel has a bar and bistro, plus the Captains Table restaurant, which offers enjoyable food. However it is the friendly and attentive staff who contribute so much to the enjoyment of a visit.
✉ Pier Road. Hotel faces Kinsale harbor, close to the Yacht Club
☎ 021 477 2135; fax 021 477 2231
🕙 Closed Christmas and Jan.   AX, DC, MC, VI

🍴 Man Friday $$
Popular long-established restaurant with a garden terrace. Seasonal à la carte menus feature seafood from local waters, duck, lamb and steak.
✉ Scilly (a 10-minute walk from town center, overlooking harbor, near Spaniard Pub)   ☎ 021 477 2260   🕙 Mon.–Sat. dinner. Closed Sun.   AX, DC, MC, VI

🏨 Trident $$–$$$
Located at the harbor's edge, the Trident Hotel has its own marina with boats for rent. Many of the bedrooms have superb views and two have balconies.
✉ Worlds End. Take R600 from Cork city to Kinsale, hotel is just beyond the pier, on the waterfront   ☎ 021 477 2301; fax 021 477 4173
🕙 Closed Dec. 25–26   AX, DC, MC, VI

LIMERICK, CO. LIMERICK

🏨 Royal George $–$$
City center hotel offering comfort and thoughtful extras. The new traditional Irish bar, An Sibín, is popular for its live music five nights

a week. Other facilities include a lounge bar, self-service bistro grill and a restaurant. Free access to fitness club. Only 15 minutes drive from Shannon airport.

✉ O'Connell Street ☎ 061 414566; fax 061 317171 ⓞ Closed Dec. 25 AX, DC, MC, VI

LISDOONVARNA, CO. CLARE

⌂ Sheedy's Country House Hotel $$

Warm, well-run family hotel providing good food from its award-winning restaurant. The hotel is beside a spa complex in well-tended gardens close to the fascinating Burren region renowned for its unique flora and fauna. Eight rooms and three junior suites.

✉ Town center, close to the sulphur wells ☎ 065 707 4026; fax 065 707 4555 ⓞ Closed Oct.–Mar. AX, MC, VI

LISMORE, CO. WATERFORD

⌂ Ballyrafter House $

A welcoming country house. Most bedrooms are pleasantly furnished in pine with suite facilities. The bar and conservatory are where guests and locals meet to discuss the day's events. The hotel has its own salmon fishing on the Blackwater river, and horseback riding is available.

✉ Half a mile from Lismore ☎ 058 54002; fax 058 53050 ⓞ Closed Nov.–Feb. AX, DC, MC, VI

MALLOW, CO. CORK

⌂ Longueville House $$$

Set in a wooded estate, this elegant 18th-century Georgian mansion has bedrooms overlooking the river valley and the courtyard maze. The situation is an ideal base for touring the scenic southwest. Long-standing reputation for excellence of restaurant. Many ingredients are home-grown. Specialties include roast lamb filled with parsley purée, blackwater salmon and gooseberry tart with elderflower ice cream. Bar food is served from 1–5 p.m., dinner reservations recommended.

✉ 3 miles west of Mallow on N72 to Killarney ☎ 022 47156 or 022 47306; fax 022 47459 ⓞ Closed mid-Dec. to mid-Feb. AX, DC, MC, VI

MIDLETON, CO. CORK

⌂ Barnabrow Country House $–$$

This is a 17th-century family-run country house set in 35 acres of parkland adjacent to the historic village of Cloyne, near Midleton. A perfect blend of old-world charm and new-world comfort with a good restaurant.

✉ Cloyne, Midleton. Take N25 from Cork to Midleton, then turning for Cloyne village ☎ /fax 021 465 2534 ⓞ Closed Dec. 24–28 DC, MC, VI

⌂ Midleton Park $$–$$$

This purpose-built hotel has fine, spacious suites, while the comfortable restaurant offers good food and attentive service. On-site parking is available.

✉ From Cork, turn off N25, hotel on right. From Waterford, turn off N25, over bridge until T-junction, turn right, hotel on right ☎ 021 463 5100; fax 021 463 5101 ⓞ Closed Dec. 25 AX, DC, MC, VI

ROSCREA, CO. TIPPERARY

⌂ Grant's $–$$

An attractive hotel opposite the 13th-century castle and Heritage Centre. Bedrooms are pleasantly furnished in warm colors and there is an excellent and relaxing, oak-paneled lobby lounge with deep leather armchairs and sofas. Restaurant, pub and café-bar.

✉ Castle Street. Off N7 Dublin–Limerick Road. Turn off for town center and follow signs to hotel ☎ 0505 23300; fax 0505 23209 AX, DC, MC, VI

ROSSCARBERY, CO. CORK

⌂ Celtic Ross $$$

This hotel overlooks a lagoon on the edge of a peaceful village and is a striking landmark on the rugged west Cork coastline. The spacious, light-filled public areas are luxurious with richly textured fabrics and highly polished Irish elm, yew bog oakwood and cherrywood. There is a cocktail bar, an Irish pub serving lunch, and an indoor fitness center. The restaurant specializes in seafood dishes.

✉ On N71 ☎ 023 48722; fax 023 48723 AX, DC, MC, VI

TRALEE CO. KERRY

⌂ The Brandon $$

This refurbished modern hotel with excellent leisure facilities is a golfer's paradise, within 30 minutes drive of six superb courses. Other facilities include an indoor heated pool, sauna, solarium, gym and spa bath.

✉ Prince's Street ☎ 066 712 3333; fax 066 712 5019 ⓞ Closed Dec. 22–29 AX, DC, MC, VI

TRAMORE, CO. WATERFORD

⌂ Majestic $$

Set a short distance from the beach, the Majestic has good sea views. Entertainment is held in the lounge during the summer months, and there is an outdoor heated pool and attractive gardens. Bedrooms are comfortable with all modern facilities.

✉ Turn off N25 through Waterford onto R675 to Tramore ☎ 051 381 761; fax 051 381 766 AX, MC, VI

WATERFORD, CO. WATERFORD

⌂ Dooley's $–$$

Located in the heart of Waterford overlooking the quayside, Dooley's is a comfortable family-run hotel. The smart public areas and bedrooms offer comfortable and stylish accommodations, and there is an elevator to all floors. Guests are very well cared for in a warm and friendly atmosphere.

✉ 30 The Quay ☎ 051 870 262 ⓞ Closed Dec. 25–27 AX, DC, MC, VI

⍾ Dwyer's Restaurant $$

Housed in an elegantly converted old barracks. The chef-owner specializes in local seafood adapted to classic French cuisine. Vegetarian choices, herbal teas, espresso and a European wine list.

✉ 8 Mary Street ☎ 051 877 478 ⓞ Mon.–Sat. 6–10 p.m. Closed Sun., Christmas week and public holidays AX, DC, MC, VI

⌂ Granville $$$

Situated on the quayside, this charming old hotel has been extensively refurbished while retaining its character Comfortable new bedrooms and the restyled public areas and restaurant are

Munster, Ulster and Northern Ireland

KEY TO SYMBOLS

- ⌂ hotel
- 🍴 restaurant
- ✉ address
- ☎ telephone number
- 🕐 days/times closed
- AX American Express
- DC Diners Club
- MC MasterCard
- VI VISA

Hotel

Price guide: double room with breakfast for two people:

$$$ over €180/UK£110
$$ €110–€180/UK£70–£110
$ up to €110/UK£70

Restaurant

Price guide: dinner per person, excluding drinks

$$$ over €50/UK£30
$$ €25–€50/UK£15–£30
$ under €25/UK£15

appointed to a high standard.

✉ The Quay. Take the N25 to the waterfront city center, opposite the clock tower ☎ 051 305 555; fax 051 305 566 🕐 Closed Dec. 25–26 AX, DC, MC, VI

⌂ Ivory's $$

This distinctive modern hotel near the Waterford Glass factory has bedrooms furnished with writing desks. The restaurant with its selection of fresh seafood is popular. The hotel has a security-monitored car park and is close to six golf courses where golfing packages can be arranged.

✉ Tramore Road. From Waterford city center take the N25 to Cork. After half a mile take exit to Trelore R675. Hotel is on right side ☎ 051 358 888; fax 051 358 899 AX, DC, MC, VI

⌂ Waterford Marina $–$$

Overlooking the River Suir, this is a smart new contemporary hotel. The Marine Bar has outdoor seating beside the river, while the colorful restaurant offers a good-value, modern cuisine. The attractive bedrooms are comfortable and well-equipped with many extras including ISDN lines.

✉ Canada Street ☎ 051 856 600; fax 051 856 605 AX, DC, MC, VI

YOUGHAL, CO. CORK

⌂ Devonshire Arms $$

This 19th-century hotel has been restored with considerable attention to detail. It offers good food in both the restaurant and the bar.

✉ Pearse Square ☎ 024 92827 or 024 92018; fax 024 92900 🕐 Closed Dec. 25 AX, DC, MC, VI

Ulster and Northern Ireland

BALLYBOFEY, CO. DONEGAL

⌂ Kee's Stranorlar $$

This former coaching inn is a comfortable hotel with bedrooms that are well furnished and offer good facilities. There is a bistro as well as a conservatory lounge and popular restaurant, plus indoor heated pool, sauna, solarium, gym, and spa bath. Mountain bikes are available for rent.

✉ 1 mile northeast on N15, in

Stranorlar village ☎ 074 31018; fax 074 31917 AX, DC, MC, VI

BALLYCONNELL, CO. CAVAN

⌂ Slieve Russell Golf and Country Club $$$

An imposing hotel on 300 acres of land, which also accommodates a championship golf course. Public areas include lounges, a restaurant and brasserie and a leisure center. Bedrooms are tastefully furnished and facilities include a beauty salon.

✉ From Cavan, head for Enniskillen, at Butlersbridge turn left toward Belturbet. Through village toward Ballyconnell, hotel is on left after 5 miles ☎ 049 9526 444; fax 049 9526 474 AX, DC, MC, VI

BALLYMENA, CO. ANTRIM

⌂ Adair Arms $$

Public areas in the Adair Arms are spacious and the lounge is inviting. The bedrooms are well presented and the refurbished restaurant offers a good choice from à la carte and fixed-price menus. There is a well-stocked bar and lighter meals are available in the Lanyon Grill.

✉ 1 Ballymoney Road ☎ 028 653 674; fax 028 2564 0436 🕐 Closed Dec. 25 AX, DC, MC, VI

BANGOR, CO. DOWN

🍴 Genoa Restaurant $–$$

Charming seaside restaurant specializing in seafood, often mixed with international recipes. Try the lamb and traditional dishes often featured on the menu.

✉ 1a Seacliff Road (at Bangor Marina parking lot) ☎ 02891 469 253 🕐 Closed Sun.–Mon., Dec. 25 and first 2 weeks in Jan. MC, VI

⌂ Royal $$

This substantial Victorian hotel overlooks the marina and offers modern comfortable bedrooms; the selection of bars and brasserie have a traditional atmosphere. Quays restaurant provides a more formal dining experience. There is weekly live entertainment.

✉ Bangor seafront. Turn right at seafront, hotel overlooks the marina ☎ 02891 271 866; fax 02891 467 810 🕐 Closed Dec. 25 AX, DC, MC, VI

BELFAST, CO. ANTRIM

🍽 La Belle Epoque $–$$
Brasserie-style restaurant displaying imaginative use of fruit- and vegetable-based sauces to complement chicken and other meats.
✉ 61–63 Dublin Road (at corner of Ventry Lane) ☎ 02890 323 244 🕐 Closed Sun. AX, DC, MC, VI

🍽 Bittles $
Small restaurant serving traditional dishes and the best place for Irish stew. Other choices are fish, pasta, vegetarian dishes and sandwiches. Lunch only.
✉ 70 Upper Church Lane ☎ 02890 311 088 🕐 Closed Sun. MC, VI

🏨 Culloden $$$
An elegant baronial mansion converted to a modern hotel with every convenience and excellent views. The day rooms include a bar and lounge areas. Facilities include indoor heated pool, tennis, squash, snooker, sauna, solarium, gym, spa, beauty salon and aromatherapy. The restaurant is a venue for some accomplished cooking.
✉ Bangor Road, on A2 ☎ 02890 425 223; fax 02890 426 777 AX, DC, MC, VI

🏨 The McCausland $$$
This exciting new hotel has been created from the conversion of two warehouses built in 1850, with the original Italianate facade retained. It is close to the city's attractions. Refined dining in the restaurant and a Continental-style café. The bedrooms are well-equipped. There is weekly live entertainment.
✉ 34–38 Victoria Street. This street is one way, turn right next to First Trust building ☎ 028 9022 0200; fax 028 9022 0220 🕐 Closed Dec. 25–27 AX, DC, MC, VI

🍽 Nick's Warehouse $$
This lively air-conditioned, two-story restaurant makes the most of a clever warehouse conversion. Cooking is seasonal and modern but with a homey feel. International influences are certainly discernible, but Irish ingredients and traditonal themes are not overlooked.
✉ 35–39 Hill Street ☎ 028 9043 9690 🕐 Closed Sat. lunch and Sun. AX, DC, MC, VI

CARRICKFERGUS, CO. ANTRIM

🏨 Dobbins Inn $$
Colorful window boxes adorn the front of this popular inn near the ancient castle. Public areas are modern without compromising the inn's original character. Bedrooms are comfortable.
✉ 6–8 High Street. From Belfast take M2, keep right at traffic circle follow A2 to Carrickfergus, turn left opposite castle ☎ /fax 02893 351 905 🕐 Closed Jan. 1 and Dec. 25–26 AX, DC, MC, VI

CARRICKMACROSS, CO. MONAGHAN

🏨 Nuremore $$$
This Victorian mansion serves as a quiet retreat, overlooking a lake and 18-hole golf course. Indoor and outdoor leisure and sporting facilities are on hand. The restaurant serves imaginative dishes, and dedicated staff ensure a pleasant stay in this friendly hotel.
✉ 2 miles south of Carrickmacross on Dublin–Londonderry road ☎ 042 966 1438; fax 042 966 1853 🕐 Closed for lunch on Sat. AX, DC, MC, VI

🏨 Zetland Country House $$$
Set in gardens featuring an unusual set of rock formations, flowers shrubs and woodland, this peaceful country house overlooks Cashel Bay and is enhanced by attractive furnishings. There is a fine lounge and smart cocktail bar, many of the bedrooms have a sea or garden view.
✉ Cashel Bay. N59 from Galway–Clifden, turn right towards Recess on the R340. After about 4 miles turn left onto R341, hotel is 1 mile ahead in the right ☎ 095 31111; fax 095 31117 🕐 Closed Nov.–Easter AX, DC, MC, VI

CAVAN, CO. CAVAN

🏨 Kilmore $$
This comfortable hotel set on a hillside on the outskirts of Cavan has a good restaurant, which is always appreciated by guests returning from a day's fishing. Golfing, windsurfing and boating are available nearby.
✉ Dublin Road. About 2 miles from Cavan on N3 ☎ 049 433 2288; fax 049 433 2458 AX, DC, MC, VI

DONEGAL, CO. DONEGAL

🏨 Harvey's Point Country Hotel $–$$
A modern hotel superbly located on Lough Eske containing spacious public rooms, excellent cuisine and a range of facilities including tennis and fishing. You can expect a warm Irish welcome at Harvey's.
✉ Lough Eske. From Donegal, take N56 then 1st right signposted Loch Eske and Harvey's Point. Hotel is about 10 minutes drive ☎ 073 22208; fax 073 22352 🕐 Closed Mon.–Tue., Nov.–Mar. AX, DC, MC, VI

DUNFANAGHY, CO. DONEGAL

🏨 Arnold's $$$
Set on the coast, this hotel has miles of sandy beaches on its doorstep. It has been in the Arnold family for three generations. There is a choice between well-equipped standard rooms and larger ones with sofas. Public areas offer comfortable seating and a choice of two restaurants, bars and weekly live entertainment. Tennis, fishing and horseback riding available.
✉ On N56 from Letterkenny. Hotel is on left entering the village ☎ 074 36208; fax 074 36352 🕐 Closed Nov. to mid-Mar. AX, DC, MC, VI

DUNGANNON, CO. TYRONE

🏨 Cohannon Inn $
Bedrooms are located behind the inn complex in a separate block. The main food and beverage areas have been smartly upgraded and food is available all day.
✉ 212 Ballynakilly Road (quarter mile from exit 14 off M1, head north towards Coalisland) ☎ 028 8772 4488; fax 028 8775 2217 AX, DC, MC, VI

ENNISKILLEN, CO. FERMANAGH

🏨 Killyhevlin $$–$$$
This hotel commands wonderful views over Lough Erne, which is visible from the comfortable public rooms. Attractive fabrics have been used to good effect in the smart modern bedrooms. The hotel makes an excellent base for exploring the many sights of Fermanagh.

KEY TO SYMBOLS

	hotel	
	restaurant	
	address	
	telephone number	
	days/times closed	
AX	American Express	
DC	Diners Club	
MC	MasterCard	
VI	VISA	

Hotel

Price guide: double room with breakfast for two people:

\$\$\$ over €180/UK£110
\$\$ €110–€180/UK£70–£110
\$ up to €110/UK£70

Restaurant

Price guide: dinner per person, excluding drinks

\$\$\$ over €50/UK£30
\$\$ €25–€50/UK£15–£30
\$ under €25/UK£15

Dublin Road. 2 miles south, off A4 ☎ 0286 632 3481; fax 0286 632 4726 AX, DC, MC, VI

FAHAN, INISHOWEN PENINSULA, CO. DONEGAL

St. John's Country House and Restaurant \$\$
A period house overlooking Lough Swilly. Gourmet meals based on Donegal mountain lamb, game in season and other local ingredients. ✉ In Fahan village on R238, Londonderry–Buncrana road ☎ 077 60289 ⏱ Closed Mon and Sun. dinner AX, DC, MC, VI

LIMAVADY, CO. LONDONDERRY

Radisson Roe Park Hotel and Golf Resort \$\$\$
In a stunning location just outside the town, this country-house complex offers superb sporting and leisure facilities. Public areas include lounges, restaurant, brasserie and colorful courtyard. ✉ On the A2 Londonderry–Limavady road, 1 mile from Limavady ☎ 028 7772 2222; fax 028 7772 2313 AX, DC, MC, VI

LONDONDERRY, CO. LONDONDERRY

Da Vinci's Bar and Restaurant \$
Dramatic pub and restaurant specializing in seafoods such as grilled seabass with tikka crust and lime-cherry relish and other creative variations of classic dishes. ✉ 15 Culmore Road ☎ 028 7126 4507 ⏱ Mon.–Sat. dinner, Sun. lunch, dinner AX, MC, VI

Trinity \$\$
Known for its interior design, the hotel's public areas include a café-bar, while the former "snug" has been converted into a bar bistro. The paneled restaurant provides a more formal food option. There is also a conservatory and roof garden. ✉ 22–24 Strand Road ☎ 02871 271 271; fax 02871 271 277 AX, MC, VI

NEWCASTLE, CO. DOWN

Enniskeen House \$\$
The Porter family's peaceful hotel enjoys superb views over the countryside to the Mountains of Mourne. Public areas and bedrooms are all traditional in style. Wholesome fare is offered in the two dining areas. ✉ 98 Bryansford Road (from Newcastle town center follow signs for Tollymore Forest Park, hotel is 1 mile on left) ☎ 02843 722 392; fax 02843 724 084 ⏱ Closed mid-Nov. to mid-Mar. AX, MC, VI

PORTAFERRY, CO. DOWN

Portaferry \$\$
Portaferry is a charming hotel with a restaurant. Many bedrooms enjoy spectacular vies over Strangford Lough. ✉ 10 The Strand (on Lough Shore opposite ferry terminal) ☎ 02842 728 231; fax 02842 728 999 ⏱ Closed Dec. 24–25 AX, DC, MC, VI

PORTBALLINTRAE, CO. ANTRIM

Bayview \$\$
Opened in late 2001, Bayview is located in the heart of this picturesque village. Overlooking the Atlantic Ocean and close to the Giant's Causeway, this small hotel of 25 rooms is an ideal destination for a leisurely break. ✉ 2 Bayhead Road ☎ 028 2073 4100; fax 028 7082 6160 AX, DC, MC, VI

PORTRUSH, CO. ANTRIM

Comfort Hotel \$\$
Sister hotel to the Bayview (see above), the Comfort opened in 2001 and can be found in the center of Portrush. It is in an ideal location for golfing, walking, cycling, angling and sightseeing. ✉ 73 Main Street ☎ 028 7082 6100; fax 028 7082 6160 AX, DC, MC, VI

ROSSNOWLAGH, CO. DONEGAL

Sand House \$\$–\$\$\$
Set in a crescent of golden sands, a hospitable hotel with good cuisine and service. Rooms with sea views, and a conservatory lounge provides a relaxing retreat.. ✉ Donegal Bay. On coast road 5 miles north of Ballyshannon ☎ 072 51777; fax 072 52100 ⏱ Closed mid-Oct.–Easter AX, DC, MC, VI

ESSENTIAL INFORMATION

"P LANNING advice and practical travel tips "

The information in this guide has been compiled for U.S. citizens traveling as tourists.

Travelers who are not U.S. citizens, or who are traveling on business, should check with their embassies and tourist offices for information on the countries they wish to visit.

Entry requirements are subject to change at short notice, and travelers are advised to check the current situation before they travel.

Ireland – Essential Information

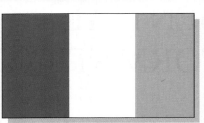

BEFORE YOU GO

PASSPORTS

The most important document you'll need before you travel is a passport. Passport application forms can be obtained from any federal or state court or post office authorized to accept passport applications. U.S. passport agencies have offices in all major cities; check the Yellow Pages. (U.S. Government, State Department) for the one nearest you. You also can request an application form by calling the National Passport Information Center at (888) 362-8668. (Note: There is a credit card charge.) Comprehensive passport information and application forms are available on the U.S. State Government internet site at www.travel.state.gov.

Apply for your passport early as processing can take several months from the time of application until arrival. Rush service is available for an extra charge. Before departure, make sure your passport is valid for at least another six months after you are due to travel: some European countries require this.

There are no border formalities between Northern Ireland and the Republic if you are crossing by car, although it is always advisable to take your passort with you.

Travel visas are not necessary for American citizens traveling to either the Irish Republic or Northern Ireland (which is part of the United Kingdom), but if you'll be traveling on to other nations, check their entry requirements before you leave home.

TRAVEL INSURANCE

Before departing make sure you are covered by insurance that will reimburse travel expenses if you need to cancel or cut short your trip due to unforeseen circumstances. You'll need coverage for property loss or theft, emergency health and dental treatment. Before taking out additional insurance, check to see if your current homeowners insurance or medical coverage already covers you for travel abroad. If you make a claim, your insurance company will need proof of the incident or expenditure. Keep copies of any police report or medical bills or statements, to submit with your insurance claim.

ESSENTIAL FOR TRAVELERS

● Required ● Recommended ● Not required

Passport	●
Visa	●
Travel, medical insurance	●
Round-trip or onward airline ticket	●
Local currency	●
Traveler's checks	●
Credit cards	●
First-aid kit and medicines	●
Health inoculations	●

ESSENTIAL FOR DRIVERS

● Required ● Recommended ● Not required

Driver's license	●
International Driving Permit	●
Car insurance (for non-rental cars)	●
Car registration (for non-rental cars)	●

*see also DRIVING section

WHEN TO GO

Weather in Ireland is impossible to predict. You can experience all four seasons in one day, but you can be certain that no conditions will last for long, and showers pass quickly. The warmest months are July and August, and rainfall in May, June and September is often lower. May and June are good months to visit, as schools are still in session and there are fewer crowds at major attractions. Temperatures rarely fall below freezing in the winter and you can pick up bargain accommodations deals during the low season, but some sights may be closed.

IMPORTANT ADDRESSES

Irish Tourist Board
345 Park Avenue
New York, NY 10154
☎ (212) 418-0800
fax (212) 371-9052

Republic of Ireland Tourist Board
Baggot Street Bridge
Dublin 2, Republic of Ireland
☎ 01 602 4000
fax 01 602 4100

Northern Ireland Tourist Board
551 Fifth Avenue, Suite 701, New York, NY 10176
☎ (212) 922-0101
fax (212) 922-0099

American Embassy (Republic of Ireland)
42 Elgin Road, Ballsbridge
Dublin 4, Republic of Ireland
☎ 01 668 8777
fax 01 668 8056
American Citizens Services: Mon.–Fri. 9–3

TIME ZONES

DUBLIN	NEW YORK	CHICAGO	DENVER	SAN FRANCISCO	215
12:00 noon	5 hours behind Ireland	6 hours behind Ireland	7 hours behind Ireland	8 hours behind Ireland	

CUSTOMS

YES

Duty-free limits on goods brought in from non-European Union countries: 200 cigarettes or 100 cigarillos or 50 cigars or 250 g. tobacco; 2 L. wine; 1 L. alcohol over 22% volume or 2 L. alcohol under 22% volume; 60 ml. perfume; 250 ml. toilet water; plus any other duty-free goods (including gifts) to the value of €164 ($162). There is no limit on the importation of tax-paid goods purchased within the European Union, if they are for your own personal use. There are no currency regulations. You can purchase $400 worth of personal goods before returning to the U.S. before a tax is levied; keep sales slips.

NO

No unlicensed drugs, weapons, ammunition, obscene material, pets or other animals, counterfeit money or copied goods, meat or poultry.

MONEY

The Republic of Ireland's currency is the euro (€), which is divided into 100 cents (c). Denominations of euro bills are 5, 10, 20, 50, 100, 200 and 500. There are coins of 1, 2, 5, 10, 20 and 50c and €1 and €2. In Northern Ireland the currency is the pound sterling (UK£) and it must be used in the following counties: Antrim, Armagh, Derry, Down, Fermanagh and Tyrone. The pound sterling is divided into 100 pence (p). The denominations of pound bills are 5, 10, 20 and 50. There are coins of 1, 2, 5, 10, 20 and 50p and £1 and £2. The pound sterling and the euro are not interchangeable. Credit cards are accepted in hotels, large stores and upscale restaurants; check first in small or rural establishments. Exchange dollars or traveler's checks at a bank, exchange office, post office or large hotel.
Exchange rate at press time: $1 =€1.02; UK£0.65

TIPS AND GRATUITIES

Restaurants (where service is not included)	10–15%
Cafés/bars	10%
Taxis	10%
Porters	€1/50p per bag
Hairdressers	€1–2/50p–£1
Tour guides	€1–2/50p–£1
Cloakroom attendants	€1/50p

COMMUNICATIONS

POST OFFICES

Buy stamps at post offices, some newsstands and tobacconists, large grocery stores and hotels. Hours for out-of-town post offices may vary. Mailboxes and vans are

green in the Republic of Ireland and red in Northern Ireland. Mail service in the Republic is notoriously slow and expensive. Postcards are cheaper to send than letters.

TELEPHONES

Older-style public call boxes in the Republic are blue and cream and marked in Gaelic *'Telefón'*. They take cash (10c/10p, 20c/20p, 50c/50p or €1/£1 coins) or pre-paid phone cards bought from newsstands, post offices and local stores.

Phoning within Ireland
All Irish phone numbers in this book include the area code; dial the number listed.

Phoning Ireland from abroad
The country code for Ireland is 353; for Northern Ireland 44. Note that Irish numbers in this book do not include the country code; you will need to prefix this if you are phoning from another country. To phone Ireland from the United States or Canada, omit the first zero from the Irish number and add the prefix 011 353; for Northern Ireland 011 44. (Note that the number of digits in Irish area codes varies.)
RI example: 01 122 3344 becomes 011 353 1 122 3344.
NI example: 01 122 3344 becomes 011 44 1 122 3344.

Phoning from Ireland
To phone the United States or Canada from Ireland, prefix the area code and number with 001.
Example: (111) 222-3333 becomes 001 111 222-3333

EMERGENCY NUMBERS

Police	999
Fire service	999
Ambulance	999

Emergency calls are free from phone booths.

Ireland – Essential Information

Ireland – Essential Information

HOURS OF OPERATION

⬜ Stores Mon.–Sat.	⬜ Museums/monuments
⬜ Offices Mon.–Fri.	⬜ Pharmacies Mon.–Sat.
⬜ Banks Mon.–Fri.	
⬜ Post offices Mon.–Sat.	

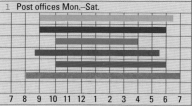

7 8 9 10 11 12 1 2 3 4 5 6 7

In addition to the times shown above, some stores stay open until 8 or 9 for late-night shopping on Thursday or Friday.

In smaller towns and rural areas some stores close in the afternoon on one day of the week.

Some banks in small towns close 12:30–1:30. Nearly all banks are closed on Saturday, and post offices close at 1 p.m. on Saturday.

Hours for museums and tourist sights vary and are subject to change; always check with the local tourist office. Many places close from October to March or have very limited opening times, although most major sights are open all year.

Pharmacies may close earlier on Saturday.

NATIONAL HOLIDAYS

Banks, businesses and most stores close on these days. Museums also may have restricted hours.

Jan. 1	New Year's Day
Mar. 17	St. Patrick's Day
Mar./Apr.	Good Friday
Mar./Apr.	Easter Monday
1st Mon. of May	May Day Holiday
Last Mon. of May	Spring Holiday (NI)
1st Mon. of Jun.	June Holiday (RI)
Jul. 12	Orangeman's Day (NI)
1st Mon. of Aug.	August Holiday (RI)
Last Mon. of Aug.	Late Summer Holiday (NI)
Last Mon. of Oct.	October Holiday (RI)
Dec. 25	Christmas Day
Dec. 26	St. Stephen's Day

RESTROOMS

 Identify restrooms in Gaelic-speaking areas by *Fir* (men) and *Mná* (women). A small charge is levied in restrooms at some railroad stations, but most other facilities are free. The standards of hygiene are moderate. You will be welcomed into any local pub if you need to use their facilities, but stop for a drink and a talk while you are there.

HEALTH ADVICE

MEDICAL SERVICES
Private medical insurance is recommended. U.S. and Canadian visitors can receive treatment in emergency rooms, but are charged if admitted to a hospital bed. A general practitioner also will charge for services.

DENTAL SERVICES
Dentists charge for treatment. Dental work is expensive, so check to see if it is covered by your medical insurance. Dentists are listed in the Yellow Pages, or ask at your embassy, hotel or at a tourist office. Alternatively, a list of dental practioners can be obtained from the Irish Dental Association; (☎ 01 283 0499).

SUN ADVICE
The sunniest months are May and June, with 5–6½ hours of sun a day (the extreme southwest is the sunniest). July and August are the warmest. During these months you should take sensible precautions against the sun.

DRUGS
Pharmacies (also called chemists) sell a range of prescription and non-prescription medicines. If you need medicine outside regular hours, information about the nearest 24-hour facility should be posted on the door of all pharmacies.

SAFE WATER
Tap water is safe to drink throughout Ireland. If, however, you prefer mineral water you will find it widely available.

PERSONAL SAFETY

Irish towns and cities are generally relaxed, safe places to be, and are regularly patrolled by police, especially in Northeren Ireland. However, it is always best to use common-sense precautions when traveling.

- Keep valuables hidden when you're on the move; a money belt or neck purse is the best option.

- Never leave bags unattended.

- Avoid walking alone in dimly lit areas at night.

- If you have belongings stolen, report the incident immediately to the police and get a written report to provide to your insurance company as evidence for your claim.

- Security forces on both sides of the border are courteous to bona fide travelers

NATIONAL TRANSPORTATION

AIR

Most European flights arrive in Dublin or Belfast; international flights land also in Shannon and Cork. Internal flights and those to the U.K. are very competitive and are a realistic option to driving. Fly with Aer Lingus (☎ 0645 737 747) or Ryanair (☎ 08701 569 569). Aer Aran (☎ 01 814 1058), operate the Aran flyer with several daily flights between the Aran Islands and Galway.

TRAIN

Ireland's rail company is Iarnród Éireann (IÉ). Trains are the fastest way of covering long distances and are generally reliable and comfortable, but the network is limited and one-way tickets cost almost as much as round-trip tickets. Midweek is less expensive than weekends, and there are many special offers on fares. The Dublin to Belfast Express takes 2 hours, and there are eight trains daily. Round-trip tickets are available; for more information ☎ 01 836 6222. Rail runaround tickets (seven days of unlimited travel) are available from main Northern Ireland railroad stations.

BUS

In the Republic, Bus Éireann operates a network of express bus routes serving most of the country and includes service to Belfast (some services run summer only); for information ☎ 01 836 6111. If you are traveling around Dublin, make sure you have plenty of change, as an exact fare policy is in operation. The number 41 bus from Eden Quay runs to Dublin Airport. Barratt Executive Travel (☎ 061 384 700) in Limerick operates day tours in the summer season and on Sundays they run a Shannon Cruise half-day tour featuring a boat trip on Lough Derg and a visit to Tipperary Crystal. In Northern Ireland, Ulsterbus Tours (☎ 028 9066 6630), has links between Belfast and 23 towns, and also run ferry and coach tours to England, Scotland and Wales; unlimited travel tickets are available.

FERRY

There are several ferries a day from Belfast and Dublin to ports on the British mainland; taxis, trains and coaches operate a regular service from the ports to the cities. Combined train and ferry or bus and ferry tickets can be an inexpensive option from London to Dublin; try National Express (☎ 08705 80 80 80). A car ferry runs between Ballyhack, Co. Wexford and Passage East, Co. Waterford (☎ 051 382 480). Another serves Killimer, Co. Clare and Tarbert, Co. Kerry, saving 60 miles on the road trip (☎ 065 953124). Traveling between Northern Ireland and London can be more expensive; for combination tickets try Scottish City Link (08705 50 50 50). There are also ferries to several islands; ask for details at a local tourist office. Ringaskiddy's Ferryport, 10 miles southeast of Cork city, provides passenger and car ferry service to Brittany (Brittany Ferries ☎ 021 427 7801).

PHOTOGRAPHY

The lush, rolling countryside is a product of a wet climate, so be prepared with 400asa film. If you are visiting in the summer period and the weather is kind, expect to use 100asa film to record Ireland's rich palette. You'll also be pleased to have a 400asa film if you wish to sum up your vacation by capturing the hospitable atmosphere inside one of the archetypal Irish pubs. There may be live entertainment and most locals will be flattered to be included in a picture, but it is polite to ask first. If landscapes are your interest , there is a large variety to choose from. You'll find a plethora of castles and intriguing ruins as subject matter, but remember, if the weather is too poor for long shots, zoom in close and study detail. Film and camera batteries are readily available in Ireland, and you should be able to find good developing and printing facilities in most large towns. Don't be concerned about your film and camera going through security equipment at the airport; it is safe for film rated up to 1600asa. It is generally illegal to take film photos of the police and military barracks in Northern Ireland.

MEDIA

The main newspapers in the Republic are the *Irish Times* and the *Irish Independent;* they both provide great insights into Irish life and politics. The *Examiner* is a serious and respected newspaper, commenting on world affairs. For arts reviews and listings, the *Sunday Tribune* is good; other Sunday papers include the *Sunday Independent* and *Sunday Business Post.* British papers are available the same day in major cities and in Northern Ireland. The local *Belfast Telegraph* is a popular evening paper. In the mornings, you can choose between the nationalist *Irish News* or the loyalist *News Letter.*

Republic of Ireland television broadcasting is operated by a state-sponsored body called RTE (Radio Telefís Éireann). It has three radio and four television channels. You can receive them all over Ireland and Northern Ireland. In much of the Republic, you can pick up BBC (radio and television) and Ulster television. Local radio, including many independent stations, offer blasts of Irish music, talk, and lilting Gaelic (also useful for traffic and weather reports and events).

ELECTRICITY

Ireland has a 230-volt power supply. Electrical sockets either take plugs with two round pins or three square pins; American appliances will need a plug adapter and will require a transformer if they do not have a dual-voltage facility.

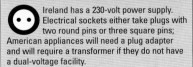

Ireland – Essential Information

Ireland – Essential Information

DRIVING REGULATIONS

DRIVE ON THE LEFT
Drive on the left-hand side of the road on both sides of the border and, at traffic circles, yield to traffic approaching from your right.

SEAT BELTS
Must be worn in front seats at all times and in the rear seats where fitted.

MINIMUM AGE
The minimum age for driving a car is 17. However, rental car firms will often stipulate a minimum age of 25.

BLOOD ALCOHOL
The legal blood alcohol limit is 0.08%. Random breath tests on drivers are carried out frequently, especially late at night, and the penalties for offenders are severe.

TOLLS
The Westlink and Eastlink bridges around Dublin require tolls of about one euro.

ADDITIONAL INFORMATION

An International Driving Permit (IDP) is recommended; some rental firms require it, and it can speed up formalities if you are involved in an accident.

A Green Card (international motor insurance certificate) is recommended if you are driving a non-rental car.

Irish Republic roads vary tremendously and the road classification gives no reliable indication of the width or surface quality – some primary roads are little better than country lanes. In Northern Ireland the major roads are fast and well-maintained and seldom congested.

SPEED LIMITS

REGULATIONS
Traffic police can impose on-the-spot fines.

Limited-access highways
(motorways)
113 k.p.h. (70 m.p.h.)

Main roads
88 k.p.h. (55 m.p.h.)
96 k.p.h. (60 m.p.h) in Northern Ireland

Urban areas
48 k.p.h (30 m.p.h.)

CAR RENTAL

CAR RENTAL
The leading rental companies have offices at airports, railroad stations and large ferry terminals. Hertz offers discounts to AAA members. If you are taking a rented car across the border from Northern Ireland into the Republic of Ireland, check with your rental company to see that you have the appropriate insurance.

Car rental is less expensive in Northern Ireland than in the Republic.

A local car rental firm is likely to offer cheaper rates than an International company, but it may not allow different pick-up and drop-off points.

Often, the cheapest way to book a car rental is to arrange a package deal in advance with a tour operator (fly and drive or rail and ferry-drive) rather than waiting until you arrive in Ireland. Early booking is advisable if you are traveling during the high season.

The minimum age for renting a car ranges from 18 to 25 depending on the model of the car. Some companies have a maximum age limit of 70.

For reservations:

	UNITED STATES	IRELAND
Alamo	(800) 327-9633	01 844 4162
Avis	(800) 331-2112	01 605 7500
Budget	(800) 527-0700	01 844 5150
Hertz	(800) 654-3080	01 844 5466

FUEL

FUEL
Gas is unleaded and sold in liters; diesel also is easily purchased. Gas stations in villages stay open until 8 or 9 p.m. and usually open after Mass on Sunday. Along main highways on both sides of the border, there are 24-hour gas stations: gas is considerably less expensive in Northern Ireland.

PARKING

In some urban areas, parking is limited to certain times and periods. Where this is signed you must buy a disk from a newsstand or garage and display it on the dashboard of your car. Multi-story and pay and display parking can also be used in cities.

Park only in authorized areas in Northern Ireland; vehicles parked in unauthorized areas may cause a security alert and be removed by security forces.

In Dublin, men called "lock'ards," carrying rolled-up newspapers may try to help you find a parking space at night. If you accept their unofficial services, a €1–2 tip is customary.

AAA

AAA AFFILIATED MOTORING CLUB
AA Ireland
23 Suffolk Street, Dublin 2
☎ 01 617 9999; fax 01 617 9400
If you break down while driving in the Republic of Ireland ☎ 1800 66 77 88
For breakdowns in Northern Ireland ☎ 0800 028 9018

Not all automobile clubs offer full services to AAA members.

BREAKDOWNS/ACCIDENTS

There are 24-hour emergency phones at regular intervals on highways: ☎ 999.

Most car rental firms provide their own free rescue service; if your car is rented, follow the instructions given in the documentation. Use of a car repair service other than those authorized by your rental company may violate your agreement.

In the event of a breakdown, the vehicle should be moved off the highway whenever possible. Hazard warning lights should be used and, if available, a red warning triangle should be placed on the road at least 165 feet before the obstruction and on the same side of the road.

ROAD SIGNS

Driving in Ireland is still, generally speaking, a pleasure. Out of the big towns the roads are uncrowded and most drivers courteous. The farther west you go, the more patience you need: roads are narrower, steeper and more winding.

Road signs in the Republic of Ireland that give road distances are in the process of being changed: Older, black-and-white signs give distances in miles, while newer green-and-white signs give kilometers. In Northern Ireland, the distance signs are always in miles.

Give way to traffic on major road

Crossroads

ROAD SIGNS (continued)

No through road

National speed limit applies

No passing

No entry for vehicular traffic

One-way traffic

Vehicles may pass on either side to reach same destination

Ahead only

Keep left

Double curve, first to the left

Two-way traffic straight ahead

Ireland – Essential Information

Ireland – Essential Information

IRISH AND AMERICAN ENGLISH

Although on the surface they are the same language, there are some quirky differences between American and Irish English. The Irish have become familiar with Americanisms through imported American television shows and movies, and on the whole will understand American visitors. However, note the possible misunderstanding if an Irish person directs you to the "first floor" of a building; the American equivalent is actually the second floor). Irish words and phrases are in the left column below; American words appear in the right column.

HOTELS

bath	*bathtub*
book	*reserve*
caretaker/ porter	*janitor*
cot	*crib*
duvet	*quilt*
foyer	*lobby*
ground/ first floor	*first/second floor*
lavatory/ loo/toilet	*restroom*
lift	*elevator*

EATING OUT

aubergine	*eggplant*
bacon butty	*bacon sandwich*
bacon rasher	*slice of bacon*
banger	*sausage*
bap	*hamburger bun*
bill	*check*
biscuit	*cookie*
broad bean	*lima bean*
chips	*french fries*
courgette	*zucchini*
crisps	*potato chips*
jacket potato	*potato in its skin*
kipper	*smoked herring*
lager	*light beer*
mash	*mashed potato*
porridge	*oatmeal*
pudding	*dessert*
runner beans	*string beans*
sweets	*candy*
jam	*jelly*
jelly	*Jell-O*

COMMUNICATIONS

call box	*telephone booth*
post box	*mail box*
post code	*zip code*
put through	*connect*
reverse charge	*call connect*
ring up	*call*

MONEY

bank note	*bill*
cashpoint	*ATM*
cheque	*check*
quid (colloquial)	*one pound (money)*
VAT	*value added tax*

SHOPPING

anorak	*parka*
bank holiday	*public holiday*
braces	*suspenders*
briefs	*jockey shorts*
carrier bag	*shopping bag*
chemist	*drugstore*
dinner jacket	*tuxedo*
ironmongers	*hardware store*
jumper	*sweater*
nappy	*diaper*
off licence	*liquor store*
pants	*briefs (underwear)*
plus fours	*knickerbockers*
public convenience	*restroom*
queue	*line of people*
tights	*pantyhose*
trousers	*pants/slacks*
shop assistant	*sales clerk*

TRANSPORTATION

coach	*long distance bus*
left luggage office	*baggage room*
lost property	*lost and found*
return ticket	*round-trip ticket*
single ticket	*one-way ticket*
timetable	*schedule*
underground/	*subway*

DRIVING

boot	*trunk (of a car)*
bonnet	*hood (of a car)*
car park	*parking lot*
caravan	*house trailer*
dual carriageway	*divided highway*
estate car	*station wagon*
filling station	*gas station*
flyover	*overpass*
gear lever	*gear shift*
layby	*pull-off*
lorry	*truck*
manual	*stick shift*
motorway	*freeway*
pavement	*sidewalk*
petrol	*gas*
roundabout	*traffic circle*
zebra crossing	*pedestrian crossing*

GAELIC WORDS AND PHRASES

Everyone in Ireland speaks English, but officially the Republic is bilingual, and Gaelic is the first language in areas of Cork, Waterford and parts of the west, where road signs are only written in Gaelic. There are around 80,000 native Gaelic speakers, making it Europe's least widespread official language, but this ancient celtic tongue is enjoying a revival. Radio, television and the internet all stir up interest in the old language, and it is being seen by the young as fashionable and a strong part of their cultural traditions. Every Irish citizen speaks the language if summoned to court, and it is usually a university entrance requirement. Understanding even a few words of this poetic language can enrich a visitor's experience.

The Irish language is not an easy one to get your tongue around. The fractured Irish pronunciation is awkward; the spelling does not appear to reflect the sound. To make matters more complicated, there are several dialects of Gaelic, and pronunciation varies from place to place. Following are pronunciations of words you may come across.

Bord Fáilte (Irish Tourist Board)	*bord falty*
Ceilidh (traditional dance night)	*kaylee*
Gaeilge (the Irish language)	*gale-geh*
Gaeltacht (Irish-speaking country)	*gale-tackt*
Garda (police)	*gawrdah*
Fleadh (traditional music evening)	*flah*
Taoiseach (prime minister)	*teeschock*

Meeting people

fáilte (welcome)	*fall-to*
le do thoil (please)	*le-do-hull*
lá maith (good day)	*law-ma*
dia hduit (hello)	*d-git*
tá (yes)	*thaw*
níl/ní hea (no)	*ha/knee*
oíche mhaith (good night)	*eha-ma*
cé mhéid? (how much?)	*k-made*
go raibh maith aguth (thank you)	*go-reve-ma-agut*
Conas taoi? (how are you?)	*konus-thaw-too*

Eating and Drinking

bialann (restaurant)	*bee-lun*
teach tábhairne (pub/bar)	*tock-tairne*
bricféasta (breakfast)	*brick-fasta*
lón (lunch)	*loan*
dinnéar (dinner)	*din-air*
tábla (table)	*taub-law*
freastalaí (waiter)	*fras-taul-ee*
uisce (water)	*ois-e*
ascailte (open)	*oscail-te*
dúnta (closed)	*doon-thaw*

GAELIC WORDS AND PHRASES

Gaelic Place Names

In Ireland the meaning of place names often refers to a natural or man-made feature of the locality or to clans and leading families. Some of the Gaelic words used in place names will tip you off as to the history, or appearance of the village or town. Here are some interesting ones.

ard	*height*
augh	*ford*
bally/baile	*town, place or farm*
bearna	*gap between hills*
boher	*road*
cashel	*castle*
carn	*heap of stones*
carraig/corrig	*boulder*
cahir	*castle*
cill	*church*
cnoc/knock	*hill*
dun	*fort or protected house*
inis/inch/ennis	*island or riverside field*
lios/lis	*circular fort*
moin/moyne	*bog*
rath	*circular fort*
slieve	*hill*
teach	*house*
tobar/tubber	*well*
tra/tray	*beach*
tulach/tullow/tully	*small hill*
uibh	*family or tribe*
iusce/isk/isky	*water*

Here are a few terms you may run across in descriptions of many archeological sites, monuments and ruins in Ireland, along with brief descriptions.

Dolmens Standing stones (usually three) surmounted by a massive capstone. One of the earliest forms of megalithic tombs, dating from 3000 to 2000 BC.

Passage graves A legacy of Ireland's Neolithic forebears: great stone tombs with a large buriel chamber, entered through a long passage. Built for someone of importance but no one knows for certain exactly who was entombed in them.

Court cairns Found mostly in the northern regions of Ireland, these are the earliest megolithic chambered tombs. Their name derives from the covered gallery used for burials, with one or more unroofed courts or forecourts for rituals.

Stone circles Early Bronze Age relics serving as temples of worship, as did large earthern circles.

Ring forts Protected dwellings, circular in design and built within stone or earthen walls. Dating from the Bronze Age, they continued to be built right up to the Norman invasion.

Crannogs Artificial islands built in lakes or marshy places, their origins are earlier than ring forts. Found mostly in the midland counties and County Clare.

Clochans Known as "behives," these remarkable stone buildings of corbel construction were erected without mortar as tiny oratories, found mostly in western Ireland where wood was a rarity.

Ireland – Essential Information

Index

Acknowledgements

The Automobile Association wishes to thank the following photographers and libraries for their assistance in the preparation of this book. ©ADAGP, Paris and DACS, London 2002. 88 James Joyce by Jacques Emile Blanche; AKG, LONDON 12; BORD FÁILTE - IRISH TOURIST BOARD 144; JAMES DAVIS WORLDWIDE 114/5; MARY EVANS PICTURE LIBRARY 182, 199; IMAGES COLOUR LIBRARY 18, 75; MRI BANKERS GUIDE TO FOREIGN CURRENCY 215; TERRY MURPHY PHOTOGRAPHY 148 (Waterford Crystal); NATIONAL GALLERY OF IRELAND 88; REX FEATURES LTD 176; SLIDE FILE 17, 20, 21, 122, 147, 166, 196/7, 198; WORLD FEATURES LTD 33; www.euro.ecb.int/ (euro notes) 215.

The remaining photographs are held in the Automobile's own photo library (AA PHOTO LIBRARY) and were taken by the following photographers:
L. Blake 26, 28, 36, 40, 40/1, 42/3, 44, 52, 53, 55; J. Blandford 110, 113, 117, 119, 120, 124/5, 126, 127, 131, 132/3, 136/7, 138, 140; C Coe 25, 150, 153, 159, 166/7, 165, 168, 192; S Day 10/1, 13, 29, 30/1, 67, 72/3, 82, 101, 108/9; M Diggin 57b, 145, 146t; D Forss 141, 142, 177; C Hill 35, 43, 47, 49, 51, 54, 57t, 180/1, 185, 187, 188/9, 190; S Hill 38, 39, 46, 124, 215b; J Johnson 143; T King 76; S McBride 3, 19, 62/3, 64, 130/1, 134/5; G Munday 9, 91, 156/7, 160, 161, 162, 163, 169, 171, 172, 173, 175, 178, 183, 193, 194/5; K Paterson 194; M Short 15, 61, 70, 77, 78, 85, 87, 93, 96, 98, 99, 103, 105, 107; Slide File 4/5, 6, 97, 104/5; S Whitehorne 58, 71, 74, 79, 80, 81, 83, 84, 88, 200, 215t; P Zöeller 94/5, 128/9.